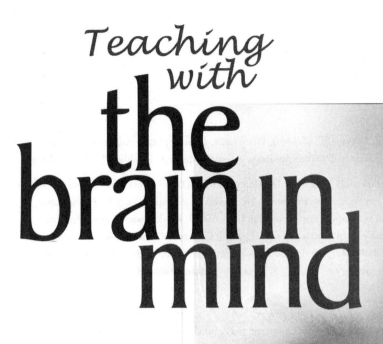

Teaching *with* the brain in mind

2nd Edition
Revised and Updated

Eric Jensen

Alexandria, Virginia USA

ASCD®

1703 N. Beauregard St. • Alexandria, VA 22311-1714 USA
Phone: 800-933-2723 or 703-578-9600 • Fax: 703-575-5400
Web site: www.ascd.org • E-mail: member@ascd.org
Author guidelines: www.ascd.org/write

Gene R. Carter, *Executive Director;* Nancy Modrak, *Director of Publishing;* Julie Houtz, *Director of Book Editing & Production;* Katie Martin, *Project Manager;* Shelley Kirby, *Senior Graphic Designer;* Jim Beals, *Typesetter;* Tracey A. Franklin, *Production Manager.*

ISBN-13: 978-1-4166-0030-5

Paperback ISBN: 1-4166-0030-2 • ASCD product #104013
s5/05

Also available as an e-book through ebrary, netLibrary, and many online booksellers (see Books in Print for the ISBNs).

e-books: retail PDF ISBN: 1-4166-0266-6 • netLibrary ISBN: 1-4166-0264-X • ebrary ISBN: 1-4166-0265-8

Quantity discounts for the paperback book: 10–49 copies, 10%; 50+ copies, 15%; for 500 or more copies, call 800-933-2723, ext. 5634, or 703-575-5634.

Library of Congress Cataloging-in-Publication Data
Jensen, Eric.
  Teaching with the brain in mind / Eric Jensen.— 2nd ed.
     p. cm.
  Includes bibliographical references and index.
  ISBN 1-4166-0030-2 (alk. paper)
  1. Learning, Psychology of. 2. Teaching—Psychological aspects. 3. Brain. I. Title.

  LB1060.J46 2005
  370.15'23—dc22
                          2005002844

15 14 13   12 11 10 9 8 7 6 5 4 3 2

Note to readers: Minor changes were made to pages 3, 4, 6, 180, and 187 when this book was reprinted in 2008.

To all the neuroscientists, psychologists, and researchers who have graciously supported my efforts to learn how we learn and how to communicate it better.

To all the educators who make such a difference in the world.

To my wife, Diane, for her support.

Teaching with the brain in mind 2nd Edition

PREFACE

For most of human history, the model for learning was simple: if you wanted to learn something new, you either had to figure it out on your own or apprentice yourself to someone who could show you how to do it. Watch, listen, and try out the new skill; this worked for peasants and royalty, parents and children, blacksmiths and monks.

So what changed all that? Massive increases in population began the first change, and the shift from plowshares to factories during the Industrial Revolution brought new models of learning. The notion developed that you could bring everyone together in a single place and offer a standardized curriculum. This paradigm of schooling, exported from Prussia, was popularized by Horace Mann in the late 1800s and early 1900s. Often referred to as the "factory model," it emphasized useful skills such as obedience, orderliness, and respect for authority. Maria Montessori commented that children often felt humiliated in this new role.

A peculiar twist to this paradigm emerged during the 1940s through the 1960s. At the time, the dominant theory of human behavior was influenced by the doctrines of psychologists John Watson and B. F. Skinner, whose thinking went something like this: "We may not know what goes on inside the brain, but we can certainly see what happens on the outside. Let's measure behaviors and learn to modify them with behavior reinforcers. If we like it, reward it. If we don't, punish it."

Considering what we knew about the brain at that time, this behaviorist approach made sense. But now, it's becoming outdated as research uncovers new understandings of how the brain works. Times have changed.

Today it's no longer suprising to see the brain on the cover of national magazines. Society in general has finally moved past the novelty stage of exclaiming, "Wow, the brain!" And collectively we've begun to grasp the endless connections between brain research and everyday life. But articles that appear in the popular media rarely offer the depth of information or point of view that today's educators need. Are the revelations and implications of brain research reaching those who work most with children? I'm not sure that they are.

If you wanted to get your car fixed, would you go to a mechanic? Certainly. If you wanted legal help, would you find an attorney? Of course. And to understand the brain and how we learn, would you go to a teacher? Probably not. Yet every year, millions of parents trust that the professionals who teach their children are knowledgeable about the brain and the processes of learning. In defense of teachers, even neuroscientists still disagree about some of the inner workings of the brain. They also disagree about how much scientific data about the brain can be applied to schools. In addition, many schools of education do not offer programs that connect neurobiology, teaching, and classroom behaviors. It's time they did.

Starting Points

I discovered for myself the concept of brain-compatible learning during a workshop I attended in June 1980. The experience was so positive, and

I became so enthusiastic (some would say zealous), that I decided to share my excitement with others. Because I was a teacher, my first response was, "Why don't my own students have this kind of learning experience every day?"

Within months, I cofounded with Bobbie DePorter an experimental, cutting-edge academic program in San Diego, California, called SuperCamp. Our purpose was to use the latest research on learning to enrich and empower young students with life skills and learning tools. I reasoned that if these strategies worked with adults, they could also work with kids. We held our first session in August 1982. It was an immediate success, and we soon offered it in other states and countries. We were flooded with media attention and were featured in more than 200 articles in magazines and newspapers including *USA Today* and *The Wall Street Journal.* Later, stories about SuperCamp appeared on CNN and *Good Morning, America.*

Students in this academic program have a nearly universal positive experience. Years of follow-up have shown that the benefits lasted long after the 10-day program itself (DePorter & Hernacki, 1992). In addition, students' grades and school participation went up, and the students reported greater self-confidence. The teaching methods used at SuperCamp have been evaluated and shown to be highly effective (Benn, 2003). The experiment we began decades ago in Southern California is now an international fixture, with more than 40,000 graduates.

In the publishing industry, the brain-based teaching revolution officially began with Leslie Hart's groundbreaking 1983 book, *Human Brain, Human Learning.* This book invited readers to make links between what we know about the brain and how we teach. Instead of leaving it all to soci-ologists, psychologists, and well-meaning educa-tors, Hart suggested we turn to biology. How exactly *is* the brain best designed to learn? This very powerful question began a lasting paradigm shift that is continually spurred by new technology, practical teachers, and the mushrooming ranks of neuroscientists, who now number more than 30,000 worldwide.

Changing Brains, Changing Minds

The first edition of *Teaching with the Brain in Mind,* published in 1998, introduced thousands of educators to links between brain research and classroom success. This revised, second edition takes a renewed and more critical look at the research connections and examines the fruits of success. Educators throughout the world credit brain-based teaching and learning with helping to raise teacher morale, increasing teacher retention, and improving student achievement. I have seen, felt, and heard firsthand the difference it makes. Students of all backgrounds and ages, with every imaginable history of failure, can succeed and have succeeded with a brain-based approach to teaching and learning.

Although it is not a panacea, this approach provides some important guidance for decision making. The brain-based revolution has already changed school start times and influenced disci-pline policies, assessment methods, teaching strate-gies, budget priorities, lunchroom choices, classroom environments, the use of technology, school architecture, and even the way we think of the arts and physical education. Brain-based learn-ing is no longer a prediction or a fad; the change

has already occurred in thousands of schools throughout the world.

Learning in ways that are compatible with the way humans naturally function is an approach that will stand the test of time. Yes, it may attract some criticism, spurred by the kind of defensive reaction that is typical among those who wish to hold on to the status quo. But if this paradigm is solid, as I believe it is, more and more people will come to realize that if you want to understand human learning, you'd better understand the brain.

Where Do You Start?

To get started, become more "consumer literate" about brain research. Learn some of the major terms and the best sources of serious research. Learn the names of prominent people who are doing the work that is most relevant to educators. Here are some of the major technical journals that are revealing new discoveries monthly:

- *Journal of Neuroscience*
- *Learning and Memory*
- *Brain and Cognition*
- *Brain Research*
- *Nature Neuroscience*
- *Brain and Behavior*
- *Journal of Cognitive Neuroscience*

Remember, one journal or one scientist's opinion is not enough. Dig for longitudinal studies that examine diverse populations and have sufficient sample sizes. Your own questions ought to be, "What's the origin of this idea? Is it still just the-ory? Where's the research on it?" You'll want to know, "What was the scientific discovery that illuminated the theory? What clinical trials have been done? Is there any evidence of successful applications in the classroom?" Don't jump to conclusions or infer something that is not stated. You may want to e-mail the scientist who did the study to find out more about it. Avoid any inferential leaps and be a critical student of the results. Here's the process I use:

- Begin with basic research. (What happens in the brain and our environment?)

- Look for clinical trials (animal and human studies) conducted under controlled conditions.

- Find educational research conducted in real classrooms. (This approach is usually but not always possible.)

- Try out the concept or strategy for yourself.

Typically, if an idea is published, someone's already tried it somewhere. But it's good to be sure. Don't embrace any idea just because someone, somewhere has labeled it as "brain based." We all want solutions to educational challenges, but we must be careful about how we apply new discoveries.

Other Considerations

First, it's unfair to expect neuroscientists to present educators with the "holy grail" of learning. That's not their job, and most of them have purposes other than education to serve. Furthermore, many paradigms have been shaken as a result of an insight from outside the field. For example, the traditional view of neurobiology is very Newtonian—a physical, matter-based explanation. The new view, the one I embrace, is equally influenced by quantum mechanics—the influence of energy and particle waves on ourselves and on

systems. Any researcher, teacher, or author who thinks he or she can explain human learning and behavior at only a micro level, by describing synapses and naming neurotransmitters, is almost 100 years out of date. The newer model shows that life forms are strongly influenced by more forces that we do not yet fully understand.

Second, remember that the learning is new, the field is young, and mistakes will be made. Many other breakthroughs will follow, and some of them *do* belong in the classroom. All of us are in this together, learning and growing as we make mistakes. If you want to move things forward in your classroom or school, you just might be the best person to do it. If the potential gain is good and the potential loss is acceptable, try out new ideas.

Third, use thoughtful action learning to test some of your own ideas. We need *more* action research, not less, and you can begin in your own workplace. The usual cautions apply. Avoid biases in the study design. Start small and keep track of your results. Tell your students what you're doing. Talk to parents about the brain, and make sure other staff members know about the information you gather. Get or give administrative backing, which helps generate the long-term resources and support needed for transformation.

Finally, begin the process with this book, which can serve as a study guide and will help you sort theory from fact. Again, brain-based learning is here to stay. You can bet it will continue to affect nearly every aspect of education, including teaching strategies, discipline policies, the arts, special education, curriculum, technology, bilingual programs, music instruction, learning environments, staff development, school design, assessment, and even organizational change. The more we understand about the human brain, the more we can apply it in our schools. Anyone who thinks this field is irrelevant is saying that the brain itself is irrelevant. Nothing could be more wrong. Understanding and applying relevant research about the brain is the single most powerful choice you can make to improve learning.

The "brain train" is leaving the station. Are you on board?

INTRODUCTION

The revolution is being televised. Countless stories on the Discovery Channel and PBS have revealed exciting new insights about the brain. Mainstream broadcast media such as ABC, NBC, CBS, and CNN and publications such as *Time* and *Newsweek* have carried stories about recent brain discoveries. Dozens of books, videos, journals, newsletters, and publishing companies have documented this burgeoning field.

Educators worldwide have taken notice, and models of how we educate are being transformed. With brain-based learning now an established paradigm, if a far from universal one, it makes sense to explore some basic questions. First, how strong and reliable is this field of brain-based learning? Second, how do we know what we know about the brain? Can we apply laboratory findings directly in a classroom? The themes implied by these questions are simple; they are about answering the critics of brain-based education, understanding the sources that underlie it, and reviewing the reliability of evidence.

Let's begin with two fundamental facts. First, students who attend school from kindergarten through secondary school typically spend more than 13,000 hours of their developing brain's time in the presence of teachers. Second, their brains are highly susceptible to environmental influences—social, physical, cognitive, and emotional. And, more important, their brains *will be altered* by the experiences they have in school. As educators, we *must*—ethically, morally, and opportunistically—pay attention to how we ask students to spend time with us. These concepts are fundamental to education, yet we often take them for granted.

Answering the Critics

Despite the mounting evidence that supports brain-based learning, some critics say, "It's no big deal; there's nothing new" or, "We don't know enough to do anything." Some even say, "Nothing will change." I wonder if those same critics would have had similar things to say at Kitty Hawk in 1903, when the Wright brothers flew the first airplane only 100 yards: "It's no big deal," "It won't change anything." We are now at the doorstep of the same kind of revolution. Instead of a mechanical one fueled by new modes of transportation, it's one of neurons, chemicals, networks, and wonderful, truly historic discoveries. For the first time in human history, we are beginning to understand how our brain works. Yes, maybe we are just at the stage of the Wright brothers' first flight. But it's a great time to be alive.

Shortly after new "brain-based" thinking began to make its way into the mainstream, critics began finding fault. For example, John Bruer, president of the James S. McDonnell Foundation, noted that "well-founded educational applications of brain science may come eventually, but right now, brain science has little to offer education practice or policy" (1998, p. 14). Armed with selected willing scientists and selective studies, the critics (Bruer, 1998, 1999; Bailey, Bruer, Symons, & Lichtman, 2001) have attempted to invalidate the integration of brain-based understandings into schools. Some claim that it's still too early and we

don't know enough for sure. But if we waited for irrefutable evidence on *everything* we did in education, we'd need to stay at home.

Some people are simply "early adapters," and others, more skeptical, are "late adapters." By nature, critics are typically late adapters. There are also those who have more personal agendas to protect, such as a pet program, an institution, or a foundation that they fear is being threatened. Having said this, some critics have raised valid points; others have raised what I see as unwarranted objections. Here are some of the criticisms and my responses.

Criticism: Many "pop" writers were not scrutinizing the sources of their information about the brain.

Response: I agree. The general news media are not always reputable sources of information about the brain. Nor is one scientist, one critic, one famous person, or a single study; anyone seeking reliable information must consider multiple credible sources. For example, I first consider material from the basic neuroscience sources, then look at clinical studies if they're available, and finally locate reports of educational practices or action research to confirm the practical applications. Readers of research on the brain should look for significant sample sizes, blind studies, well-designed experiments, and plausible conclusions. For every source that appears in the References section of this book, there are a half dozen that I left out, just to keep the length of the list reasonable. In short, what I state in this book is solid information.

Criticism: There's nothing new here—all this brain-based stuff is a bunch of hype.

Response: I strongly disagree. Whenever someone claims there's nothing new, I reply with this abbreviated list of "Top 10 New Discoveries About the Brain," all of which have come to light during the past 10 years:

1. We have discovered that the human brain can and does grow new neurons, that these neurons become functional and are highly correlated with memory, and that this process can be regulated.

2. We have discovered that there is no stable baseline for stress. Unlike other systems of the body, which usually revert to a prior, healthy state after suffering trauma (a process called homeostasis), the brain responds to extended periods of stress by developing a new, less healthy baseline. These "allostatic"—or adjusted—stress loads are becoming increasingly common and are associated with serious health, learning, and behaviorial risks.

3. We have discovered that aggressive behavioral therapies, new drugs, and revolutionary stem-cell implantation can be used to influence, regulate, and even repair brain-based disorders, including fetal alcohol syndrome, autism, retardation, strokes, and spinal cord injury.

4. We have discovered that "teenage behavior" may result from a complex array of fast-changing factors—not just hormones.

5. We have discovered that genes are not fixed. Evidence suggests that both gene expression and genetic makeup can be altered.

6. We have assembled tomes of evidence to support the delicate interplay between emotional states and cognition.

7. We have confirmed that music can affect cognition.

8. We have confirmed that software programs that use brain plasticity to retrain the visual and auditory systems really can improve attention, hearing, and reading ability.

9. We have discovered that exercise is strongly correlated with increased brain mass, better cognition, mood regulation, and new cell growth.

10. We have discovered that humans with implanted "brain chips" can operate thought-controlled mechanical interfaces; in other words, they can guide a robotic arm merely by thinking. The implications of these findings could revolutionize life for the physically disabled.

Anyone who says there's nothing new in brain research must have been living in a cave. The past 10 years have been the most explosive and hopeful in the entire history of neuroscience.

Criticism: Research findings are being misinterpreted; unwarranted leaps are being made.

Response: This criticism is often valid. The best-known example of this kind of extrapolation is hearing about the Mozart effect and then concluding, for example, that all music makes you smarter or all music is good for all students. Another is making an unwarranted leap from the understanding that new learning creates new synapses to the conclusion that more synapses must necessarily be a good thing. Untrue. Children with Fragile X syndrome actually have too many synapses. The best advice here is to read the studies and *wait for corroborating studies* before hopping onto a bandwagon. In addition, just because a study suggests that a certain instructional strategy may work well, the possibility remains that other strategies also work as well or better.

Mysteriously, most brain-based education books have not addressed the kinds of revolutionary discoveries found in my Top 10 list. Books on nearly every topic, including parenting, leadership, and specific curriculum topics have been published. Some reveal excellent connections and others need better scholarship. Having said that, I'll add that an author *is warranted* in drawing practical conclusions when there's little or no downside risk and the conclusions are reasonable.

Criticism: Some of the brain studies cited involved animals, not humans.

Response: This is true, but not a definitive reason to discount those studies' findings. Animal studies *do* offer much that we can transfer and learn from. Lab experiments with rats or primates are clearly more credible than those with sea slugs or fruit flies. Some studies may never be done on humans for ethical reasons. And although obvious differences distinguish humans and rats, science tells us that there are more similarities than differences (Cenci, Whishaw, & Schallert, 2002).

Overman & Bachevalier (2001) have studied the question of animal models versus human models, designing and testing learning trials in which humans and animals negotiated comparable mazes. They concluded, "In most instances . . . the procedures of animal testing can be directly applied to children . . ." (p. 120). This is not a blanket justification for applying the results of all animal studies to human situations. But neuroscientists study Norway rats and macaque monkeys for a reason—these animals have

significant neuroanatomical similarities compared to humans. Yes, whenever possible, human studies are ideal, ensuring greater reliability and confidence in the results. But, as noted, for ethical reasons, it's not always possible to conduct human studies.

Criticism: The field of brain-based education is not "brain based" enough; many ideas are actually from psychology, sociology, or psychiatry.

Response: The error in thinking that it's not "brain based" *enough* is simple: it's *all* about the brain. The disciplines of psychology, biology, sociology, psychiatry, and pedagogy are all concerned, to some degree, with understanding human behavior. And, increasingly, those looking to understand human behavior are looking at the brain. Most of the newer books in these fields include chapters on brain function, anatomy, or processes. We cannot explore learning and the brain without having our inquiry overlap those of these other disciplines. Besides, where's the wisdom in studying ways to improve student learning without considering issues that affect it, such as nutrition, racism, poverty, trauma, and stress?

A slightly different problem occurs when some "brain-based education" presenters simply recycle their favorite pedagogy—such as that of Dewey, Piaget, Montessori, Kolb, Hunter, Lozanov, McCarthy, or Gardner—with a brain-based spin. "Brain-based" rightfully means that the actual work and conclusions were based on recent findings about the brain. Dewey, Piaget, and Montessori have much to offer, but their models might more correctly be called "brain compatible," meaning that the work and conclusions are *aligned with* or *compatible with* recent brain research. Besides, if the work of these giants was valid before, it's still valid now; we don't need to look for proof in the latest brain scan.

For the critics of brain-based learning, my message is this: you are fighting a losing battle. Thousands of neuroscience studies are being produced every year, and some of them *do* apply to the classroom. In the classroom are millions of teachers who need real-world solutions today, not 50 years from now. Educators are practical; they will try out almost any reasonable, ethical strategy, but they will keep using it only if *it works*. And thousands of educators are already using brain-based strategies with great success. To the critics in an office or a laboratory I say, "Get out in the real world—and teach for a week!"

One developmental neuroscientist recently stated, "If the likely risk-reward ratio is good, I see nothing wrong with classroom teachers trying out new ideas straight from neuroscience" (Jernigan, 2003). Sufficient studies support the things that I argue for in this book, and the references are solid. Many teachers are already doing action research to find out for themselves what works and what doesn't. They know brain-based teaching works.

I believe that over time the ideas and approaches I advocate in this book will become the standard. Why? Because when we teach in ways that make sense for the brain, that match how we were designed to learn, everyone wins.

Making Sense of Brain Research

A new breed of science of the brain is developing: educational neuroscience. No current journal carries that title, but one will probably appear soon. How else will we be able to integrate fields like psychiatry, sociology, nutrition, learning, emotions, and memory into a single social construct? Today dozens of new disciplines serve as examples of things to come. They have multiplied within the thriving biological community and find expression in journals such as *Social Neuroscience, Biological Psychiatry,* and *Nutritional Neuroscience.* Education will soon be part of this trend. The key to introducing and integrating these new fields is visionary researchers with a multidisciplinary approach.

The prevailing belief is that information is doubling in our society about every 18 months. In the field of neuroscience, the pace seems even faster. In short, we are learning about the brain at an unprecedented rate. It's generally acknowledged that research more than two years old is already "old information." In the coming years, we can expect new and more accurate technologies to further illuminate the brain's mysteries.

Even with all the exciting new research, it's easy to understand why many educators were turned off by the early attempts at applying it in the classroom. Typically, select and qualified "translators" of brain research shared their knowledge with staff developers and administrators who, in turn, set up professional development sessions to share the translated knowledge with classroom teachers. If these professional development sessions used role modeling and other effective techniques, the teachers often had reactions like "Wow! This is great stuff!" But if "application of brain research to the classroom" was presented as dry science, the responses were more along the lines of "Ho-hum. Tell me something new." Some educators got such a shallow, trivialized version of (mis)understanding—advice like "put water bottles in the classroom"—that it was difficult to have a serious conversation about the value of the research.

Let's remember, too, that errors of omission, commission, or enthusiasm come with every major paradigm shift. Educators have also seen laughable "translations" of learning styles, cooperative learning, multiple intelligences, and differentiated instruction. Early in any movement, it's tougher to separate the wheat from the chaff. But it's important to stay the course and consider recent brain research as part of the major rationale for today's educational practices. Why? Because *all learning involves the brain*. The more we can understand how the brain naturally works, the better we can structure educational practices to align with that functionality.

Here's a simple example. A good bit of evidence from studies of both animals and humans suggests that 30 minutes of vigorous exercise at least three times a week can contribute to enhanced mood, increased brain mass, better circulation, more brain cells, and improved cognition (Adlard, Perreau, Engesser-Cesar, & Cotman, 2003; Churchill et al., 2002; Markakis & Gage, 1999; Sutoo & Akiyama, 2003; Tomporowski, 2003; Van Praag, Kempermann, & Gage, 1999). This research suggests that schools that eliminate physical education programs may be more than shortsighted; they may be reckless and hurting their own causes.

Here's another example. Each year, tens of thousands of students are helped by a computer software program called FastForWord, which helps them develop phonological awareness (Temple et al., 2003). Several neuroscientists developed this educational program as a direct result of brain research.

After years of pushing for brain-based education, I am encouraged that the tide has turned. Harvard University now offers advanced degrees in its Mind, Brain, and Education (MBE) program. This interdisciplinary brain-based education degree has already graduated many with a masters and Ph.D. in brain-based education. The goal of the new movement is a marriage of cognitive science, neuroscience, and education that creates an integrated synergy of research and practice. There's now a peer-reviewed scientific journal on brain-based education. The journal, which is published quarterly by the reputable Blackwell Publishers and the International Mind, Brain, and Education Society (IMBES), features research reports, conceptual papers, reviews, debates, and dialogue.

Yet, despite all that we're learning from brain researchers, school boards and shortsighted policymakers continue to scream "budget cuts" and eliminate the things that can make the biggest difference. If your physical education program is ineffective, don't throw it out, fix it. When done right, PE can improve health, increase brain mass, reduce the likelihood of childhood-onset diabetes and teen depression, boost neurogenesis, and provide a host of other benefits. I know of no other subject or discipline that can make those claims. Choosing to keep a physical education program is choosing well— *with the brain in mind*. Although every school decision does not need to be made by consulting recent studies from neuroscience, we should be paying more attention to what the research says. Brain-based learning is a force to be reckoned with, and it's here to stay.

Meet Your Amazing Brain

You've heard for much of your life that the human brain is amazing. It's true. That soft, squishy blob between your ears—the blob that runs your life—*is* pretty amazing. Every day in classrooms around the world, teachers are amazed by what the human brain can do. Because exploring *all* the facets of the brain is beyond the scope of this chapter, we'll focus on three relevant and essential features:

- *Adaptability.* The brain changes constantly.
- *Integration.* Brain structures compete and cooperate.
- *Sophistication.* The brain is highly complex.

These themes help to establish the nature of the brain: it is constantly working; it operates with a high level of structural cooperation; and seemingly simple processes, like learning to read, are actually highly complex. This dynamic and versatile structure is unlike anything else on earth. That may be why we are so attracted to the study of the brain—it evokes both wonder and curiosity. At the simplest level, the brain is an

Key Concepts

- Basic brain anatomy
- How the brain changes over time
- Cooperation and competition in the brain
- How the brain learns

7

organ that we are all born with, and we'll explore that concept first. But the brain is much more than an anatomical structure; it is also an active processing center, always at work.

The Raw Material

To begin learning about the brain, consider a grocery store's produce and dairy departments. In shape, the brain closely resembles a head of cauliflower. In size, it's similar to a large grapefruit or cantaloupe (see Figure 1.1). The brain is mostly water (78 percent), fat (10 percent), and protein (8 percent). From the outside, the brain's most distinguishing features are its convolutions, or folds. The wrinkles are part of the cerebral *cortex* (Latin for "bark" or "rind"), the brain's outer covering. The cerebral cortex is about as thick as an orange peel. The folds allow the covering to maximize its surface area (have more cells per square inch). In fact, if the cortex were laid out flat, it would be about the size of an unfolded, single page from a daily newspaper. Remember, the brain is only a grapefruit-sized organ. It's general texture is about the same as soft butter, but some parts are as gooey as raw eggs or yogurt.

Brains have both neurons and glial cells (see Figure 1.2). The most well-studied brain cells are *neurons*, which consist of a cell body with fingerlike input extensions, called *dendrites,* and a single output, called an *axon*. Neurons have different shapes depending on the part of the brain they're in and their function. There are many types of glial cells, each with different functions. Recently, scientists have discovered that glia—also known as interneurons—are not, as once thought, just a "support" or "housekeeping"

Figure 1.1

THE HUMAN BRAIN

cell, but are quite important in brain development, function, and growth.

Estimates vary on the actual number of neurons and glia in the human brain. One researcher who has done detailed studies in this area, William Shankle of the University of California–Irvine, asserts the human brain has about 30 to 50 billion neurons. His studies (Landing, Shankle, Hara, Brannock, & Fallon, 2002) also show a 20 to 40 percent variance among humans, meaning the real numbers vary by *billions* from one person to another. No wonder differentiation in teaching makes sense!

A more mainstream view is that we're born with about 150 to 200 billion neuron cells and keep about 100 billion of them. (The rest disappear for various reasons, as explained later.) By the time we're adults, we also have about 500 billion to 1,000 billion glial cells. For the sake of comparison, a fruit fly has 100,000 neurons, a mouse has 5 million, and a monkey has 10 billion. A single cubic millimeter (1/16,000th of an inch) of human brain tissue has more than 1 million neurons.

Humans have large brains relative to body weight. The adult human brain weighs about three pounds (1,300–1,400 grams). But would a

Figure 1.2

Neurons and Glial Cells

Both neurons and glial cells integrate neural outputs, release transmitters, have long-range signaling, can enwrap synaptic terminals, and are connected by gap junction.

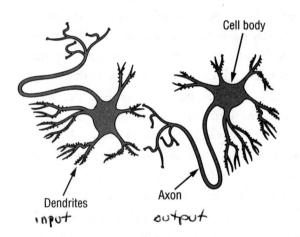

Cell body

Dendrites
input

Axon
output

Typical neurons

Neurons receive stimulation from their branches, known as dendrites. They communicate with other neurons, creating a network with millions of other by firing a nerve impulse along an **axon**.

Various types of glial cells *interneurons*

Glia carry nutrients, speed repair, provide myelin for axons, support the blood–brain barrier, and may form their own communication network. They are also involved in neurogenesis.

---

bigger brain make you smarter? That's unlikely. A sperm whale's brain weighs about 17 pounds, or 7,800 grams.

The brain's various parts and its nerve cells are connected by nearly 1 million miles of nerve fibers. The human brain has the largest area of uncommitted cortex (with no specific function identified so far) of any species on earth. This gives humans extraordinary flexibility for learning.

Scientists divide brain areas into lobes (see Figure 1.3). The *occipital lobe* is in the middle-back area of the brain, and it's primarily responsible for vision. The *temporal lobes* are located above and around the ears on the left and right sides of the brain. These areas are primarily responsible for hearing, memory, and language. Connect visual areas to language areas, and you can "see" what you hear and say. That's part of the essence of reading: high visual-auditory connectivity. The *frontal lobe* is the area around your forehead. It's involved with purposeful activities like judgment, creativity, problem solving, and planning. It also holds short-term memory so you can juggle two or more thoughts at once. The *parietal lobe* is at the top and back areas of your head. Its duties include processing higher sensory and language functions. It also has a cool tie-in with the Sci Fi Channel in that it's highly active in subjects who claim to have seen hallucinations or UFOs, or have had "near death" experiences.

The territory in the middle of the brain includes the *hippocampus, thalamus, hypothalamus, cingulate, basal ganglia, fornix, striatum,* and *amygdala* (see Figure 1.4). You could call this area both the chemistry lab and the drama department of the brain. Sometimes known as the *limbic system,* it represents 20 percent of the brain by volume and is partly responsible for emotions, sleep, attention, body regulation, hormones, sexuality, sense of smell, and production of many brain chemicals. However, noted neuroscientist Joseph LeDoux (1996) contends that there is no real "limbic system," only specific

structures that process emotion, such as the amygdala. In either case, this middle area of the brain, along with the parts of the cortex, helps you feel what you feel about the world.

The location of the brain area that allows you to know that you are "you" (consciousness) is disputed. It may be dispersed throughout the cortex, or it may be in the thalamus, or it may be located near the reticular formation, a structure atop the brain stem (Crick, 1994). You'd think that this part of the brain would be easy to find—just cut away brain areas until a person loses awareness, right? But it's not just a simple case of Jack the Ripper meets the Nutty Professor. Remember, the second essential feature of the brain is integration, or strong connectivity. That means many areas connect to and influence other portions, so that specific sections of the brain may contribute separately and collectively to your sense of self. In short, one critical quality that makes the brain work so well is its degree of connectivity, not its individual structures.

Figure 1.3

MAIN AREAS OF THE HUMAN BRAIN

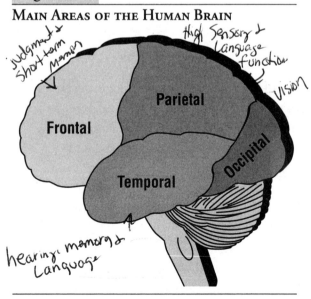

Adaptability: The Constantly Changing Brain

Not long ago, the prevailing view of the brain was that it remained fairly constant throughout a person's life. We knew that the brain was smaller in childhood; once it reached maturity, we thought it remained more or less stable over many years before beginning to deteriorate somewhat with age. This view of a "static" brain is decidedly out of date. Yes, the most amazing new discovery about the brain might be that *human beings have the capacity and the choice to be able to change our own brains.*

It's now understood that environmental events at one level of an organism (molecules, cells, organs, systems, individual behavior, society) can pro-foundly influence events at other levels (Cacioppo, Berntson, Sheridan, & McClintock, 2001). This finding suggests that your experiences and the actions you take can lead to changes in your brain. These changes, in turn, change you. We also know that your life influences your genes at the same time that your genes regulate your life. Researchers have found evidence of social influence on both genetic constitution (Reik, Dean, & Walter, 2001; Wilson & Grim, 1991) and genetic expression (Suomi, 1999)—meaning the substance of the genes and how the genes function. New evidence suggests that environmental triggers, even things like stress (Foster & Cairns, 1994), can "reprogram" our genes. In short, we can and do influence our own genetic material; this is a profound revelation!

The result of the various interrelation of humans shaping environments and environments shaping humans is that there is no fixed human brain; it is always a work in progress. Another way to put it is that your brain is dynamic and constantly changing as a result of the world you live in and the life you lead. Whether you are 2 or 92, your brain is a cauldron of changing chemicals, electrical activity, cell growth, cell death, connectivity, and change.

This dynamism makes it very challenging to get clear data on what's happening in the brain. From birth to the teenage years, the brain undergoes a fourfold increase in volume (Johnson, 2001). Infants are born with roughly a trillion connections (synapses) already in place. The infant's interaction with his or her environment helps create many additional connections within the cortex. At the same time, the genetic process called "pruning" eliminates countless unnecessary connections. Throughout life, your brain is losing connections at

the same time it is creating new connections. It's a bit like going out shopping for new clothes at the same time that someone is raiding your closet back at home. This ongoing refinement results in a highly adapted, highly specialized brain (see Figure 1.5).

Longtime neuroscience dogma held that the mammalian brain couldn't grow new brain cells, and mainstream science was absolutely certain that new brain cell growth (neurogenesis) was impossible in

Figure 1.4

MEDIAL AND CORONAL VIEWS OF THE BRAIN

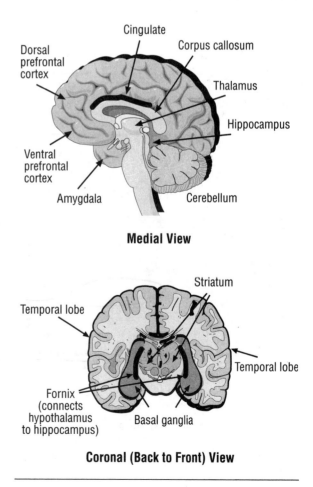

Medial View

Coronal (Back to Front) View

the human brain. However, the groundbreaking research of Kempermann, Kuhn, and Gage (1998) showed not only that humans *do* grow new neurons, but also that these new cells survive and become functional and integrated. Just as important, a follow-up study (Van Praag et al., 1999) found that humans can influence the rate of new brain cell growth. In fact, researchers have identified more than 15 factors that either enhance or impair neurogenesis. Again, the complexity of the brain comes into play. Although factors such as excess stress can inhibit growth, exercise can encourage it, as we'll see in later chapters. All of this paints a

complex picture of what exactly you have in your brain at any particular moment.

Inside your brain, cells are being eliminated at the same time new cells are being born. You lose some brain cells every day through attrition, decay, and disuse, and we know that certain behaviors affect the loss of brain cells. For example, although there's no evidence that an occasional glass of wine or beer destroys brain cells, it's clear that alcoholism does substantial damage (Eckardt, Rohrbaugh, Rio, Rawlings, & Capola, 1998). Scientists differ on what your daily net gain or loss in brain cells might be. But even if you lose a half-million neurons per day, it would take centuries to literally lose your mind.

Some of the most interesting recent research on the brain's adaptability shows how activities can influence the actual mass and organization of the brain. For example, playing a musical instrument consistently over time can literally remap the brain's "real estate." It's as if there's a big "Texas land grab" going on. Neuroscientist Arnold Scheibel of UCLA did an autopsy on a renowned violinist and found that the area of the brain responsible for hearing reception (layer four, auditory cortex) was twice as thick as normal (Diamond & Hopson, 1998). Michael Kilgard found that areas of the auditory cortex increased in size with specific auditory trainings over time (Kilgard & Merzenich, 1998). It's as if the brain said, "We need more space for what you're doing. We'll just use this nearby spot." Another study found that the cerebellum, the brain structure that contains almost half of the brain's neurons and that is also involved in keeping beat and rhythm, was 5 percent larger in musicians than in the general population (Gaser & Schlaug, 2003; Hutchinson, Lee,

Figure 1.5

CONSTANT CHANGE IN THE BRAIN FROM BIRTH THROUGH ADULTHOOD

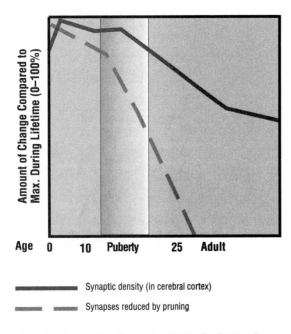

Synaptic density (in cerebral cortex)

Synapses reduced by pruning

Source: Based on data from Huttenlocher & Dabholkar (1997) and Bourgeois (2001).

Gaab, & Schlaug, 2003). These studies and others provide evidence that many years of specific fine-motor exercise prompts brain reorganization and nerve growth.

What's truly amazing is that this constant reorganization of the brain is always purposeful—driven not by a mysterious signal but by real-life use and disuse. The brain has no single command center; it's a system of systems governed by life experience and by complex processes, which appear to be both variable and fixed, random and precise. Your constantly changing brain is shifting your moods, your thinking, and your actions through countless electrical and chemical changes. Each of these changes results in a shifting state of mind.

In summary, the brain is a dynamic, opportunistic, pattern-forming, self-organized system of systems. That's a mouthful. It's also mind-boggling. So why is this new view of the brain so important to you, as a teacher? Because it reinforces that every student in your classroom has the capacity for change. Yes, genetics plays a part in who students are and how they behave and reason, but each of them can change. Even your most frustrating student can improve. Now that should be the best news you've gotten all day.

Integration: How Brain Structures Cooperate and Compete

How does your brain cooperate with itself? Brain cells are "connected" to other brain cells by physical structures such as axons, which are extensions sent out by neurons. Brain areas and structures can communicate via glial cells too. And certainly the bloodstream creates a common network, circulating brain chemicals known as *neurotransmitters*

(e.g., serotonin, dopamine, and acetylchoine) and hormones known as *neuromodulators* (e.g., cortisol and adrenaline). Information is also communicated through the immune system and "messenger molecules" known as *peptides*. It's fair to say that very little happens in one part of the brain without some kind of potential effect in other areas. It's just a matter of degree.

The two sides of the brain, the left and right cerebral hemispheres, are connected by bundles of nerve fibers. The *corpus callosum* (see Figure 1.6) is the largest of these connective pathways, with about 250 million nerve fibers. In healthy brains, this interhemispheric highway allows each side of the brain to exchange information freely. Patients whose corpus callosum has been severed can still function in society, but suffer an inability to integrate certain brain functions. For example, a subject who is shown an apple in his right field of vision might know what it is, but not be able to come up with the correct name for it. Switch the apple to the right field of vision, and the subject might be able name it correctly, but not be able to explain what an "apple" is.

Although each side of the brain processes things differently, some earlier assumptions about the "left" and "right" brain—that the left brain is "logical" and the right brain is "creative"—are outdated. In general, the left hemisphere tends to process information in parts, in a sequence, and using language and text representations. But none of these tendencies guarantees that the left brain will be logical. If a learner sequences words and then assembles the parts of sentences, there's no guarantee that the written material is logical. Any high school English teacher will confirm this. The use of logic is not a given; it's a learned, highly complex, contextually based, and rule-generated subskill that probably uses many brain areas. Again speaking generally, the right hemisphere tends to process information as a whole, in random order, and within a spatial context. But, like the left-brain tendencies, none of these tendencies guarantees that the right brain will be creative. Creativity can be either more right- or more left-hemisphere dominant. Logic can be either more left- or more right-hemisphere dominant.

Figure 1.6

Three Views of the Corpus Callosum

The approximately 250 million nerve fibers of the corpus callosum connect the brain's two hemispheres.

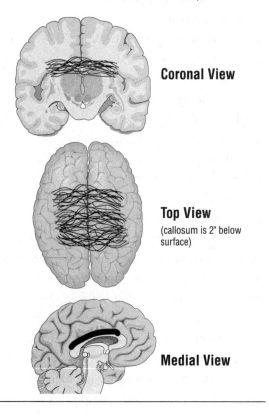

Coronal View

Top View
(callosum is 2" below surface)

Medial View

For all these reasons, it's best to avoid the labels of "left-brain" and "right-brain" thinking. Clearly, some people do *prefer* linear processing and others do *prefer* randomness. But that's all it is—a preference. And there's no scientific support for music and arts being "right-brained frills" (Jensen, 2000). Many of the greatest scientific and mathematical discoveries of the last 500 years fit the qualities of both right-hemisphere processing (random, focused on the whole, having a spatial context) and left-hemisphere processing (sequential, focused on the parts, relying on language).

Recent discoveries in cognitive neuroscience have shown many nuances in the left- and right-brain preferences. Trained musicians process music more in their left hemisphere, while novice musicians process it more in the right hemisphere. Why? The brain of a more-experienced musician is trained to recognize the elemental parts of music more than a beginner's brain. Among left-handed people, almost half use their right (not left) hemisphere for language. And here's something odd: those chess players who battle IBM's "Big Blue" computer for big bucks have more activity in their right (not left) hemisphere during their games. But beginning chess players usually have more activity in the left hemisphere.

Richard Davidson (1992) at the Laboratory for Affective Neuroscience at the University of Wisconsin has shown that the right hemisphere is activated with negative emotions and the left hemisphere is activated with positive emotions. People with more left-hemisphere activations tend to be happier and more positive than those with a right-hemisphere dominance. We also know that the left hemisphere controls movements on the right side of the body, and vice versa.

As you may have guessed, it would be difficult to have a left- or right-brained school. Although a teacher could structure an activity so that it was hemisphere-dependent, on most typical schooldays, students use both sides of the brain. Let's put aside the notion of right brain versus left brain and move on.

Competition

"Competition within the brain" sounds a little like malfunction to be corrected. Actually, the brain has a problem to solve. Because humans have so much uncommitted brain tissue at birth (proportionally more than any other species), our brains have an extraordinary opportunity to become customized by life experiences. Put another way, the human brain has a great deal of uncommitted postnatal "real estate." These undeveloped brain areas are waiting for signals from the environment to tell them whether they should "set up camp" or wait for further signals. The competition concept is simple: whatever is first, whatever activities are more frequent, and whatever actions are more coherent will "win" the competition for network wiring and signal the brain to allocate space and resources to that set of behaviors.

Sophistication: How the Brain Learns

Although there are many examples we could look to for an illustration of the brain's complexity, it's the learning process that we want to focus on. At the most general level, the brain processes for learning are deceptively simple (see Figure 1.7).

Figure 1.7

HOW THE BRAIN LEARNS NEW CONTENT

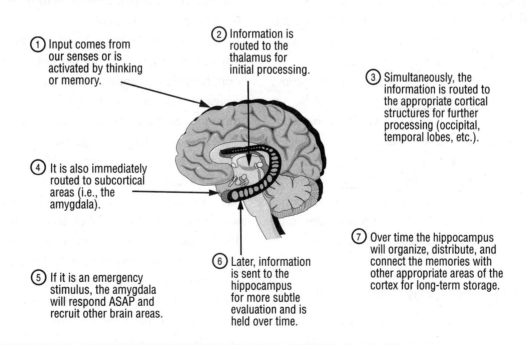

① Input comes from our senses or is activated by thinking or memory.

② Information is routed to the thalamus for initial processing.

③ Simultaneously, the information is routed to the appropriate cortical structures for further processing (occipital, temporal lobes, etc.).

④ It is also immediately routed to subcortical areas (i.e., the amygdala).

⑤ If it is an emergency stimulus, the amygdala will respond ASAP and recruit other brain areas.

⑥ Later, information is sent to the hippocampus for more subtle evaluation and is held over time.

⑦ Over time the hippocampus will organize, distribute, and connect the memories with other appropriate areas of the cortex for long-term storage.

Input to the brain arrives from the five senses or is generated internally through imagination or reflection. This input is initially processed in the thalamus, but it's also routed simultaneously to other specific areas for further processing. Visual information is routed to the occipital lobe, language to the temporal lobe, and so on. Quickly, the brain forms a rough sensory impression of the incoming data. If any of the data are threatening or suspicious, the amygdala (the "uncertainty activator") is activated. It will jump-start the rest of the sympathetic nervous system—the part of the nervous system that helps us deal with emergencies—and enable a quick response.

Typically, however, the frontal lobes hold much of the new data in short-term memory for 5 to 20 seconds. Most of the new information is filtered, dismissed, and never gets stored. It may be irrelevant, trivial, or not compelling enough. If it's worth a second consideration, new explicit learning is routed to and held in the hippocampus. There the information is processed further to determine its value. If the new learning is deemed important, it will be organized and indexed by the hippocampus and later stored in the cortex. In fact, it will be stored in the same lobe that originally processed it—visual information in the occipital lobe, language in the temporal lobe, and so on. The original processing takes place at lightning speed, but the subsequent stages and storage process can take hours, days, or even weeks. To better appreciate the brain's complexity, let's take a closer look at learning.

The Mechanics of Learning

Have you ever fallen in love? The mechanics of learning are a bit like human relationships.

Initially, there's some attraction. Early on, dating is more effortful, with one person often trying harder to "make it happen." Either there are some "sparks" or there aren't. If the sparks don't reach the threshold needed to continue, the dates are no fun and the two people go their separate ways. If the dating goes well and becomes more intense, it may become exclusive. The couple may decide to become engaged and get married. The relationship deepens. Whereas early on in a relationship little things were often misinterpreted, at some point, the relationship is close enough so that a kind word, a smile, or a touch goes a long way toward saying "I love you." We could say that the relationship has matured. Less contact goes further, whereas early in the relationship it took more contact to get the same partner reaction. So, what do attraction, lust, love, consummation, and maturity have to do with the brain and how we learn?

First, it's important to know that humans learn in many ways, including through sensitization, habituation, conditioned responses, semantic learning, imitation, and by doing. Many of these processes are not well understood. For the most part, long-term potentiation (LTP) has been accepted as the physical process of learning. The foundation for LTP was built on the work originally done by Donald Hebb in 1949. Since LTP was first described in 1973 (Bliss & Lomo, 1973), countless experiments have explored this process of memory formation. LTP means a neuron's response to another neuron has been increased. It has "learned" to respond. Each future event requires less work to activate the same memory network.

Briefly, the process goes like this. The units in the brain that are largely responsible for information processing and storage are the neurons and the glia. The brain has at least two dozen types of neurons. As mentioned on page 8 (and illustrated in Figure 1.8), neurons have a cell body, a tail-like extension called an axon, and branchlike structures called dendrites. The junction between two connected neurons is called a synapse. Neurons use both chemical and electrical signals for processing. Each brain cell acts as a tiny electrical battery. A normally functioning neuron is continuously firing, integrating, and generating information; it's a virtual hotbed of activity. The connectivity is powered by the electrical-to-chemical-to-electrical activity within each nerve cell. Information flow in the cortex always goes in two directions. Receiving neurons "talk back" to the neurons that are providing the information. This "dialogue" produces a large amount of internal feedback for error correction.

The electrical charge is generated by the difference in concentration of sodium and potassium ions across the cell membrane of each nerve cell. Neurotransmitters are chemicals stored in the ends of the neuron's axon, which nearly touch the dendrites of another cell (see Figure 1.9). Typically, the neurotransmitters are either excitatory (glutamate is the most common) or inhibitory (an example is GABA, or gamma-aminobutyric acid). Glutamate is highly excitatory—something like zoo monkeys teased by a hyperactive class of 4th grade boys. At first, the monkeys may simply ignore the visitors, but with just enough activation, all heck breaks loose. The sum total of all the neurotransmitters arriving from all the dendrites to the cell body at any moment determines whether or not that cell

will, in fact, fire. The electrical discharge that comes down the axon stimulates the release of that final "oomph" of stored glutamate into the synaptic gap—the "playing field" or "common activity area" defined by the area just outside the end of the outputting axon and just outside the surface of a receiving dendrite—and a glutamate threshold is reached. This "climax" in the synapse releases neurotransmitters such as serotonin and dopamine into the synaptic gap.

Once chemicals have been released into the synaptic gap, a chemical reaction triggers (or inhibits, depending on which chemical is involved) a new electrical reaction in the receptors of the contacted dendrite. Thus, the process is electrical to chemical and back to electrical. The process is repeated as it moves on to the next cell. But it's also important to suppress unwanted neural firings. Long-term depression (LTD) occurs when a synapse is altered so that it is *less* likely to fire and it's promoted by making the wrong connection less likely and eliminating possible "false positives."

Figure 1.8

TWO NEURONS CONNECTING

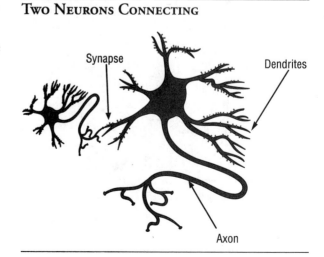

Synapse

Dendrites

Axon

This occurs when you make mistakes and then learn from them. A good example is trial-and-error learning (Siegfried, 1997). So learning is not just about being able to "throw the switch" on the right neurons. You also have to be able to shut down other neurons. Learning involves both excitatory and inhibitory processes.

When learning occurs, specific neurons connect and form a "junction box" at the synapse. When we say cells "connect" with other cells, we really mean that they are in such close proximity that the synapse is easily, almost effortlessly, "used" over and over again; the cells have changed their receptivity to messages based on previous stimulation and have "learned." In short, learning happens at a micro level through the alteration of synaptic efficacy. Excited cells will excite other nearby cells. Technically, a specific type of contact occurs

between an axon and a dendrite. A process known as synaptic adhesion helps "bind" the two together (Goda & Davis, 2003) in close proximity with protein strands. Without these strands, the axon and dendrite would drift apart.

To understand what happens beyond the micro, cell-to-cell level, consider this analogy. Individual students may have a small influence on a school, but assemblies of students (clubs, sports teams, special interest groups) can change the school's entire nature. Likewise, the brain multiplies the individual cell-to-cell learning process by thousands, even millions. These network codes are robust; damage to one neuron will not damage the entire "coded" network (Pouget, Dayan, & Zemel, 2000). The brain has what we call population codes or neural networks—entire "forests" of neurons signaling other neurons, many with massive proliferations of dendrites. An individual cell may be connected, through its synapses, to tens of thousands of other cells. At the simplest level, learning may seem microscopic, but each neuron plays its part in larger assemblies of cell networks. Inside the brain, several conditions show that learning has taken place:

Figure 1.9

THE SYNAPSE—WHERE LEARNING TAKES PLACE

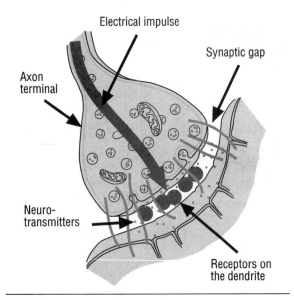

- *Modification of existing connections.* The connections are strengthened, weakened, or reprogrammed to new neurons. Location is unimportant; the dendritic connections are equally potent whether they are at the farthest end of the neuron or right next to the cell body (Magee & Cook, 2000).

- *Elimination of synapses.* Synapses are eliminated through pruning and experience. What you don't use is usually eliminated in the competitive neural world.

- *Growth of new connections.* This process, called synaptogenesis, is typically the result of new learning.

• *Retention of exuberant connections.* Although some synapses are normally eliminated, unusual conditions such as trauma or prenatal insult (e.g., poor nutrition or exposure to dangerous drugs in utero) can prevent this from happening—meaning the brain will retain those "extra" synapses.

• *Compensatory reorganization.* In cases of lesions or insults, areas of the brain may reorganize. For example, in some brains with damage to the left hemisphere, language repositions itself in the right hemisphere. In nontraumatic cases of experience-driven learning (such as playing a musical instrument over time), the brain may "remap" itself, using up abnormal areas of neural real estate.

The repeated mention of "synapses" may lead you to think they are the holy grail in learning. Although synapses are certainly key players, learning is far more complex. No causal relationship exists between the number of neurons and either learning or intelligence. Researchers also now know that learning is not simply "stored" at the synapse. If that were the case, activation of a particular synapse would *always* activate a particular memory. Other factors come into play, and the brain's enormous sophistication begins to reveal itself. Even with the learning stored properly, only the right "state activations" (meaning the right neuronal assemblies) and the appropriate chemical mix will retrieve the learning.

Whole-body "states" activate these networks. When you're in a clear-thinking, level-headed frame of mind (a good state for learning), you learn and recall more than when you're depressed, tired, or angry. This conclusion seems straightforward, doesn't it? We'll learn more about states and learning in later chapters.

Applying What We Know

So what should we do with our knowledge about the brain? Is it useless theory? Just trivia? Not for the professional educator. As long as we are in the business of learning, the brain is relevant. Many studies present enough clear and solid information to be transformed into classroom practice. In *Minds, Brains, and Learning,* Byrnes (2001) suggests that any ideas from neuroscience that we want to implement should be integrated and consistent with other models from psychology and behavioral sciences. This is a good approach. Many of the studies cited in this book are multidisciplinary.

It's also a good idea to share information with your students about how their brains learn and work. Talk about how their lives influence their brains' adaptability. Help them make connections. And acknowledge the complexity of the brain by allowing a wider range of what we call learning. To paraphrase Einstein, today's problems cannot be solved with yesterday's thinking. Allowing learners to think outside the box is a good occasional strategy. Talk to interested parents about the brain too.

The following chapters present many solutions to everyday problems in teaching and learning. But be prepared: there also will be many questions.

Preparing the Brain for School

Most educators would love to have all their students arrive at school with attentive, cooperative, trauma-free, drug-free, healthy brains. These young learners would be brimming with positive life experiences and a love of learning. But such an ideal state rarely happens by accident. To improve the odds, parents, teachers, and students need to know what to expect and what to do. This chapter considers how each individual can better manage various influences on the brain. It's organized around four stages of brain development:

- Conception to birth.
- Birth to age 2.
- Ages 2 to 5.
- Age 5 through the teen years.

Conception to Birth: Parenting with the Unborn in Mind

It's no exaggeration to say that the first opportunity to get children ready for school is in the womb. We know that drugs, smoking, nutrition, and stress all affect the embryo

KEY CONCEPTS

▶ **What to do to get a child's brain ready for school**

▶ **Sensitive periods in brain development**

▶ **Developing social and emotional skills**

▶ **The importance of nutrition**

▶ **The dynamic teenage brain**

(Van Dyke & Fox, 1990). The most important things a pregnant woman can do for her developing fetus are to eat well, to avoid drugs and smoking, and to minimize stress. Each developing fetus is highly sensitive to stress and poor nutrition (Georgieff & Rao, 2001). The causes of fetal sensitivity are threefold: a small, enclosed environment; high, unbuffered exposure to toxins; and rapid proliferation of new cells.

Most brain cells are produced between the fourth and seventh month of gestation. (See Figure 2.1 for a snapshot of the rate of prenatal brain development.) Those fast-developing brain cells (neurons) first travel up through the neural tube, then migrate, and eventually form a vast network, connecting to other cells. The developing brain grows so fast that counting brain cells is hopeless—like counting snowflakes in a blizzard or drops of water in a hurricane. At its peak, the embryo is generating 250,000 brain cells a minute, or 15 million cells per hour.

By birth, a baby's brain has more than a trillion connections (and has reached 60 percent of the peak number of synapses that will develop over a lifetime. If you knew your child's brain was being shaped at that rate, wouldn't you be cautious about what you did to it? Educators must help parents understand prenatal brain development. These future children are also future students.

Birth to Age 2: Early "Critical" Versus "Sensitive" Periods

This stage of development has had a good deal of coverage in the popular press as a critical, do-or-die "biological window of opportunity" for children's brain development, leading some parents to worry excessively about whether or not they are doing the right things. It doesn't help that some of the well-publicized information is misleading and that there are critics who are vehemently *opposed* to the notion that "development windows" even exist (Bailey et al., 2001). The primary argument against critical development periods goes something like this: Because we cannot say definitively that birth to age 2 is the *only* time the brain's able to learn certain things, we should back off on the urgency. Some of these critics suggest that we use the phrase "sensitive periods" instead. I like that alternative, and I suggest using it to describe most (but not all) early developmental periods.

Although I agree that many things, such as certain motor skills or a second language, *can* be learned later in life, I believe that starting earlier is often better. Why? Because of two reasons: the "scaffold effect" and the "mañana effect." The scaffold effect reasons that although your child *could* learn many motor skills at age 15, she needs them earlier because they are the foundation for other important early skills, such as reading, writing, and reasoning. From cross-crawling (using opposite arms and legs to move forward) to balancing, there's a cascade effect—either up or down—in the brain's development, depending on the later cognitive demands for that "neural scaffold." The other reason is that almost anything that we can postpone ("let's do it mañana") *will be* postponed. Yes, your child is capable of learning many motor skills, a second language, and for that matter, all of the arts, at age 20, but *will* she? These skills may not have definite, biological critical periods, but they do have preferred periods, meaning there's no better time to start developing them. In addition, children in their earliest years are a captive audience. Even though a biological window of opportunity may not slam shut after age 2, it makes sense to take advantage of the social, economic, and practical windows.

All of that said, there *are* certain essentials in the child's developing brain that cannot wait a few years. The four aspects of development for which the labels "window of opportunity" and "critical periods" *are* legitimate are emotions, sensory motor development, auditory development, and vision.

Figure 2.1

THE RAPID PACE OF PRENATAL BRAIN DEVELOPMENT

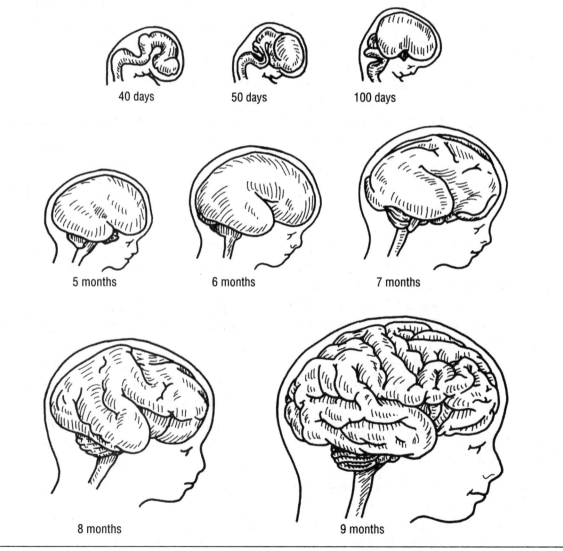

40 days   50 days   100 days

5 months   6 months   7 months

8 months   9 months

Emotions

Healthy emotional attachment during a child's first 24 months helps develop the social and emotional skills fundamental for life (Siegel, 1999). Because this is the time frame during which a child learns how to express emotions in a social world, it is important for the primary caregiver to set a good example in demonstrating proper emotional responses. These demonstrations help the child understand when it's appropriate to be disappointed, pleased, anxious, sad, fearful, proud, ashamed, delighted, apologetic, and so on. The early attachment behaviors shown by the mother (or other primary caregiver) begin shaping the child's emotional systems early on (Polan & Hofer, 1999). Even when children have quality relationships with nurturing parents in adolescence, if they had poor attachments from birth to age 2, their relationships suffer (Hodges & Tizard, 1989). Of course, attachment occurs both to supportive caregivers and abusive caregivers. According to one theory, it may be better to have a bad caregiver than no caregiver or too many caregivers (Helfer, Kempe, & Krugman, 1997).

Research tells us that early childhood exposure to stress, neglect, abuse, or violence can cause the brain to reorganize itself, increasing receptor sites for alertness and stress chemicals (McEwen & Schmeck, 1994). Troubled early relationships cause a child's brain to use glucose to deal with stress rather than to support cognitive functions. Scary, abusive, or neglectful circumstances may lead to errant synaptic pruning in the frontal lobes and impaired emotional development that can reduce the child's future ability to regulate emotions (Perry, 1997).

If children aren't exposed to proper emotional models during their early childhood years, can they develop emotional skills later in life? This issue is well researched, and the answer is ambiguous, but it leans toward no (Gunnar, 2001). Some studies suggest that the brain could be wired emotionally later on but that it's far from a sure thing, owing to additional resources required—things like parental training, social services, and school programs. In addition, it's far easier to develop emotional skills with a 2-year-old than with an independent-thinking teenager. Parents must take the time to engage in healthy emotional give-and-take if they want an emotionally and socially healthy child (Greenspan, 1997).

Sensory Motor Development

Because sensory experiences (seeing and hearing, for example) and motor experiences (movement) are so closely intertwined in the brain, scientists commonly use the term "sensory motor systems" to describe how the brain processes and controls these activities. The sensory motor systems (especially visual, motor, and auditory systems) develop through exploration during the first two years of life. Consider, though, that many infants today are in a child care center within three months after birth, and only one child care facility in seven "provides a level of child care that promotes healthy development and learning" (Galinsky, Howes, Kontos, & Shinn, 1994, p. 2).

The vestibular system is the system in the inner ear that controls the sense of movement and balance; it strongly influences the other sensory systems. Many scientists link the lack of vestibular stimulation with dozens of learning problems, including problems with reading, writing, and math. Vestibular stimulation occurs through activities involving movement—even such simple movements as rocking.

Are today's children getting enough sensory motor stimulation? Probably not. Today's infant is placed before a TV, seated in a walker, or strapped in a car seat for hundreds of precious motor development hours. In 1960, the average 2-year-old had spent, since birth, an estimated 200 hours in a car. In comparison, today's 2-year-old has spent an estimated 500 hours in a car seat! Although car seats are vital for infant safety, few parents ever compensate for the hours their child spends confined by providing additional sense-stimulating activities later on.

Lyelle Palmer, professor of special education at Winona State University in Minnesota, has clearly shown the positive effects of such activities. His innovative pre-K and K–2 programs (Smart Start) stimulate children's sensory motor systems to develop higher levels of academic success. For more than 20 years, he has shown that early motor stimulation leads to better attention, listening skills, reading scores, and writing skills (Palmer, 2003).

Auditory Development

The auditory cortex undergoes dramatic growth and stabilization from the beginning of the last trimester of gestation through the first year after birth. Infants can discriminate most sounds in their normal environment by 6 months (Aslin & Hunt, 2001). Several developmental thresholds occur between birth and 6 months and again between 6 months and 24 months. These

milestones suggest how the infant's auditory system matures toward adult levels in range of sounds (decibels) heard, ability to discriminate among sounds in the presence of a "masking" noise, and ability to distinguish sounds from one another. When there are problems with the developing auditory system, children often have academic difficulties because they struggle with concentration. They may have difficulty hearing the prefixes or suffixes when a speaker is talking quickly. These auditory skills are essential when it comes to understanding material that is being read aloud, developing phonemic awareness, and learning to read.

There is no biological mandate for language in the left brain, but there are "soft biases" in information processing that give preference to the left hemisphere in the development of language skills. Between birth and age 5, experience develops the language capacities in the brain, but the biggest burst in vocabulary occurs between 19 and 31 months. The development of language is primarily stimulated by the following:

• *Hearing it.* The more words a child hears, the better. The highly fluctuating tonality of "parentese" is helpful from birth to 12 months.

• *Speaking it.* The more a child speaks, the better.

• *Hearing parents speak normally.* Normal "grown up" talk is beneficial for babies at any time after 6 months.

Vision

Neurobiologists tell us that vision develops largely during the first year, with a major advancement taking place sometime after the fourth month. The density of synapses in the visual system reaches a peak at 10 months (Wilson, 1993), after which the brain begins to prune unneeded connections rapidly. With more than 15 distinct visual areas in the brain (including areas related to the perception of color, movement, hue, and depth), the developing infant needs a variety of stimulating inputs. Babies should get plenty of practice handling objects and learning about their shapes, weights, and movements.

A study by Fine and colleagues (2003) provides a striking illustration of how early stimulation affects visual development. A man who had been blinded at age 3 had his sight restored at age 43. After two years, he found that he still couldn't recognize his wife by sight, only by the sound of her voice. In addition, most of the world remained a confusing blizzard of shapes.

Although the specifics of the visual system are highly complex (see Figure 2.2 for a simplified depiction), psychologist Daphne Maurer says, "Whatever the underlying mechanisms, it is clear that experience and competitive interactions play a prominent role in the development of spatial vision" (Maurer & Lewis, 2001, p. 237). The experience and interactions should not come from television, which often is used as a babysitter (Tonge, 1990). Television is two-dimensional, and the developing brain needs visual depth, says V. S. Ramachandran, a neuroscientist and vision specialist at the University of California–San Diego. Television images appear rapidly, allowing the eyes no time to relax. In addition, people on TV are often talking about abstractions that are nonexistent in the child's environment. The stress caused by trying to process the images can aggravate learning difficulties.

Nutrition

Although good nutrition is advisable at any time in life, it is especially important during the early years of brain development (Georgieff & Rao, 2001), when specific nutrients help ensure stable, successful growth. Food must supply the nutrients necessary for learning, which include proteins, unsaturated fats, complex carbohydrates, and sugars. The brain also needs a wide range of trace elements such as boron, iron, selenium, vanadium, and potassium.

Prior to the 1990s, many of the studies on the role of improved nutrition in cognition were

Figure 2.2

VISUAL PATHWAYS

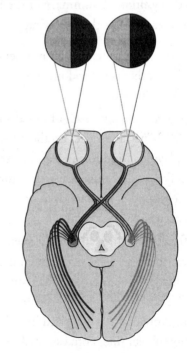

Visual pathways cross sides of the brain and go front to back to front. What we see is processed in multiple areas of the brain.

hopelessly flawed. But in the past decade or two, compelling longitudinal studies (with variables well separated) have shown the clear effect of better nutrition. In fact, the long-term impact on cognition of nutritional supplements (given to children from birth to age 7) is significant. Not only did children who received supplements score higher in quantitative thought and expression, reading, and vocabulary 10 years later, but also, when researchers followed up with these children between the ages of 11 and 26, they had improved socioeconomic status compared to the control group (Pollitt & Gorman, 1994; Pollitt, Gorman, Engle, Rivera, & Martorelli, 1995; Pollitt, Watkins, & Husaini, 1997). Research strongly indicates that improved nutrition leads to improved cognition. A summary of the best-designed studies suggests the following:

• Nutrition should begin with mother's milk. As long as the mother gets good nutrition, it's the best source of early food.

• Hypoglycemia (low levels of blood sugar) has a profoundly negative effect on the hippocampus, which plays a critical role in learning and memory. Children need nutrition-rich complex carbohydrates found in such foods as cereal, pasta, and rice to prevent hypoglycemia.

• Sufficient protein is absolutely essential in the early years because, aside from water, the growing body is made of more protein than any other substance. The body needs it for growth and mental function. Proteins are synthesized into dopamine and norepinephrine, both essential for quick reactions, thinking, and working memory.

• Minerals and trace elements, including iron, zinc, iodine, and selenium, are essential to ensure proper mood regulation, reduce fatigue, and improve concentration.

• Vitamins A, B, C, and E are essential for brain maintenance, protective effects, vision strength, and memory.

• Essential fatty acids (EFAs), especially omega 3 and 6, are needed, too. They play an integral role in cell membrane function and the development of the brain and eyes.

Taken as a whole, the data suggest that we need much better parent education and more nutritional resources available for the pre-K child. Making low-cost or free nutritional supplements available for the child's developing brain may be a wise long-term government investment. The next section has more information about nutrition and "brain-friendly" foods.

Ages 2 to 5: Getting the Brain Ready for School

Getting children ready for school is not an easy or "automatic" task. It requires thoughtful effort and some tough choices on the parent's part. And it involves getting children ready on all three fronts: academics, emotional and social skills, and nutrition and health.

Prepping for Academics

We consider many capacities to be built into our brains. For example, we flinch when a fast-moving object approaches us unexpectedly. But what about the more academic capacities? Are certain aspects of math, science, or language built in? Although some researchers, such as Steven

Pinker (1994), view language as an instinct, others disagree. Many of today's researchers support an emergent view that suggests that the developing brain has some "cheap tricks" that allow it to learn so fast that infants can appear to know instinctually things that they actually just learned. The key role of neural networks that "learn to learn" may have more support from a biological point of view (Elman et al., 1996) than the "built-in," or nature, viewpoint. But these fast-learning networks require, without exception, a rich variety of coherent life experiences.

As in the birth-to-2 stage, one of the first rules for parents of 2- to 5-year-olds is to limit television; it's a poor replacement for time spent on sensory motor development, exploratory play, and development of key relationships. Instead of a diet of TV, video games, and DVDs, parents should provide children this age with plenty of free, creative, exploratory playtime. (The benefit of this unstructured, exploratory time is also an argument against "overscheduling" children with an unrelenting stream of organized activities.)

We've all heard that one of the best ways to help children become readers is to read to them often during the preschool years. That advice is as good as ever. Surprisingly, no absolute timetable dictates when children are developmentally ready to read. Generally boys will be ready later than girls. Differences of one to three years are normal, meaning that some children will be ready to read at age 4 and other children, just as normal, will not be ready to read until age 7 or later. Is whole language or direct phonics instruction better for the developing brain? Research suggests that each approach has value, and either may be more effective for the individual child. A combination is best.

Here's a list of some of the most important things parents should do to better prepare preschoolers for the academic requirements of school:

- Read to them.
- Give them time to discover and learn on their own.
- Teach them rhyming games and the alphabet.
- Avoid all toys with batteries until age 4; choose "high-touch" toys instead.
- Provide simple toys that encourage imagination.
- Talk to them and ask them questions.

Prepping for Emotional and Social Skills

To help preschoolers develop emotional and social skills, parents should replace television time with interactions with real people. Adding some problem-solving activities is also helpful. So is speaking to babies and young children about everyday activities and explaining the processes involved: the steps undertaken to fix something, do laundry, or go shopping. When I am in the supermarket, I too often see parents with children spending this precious interactive time admonishing them about their behavior and making dire threats about the consequences of their next wrong move. Instead of focusing on the negatives, it's better to find ways to reinforce what's good. Strengthen self-concept through the positives.

During this highly sensitive time, it's critical for parents to continue to influence their children's emotional development in a positive way. Much research has examined the mechanisms of and influences on chronic aggression. Researchers generally agree that evidence of aggressive tendencies can be detected in the first four years of life (Huesmann, Moise-Titus, Podolski, & Eron, 2003). In fact, in one study, 80 percent of parents plagued by aggressive teens actually noticed the onset of aggressive behavior—including the early stages of oppositional personality disorders and hyperactivity— by the time the child was 17 months old (Tremblay et al., 2002). These findings imply either strong genetic factors or the existence of a sensitive period for learning to inhibit physical aggression, generally between birth and age 4. The brain's cognitive–emotional map is being drawn early on, and parents can either be the cartographers or the victims. One simple thing parents can do is to reduce violent visual images. Compelling evidence links violent video games with aggressiveness in children (Anderson & Bushman, 2001).

Here's a list of suggestions for helping preschoolers develop good social and emotional skills:

- Provide opportunities for social games and activities.
- Role-model emotional stability and kindness.
- Teach children how to behave with their peers.
- Help children learn how to be comfortable away from parents.

Nutrition and Health

Fast-paced lifestyles leave many us with little time to prepare nutritious home-cooked meals. In a fast-food society, it should come as no shock to us that preschool children consume soft drinks regularly. A study of children under age 2 showed that 11 percent eat french fries daily, and 24 percent eat hot dogs daily (Fox, Pac, Devaney, & Jankowski, 2004).

Are there specific foods that are particularly good for the brain? Yes, there are many—including leafy green vegetables, salmon, nuts, lean meats, and fresh fruits—and children rarely get enough of them. Recently researchers found that vitamin A, found in sweet potatoes and other orange vegetables, supports learning and memory (Misner et al., 2001). To work fast, brain cells need a fatty coating called myelin. Deficiencies in protein, iron, and selenium impair myelination of axons, which reduces mental efficiency (Georgieff & Rao, 2001). Although food sources are the best way to get the vitamins and minerals that support optimal brain function and development, supplements can help to make up for a diet that is lacking.

We may not think of water as a nutrient, but from the brain's perspective, it is. Hydration is important to the brain's normal development and functioning (Maughan, 2003). Water should be available for drinking throughout the day, and the recommended amount is 8 to 12 glasses per day.

Nutrition is an area where we can easily make a positive difference. Most of the children in our schools are not malnourished; they are improperly nourished. Parents need to take nutrition more seriously. Among the things they can do is to stop giving kids total control over their food choices. Instead, let children choose from among desirable alternatives ("Do you want beef, tofu, or grilled chicken?"). Offer nutritious snacks (see Figure 2.3) or no snacks. Push water instead of soft drinks and reduce soft drink consumption each week until soft drinks become a treat, not a staple. These early habits can have a positive lasting effect throughout children's schooling. The foods we serve are not just feeding a child's daily energy requirements, they are shaping the child's brain.

Age 5 Through the Teen Years: The School-Age Brain

By age 5, the brain has learned a language, has developed sensory motor skills, and is concerned with active exploration. Although the rapid changes of the first five years of life have slowed, the brain is continuing to grow, and over the next five years it will reach 90 percent of its adult weight. During this time, as the child engages in more active exploration of the world, neurons are developing massive and detailed dendritic branching, and synaptic density reaches a lifetime peak (Huttenlocher, 1994; Huttenlocher & Dabholkar, 1997). At the same time, the child's brain is pruning itself like there's no tomorrow. Weak, rarely active synapses are eliminated. Everything the child *doesn't* do sends a message to the brain, "You may not need these connections; it's okay to pull back on resources in this area. Something else more important is going on elsewhere."

It's perhaps clearest to talk about the school-age brain in two substages: the elementary and middle school years, and the teenage years.

The Elementary and Middle School Years

The brain of a child between the ages of 5 and 12 is a brain of wonder, ready to take on new challenges, including reading, writing, arithmetic, and the world of reason.

Kurt Fischer at the Harvard Graduate School of Education says that children experience two growth spurts during this time. The first occurs around age 6 or 7 and the other around age 11 or 12. Both, he says, appear to support emerging cognitive capacities, including the ability to reason, to understand cause and effect, and to grasp abstractions—concepts like honesty, liberty, or hope (Fischer & Bidwell, 1991). In addition, between the ages of 5 and 10, children are developing a wider sense of what the world offers. Novelty abounds, and things like exposure to music, new classmates, different options in clothing, an active classroom at school, and opportunities to bicycle and explore the neighborhood are all building a young brain. Typically, it's in these years that children first become interested in computers, hobbies, sports, and yes, sexuality. They develop more of their social sense and more interest in friendships, though the criteria for friends ("She likes my clothes" or "He's got really good video games") can seem a bit whimsical to parents.

Elementary and early middle school–age children also have definitive ideas about what they like to eat. They often consume nonnutritious foods they've chosen from vending machines, school lunch counters, and enticing supermarket displays.

Figure 2.3

NUTRITIOUS SNACKS

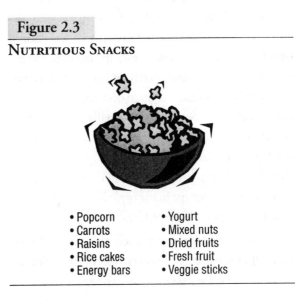

- Popcorn
- Carrots
- Raisins
- Rice cakes
- Energy bars
- Yogurt
- Mixed nuts
- Dried fruits
- Fresh fruit
- Veggie sticks

But does all this junk food really matter in the learning process? Yes. Nutritional deficits have been known to decrease test scores, and nutritional supplementation has improved them (Lozoff et al., 1987). One study (Halterman, 2001) has shown that school-age children with an iron deficiency (an estimated 1 in 12 children) were twice as likely to score below average in math compared with children with normal iron levels. Another (Louwman et al., 2000) found that students with diets low in vitamin B-12 have reduced learning ability. In addition, both too much dietary fat (Greenwood & Winocur, 2001) and unbalanced diets in general (Ramakrishna, 1999) can impair cognition.

The Teenage Years

The everyday experience of adults who either live or work with teens is often that of bewilderment and exasperation. Teens often make bad choices and then lie to cover them up. In some cases, the average 9-year-old can make a better decision than an adolescent can. The traditional explanation has been "it's hormones." But recent neuroscience is shedding new light on teen behaviors, and the bottom line is that hormones are only partly to blame. The rapid and massive structural change occurring in the brain during the teen years is actually the biggest reason for often-bizarre teen behavior. Teens may need time to "catch up" to what's happening in their brain. Sleep is when this catch-up takes place, and when the teenage brain organizes and stores new learning (Wolfson & Carskadon, 1998).

On a gross anatomical level, most areas of the brain are under major construction during adolescence. In fact, the changes are similar to those

happening in an infant's brain. The parietal lobes undergo major changes, with areas doubling or tripling in size. The frontal lobes, a big chunk of our "gray matter" and the area of the brain responsible for thoughtful, reflective reasoning capabilities, are the last areas of the brain to mature (see Figure 2.4). Brain cells first thicken between ages 11 and 13 and then thin out by 7 to 10 percent between the ages of 13 and 20. In some cases, the process may extend until around age 30, suggesting that the teen brain is especially immature.

A study that used MRIs to examine the developing brain (Durston et al., 2001) suggests the thickening of adolescent brain cells is due to massive changes in synaptic reorganization, meaning many more connections are being formed. The cells involved in this reorganization become highly receptive to new information. But although this nearly exploding brain has more choices, it is often paralyzed by inefficiency. Just like the infant brain, the adolescent brain relies on the pruning of synapses for more efficient decision making. Elizabeth Sowell's work at UCLA suggests that the frontal lobes of girls mature faster than those of males during puberty (Sowell, Thompson, Holmes, Jernigan, & Toga, 1999). Although most brains become physically mature between the ages of 18 and 30, it takes boys until about age 24 to catch up to girls' brain development. These processes suggest that the "under construction" brain areas may be highly unstable, volatile, and unpredictable.

On the chemical level, the teen brain is influenced by volatile levels of the feel-good neurotransmitter dopamine. Some researchers argue that dopamine levels are too low during adolescence, and others argue that dopamine levels are actually very high during this time frame—even higher than the levels found in adults. In either case, the teen brain *is* different. It is more sensitive to the pleasurable effects of nicotine and alcohol and less sensitive to the adverse effects, says Frances Leslie of the University of California–Irvine. Leslie and colleagues (2004) note that risk taking, drugs, and sexual activity activate dopamine levels. Students become predisposed to these novelty-seeking behaviors. They often choose activities with smaller, more immediate rewards rather than larger, more delayed rewards. It may be nature's way of encouraging mate selection during our most energetic and fertile time.

Other chemicals are also fluctuating wildly during the teen years. The hormone melatonin is associated with regulating the sleep schedule, and levels are typically too low during the teen years. Most teens want to stay up later and get up later. As a result, early school-start times are associated with significant sleep deprivation and daytime sleepiness (Carskadon, Wolfson, Acebo, Tzischinsky, & Seifer, 1998). Psychosocial influences, such as peer groups, and changes in

Figure 2.4

The Orbitofrontal Cortex

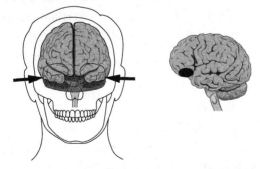

In the orbitofrontal cortex, thinking and emotions are integrated with sensations. This area matures between the ages of 16 and 30—much later than other areas.

bioregulatory systems (melatonin levels) controlling sleep may limit teenagers' capacities to make adequate adjustments to an early school schedule. The result is classrooms full of drowsy teens and academic underperformance (Maquet, 2001).

These various findings from recent brain research tell us that teenagers are probably undergoing even more changes than we once thought. For parents and teachers, they suggest a slew of practical implications regarding mood, attention, sleep, learning, and memory:

- *Be succinct.* Teens' frontal lobes may not be good at storing many ideas at a time. When giving directions, give just one at a time. Be straightforward, not sarcastic, circuitous, or patronizing.

- *Use modeling.* Early teens need concrete and realistic models in the classroom. Use hands-on, working models, and let students debrief and think through explanations in guided discussions.

- *Be a coach.* The increased synaptic exuberance (too many unpruned connections) of the teenage brain may impair decision making. Repeat decisions and offer options to be brainstormed with coaching. Expect that most teens will be unable to recognize the universe of options available. As a result, they lie more—they can't see options, so they assume the lie will help them get out of a bind. Help guide them through the tougher decisions with discussion, not lecture.

- *Be understanding rather than judgmental.* Socially, teens are less able to accurately distinguish between the emotions conveyed by facial expressions (Killgore, Oki, & Yurgelun-Todd, 2001). Their ability to recognize the emotions of others is weaker by 20 percent up until age 18 (McGivern, Andersen, Byrd, Mutter, & Reilly, 2002). In fact, it's weaker at ages 11 and 12 than at age 10! Not surprisingly, adolescents are also less than adept at identifying their own emotions. But don't tell them how they feel. Simply identify what behaviors you see and let them reach their own conclusions.

• *Be tactful.* Until ages 16 to 18, students have difficulty grasping nuance. They don't understand certain implications or jokes with social inferences, and they often can't predict others' behaviors well. They will not want to look ignorant (when they don't get an inference, for example), but they will need an explanation.

• *Cut them some slack.* Although teens need to feel the consequences of their mistakes, punishment should be approached carefully. Sometimes their brain just can't help them avoid doing seemingly stupid things.

• *Sometimes, just let them sleep.* As a rule, adolescents need more sleep—seven to nine hours a night. During sleep the brain is massively reorganizing, pruning synapses and organizing newly stored experiences.

• *Be clear about the dangers of substance abuse.* The young brain is highly receptive to the effects of drugs at this age, underlining the need to be clear and stern about avoiding both the use of illegal substances and the misuse of over-the-counter drugs. The greatest risk for alcohol and tobacco addiction occurs between the ages of 12 and 19.

Summary

We know that extreme experiences during the first year of life can significantly change the way a child turns out (Gunnar, 2000). But generally, recent brain research does not overturn any long-held beliefs about child-rearing practices. The recipe remains the same: lots of love, talking, bonding, healthy stimulation, exploratory games, and good nutrition. It may seem as if educators can't do much to influence brain development; after all, it's parents who get children ready to learn. But this issue is so important that educators must do something. We can't afford *not* to take action.

We ought to engage both school and community resources to educate parents on how to get their children ready for school. Many parents simply don't have access to critical information, or they think they already know it. Create alliances with local hospitals, the chamber of commerce, or local businesses to get the word out. Refer them to trusted Web sites, such as www.ascd.org. Prepare flyers and provide free sessions for parents on the benefits of getting their children ready to learn. Talk to parents about motor development, crawling, and how movement affects reading and writing skills. Provide them with information about good nutrition and how it relates to healthy brain development. Encourage them to talk more, play music, and solve more problems with their children. Share with parents the negative impact of television and suggest some easy-to-use alternatives.

By working with parents and others, educators can help ensure that students come to school ready to learn. With healthy brains as the outcome of such an effort, *everyone* benefits.

Rules We Learn By

For years, educators assumed that if students paid attention, took notes, and did their homework, eventually they would learn. Although there's some truth to that assumption, at least for most learners, we now know that learning is governed by a more complex set of variables, some of which are the result of nature and others, the result of nurture. The "nature" influence is actually quite significant: genetics accounts for *almost half* of all student learning and intelligence (Bacanu, Devlin, & Roeder, 2000; Bouchard, 1988). But that leaves a huge chunk up to nurture (you and me). Yes, educators *can* influence learning a great deal. That premise helps form the theme for this chapter: *You have much, much more to do with how your students turn out than you may have thought.*

Before we find out what the brain needs in order to learn successfully, let's define what *learning* really is. Learning is commonly divided into two broad categories: explicit learning and implicit learning. Explicit learning consists of what we commonly read, write, and talk about. It is conveyed via such means as textbooks, lectures, pictures, and videos. Implicit learning consists of things we learn through life experience, habit, games, experiential learning, and other "hands-on" activities. Surprisingly, most explicit learning revolves around task prediction (Thornton, 2000). When we say students have "learned" something, we might say that they can

• Identify or predict the relevant associations among variables in the learning situation.

• Predict and express accurately the appropriate concepts or actions.

• Store, retrieve, and apply that prediction in context next time.

If the learner can't do all three of these things, we might say the material has either been learned partially or not at all. Better learners can accurately and quickly identify relevant properties in the material to be learned (usually through the discovery of cognitive patterns or procedural sequences), then can predict and master favorable outcomes repeatedly. At the micro level, inside the brain, simple properties manifest themselves as connections at the synapses between neurons. The biological evidence of this behavior is what we call memory.

Complex learning typically involves multiple neural networks, consisting of hundreds of thousands, or even millions, of neurons. The result is still the same: smarter learners are better predictors, even with the complex variables. This process goes by many names: higher-order thinking skills, intelligence, street smarts, or school savvy. If you understand how to enhance this process, you can dramatically increase student learning and, hence, student achievement.

Many things matter in the learning process; some of them are external (such as support from peers, temperature of the room, relationship with

the teacher), and others are more internal. This chapter focuses on seven critical factors in the learning process that are more a function of the brain's design than what the environment provides. Each has been shown to dramatically influence learning. The factors are

• *Engagement* (goal-oriented attention and action).
• *Repetition* (priming, reviewing, and revising).
• *Input quantity* (capacity, flow, chunk size).
• *Coherence* (models, relevance, prior knowledge).
• *Timing* (time of day, interval learning).
• *Error correction* (mistakes, feedback, support).
• *Emotional states* (safety, state of dependency).

Engagement

The first thing that's important to know about engagement is that it is *not* a requirement for all learning. Most of what we learn—probably more than 90 percent of it—is the result of unconscious acquisition (Gazzaniga, 2001), and we can learn even complex patterns unconsciously (Nissen & Bullemer, 1987). Even when we go for a walk, our brain "learns" a great deal. But what we're talking about here is not an in-depth type of learning; it's what is known as *priming*. There's value in priming, as you'll see later in this chapter. For typical, word-based classroom learning, however, more focused and engaged attention is better than less of it. That's no news flash to most teachers. Yet many of us still struggle to get and sustain student attention. Why?

To the student's brain, biologically relevant school stimuli include opportunities to make friends (or find mates), quench thirst or hunger, notice a change in the weather, or interact with classroom visitors. All the while, the student's brain is concerned with avoiding the dangers of embarrassment, failure, or harm. These last three are actually what typical students care about the most! Yet we ask them to orient their attention on the curriculum topic at hand and to maintain that attention until instructed otherwise, even if this means continuing to listen, read, or work on a single task for up to an hour. They're supposed to do this day in and day out in the midst of a gossip-ridden, physically active, emotionally sensitive, and highly social environment. It's challenging, to say the least!

The expression "pay attention" is appropriate. Attention is a "payment" of the brain's precious resources. It requires that we *orient, engage, and maintain* each appropriate neural network. In addition, we must *exclude or suppress* external and internal distracters. Maintaining attention requires highly disciplined internal states and just the right chemical balance (Wang, Zhong, Gu, & Yan, 2003). In short, paying attention is not easy to do consciously. The areas of the brain dedicated to attention are highly complex and somewhat variable (see Figure 3.1). Neuroimaging methods have shown increased neuronal firing in the prefrontal and posterior parietal lobes and in the thalamus and anterior cingulate when someone is working hard to pay attention (LaBerge, 1995).

From an observer's perspective, engagement is a simple, easily understood concept. It means that, as learners, we "bring more to the table." We focus our sight, pitch our ears, and physically attend to the process at hand. All teachers know that engaged students are usually happier than disconnected ones who have isolated tasks to do, and

research confirms that engagement activates more of the pleasure structures in the brain than do tasks of simple memorization (Poldrack et al., 2001). More attention to the learning also usually means better results. In fact, experiments with monkeys showed that only when they paid close attention did their brains make changes corresponding to the learning at hand (Merzenich, Byl, Wang, & Jenkins, 1996). So there's clear value to paying attention—but we all have our limits.

Paying attention requires that the visual and auditory systems lock into the work. Neuroscientist Michael Kilgard, in his studies on auditory

Figure 3.1

BRAIN AREAS INVOLVED IN ATTENTION

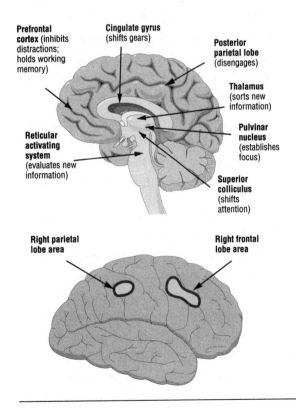

Prefrontal cortex (inhibits distractions; holds working memory)

Cingulate gyrus (shifts gears)

Posterior parietal lobe (disengages)

Thalamus (sorts new information)

Pulvinar nucleus (establishes focus)

Reticular activating system (evaluates new information)

Superior colliculus (shifts attention)

Right parietal lobe area

Right frontal lobe area

processing, suggests characteristics of input that influence the human brain's reorganization. Specifically, he says they are engagement and goal-oriented procedures (Kilgard & Merzenich, 1998). You can reasonably expect focused attention when the following conditions are met:

• *Students choose relevant, meaningful learning.* This approach supports what Csikszentmihalyi (1991) calls the "flow" state, in which learners become engrossed in learning without regard for time. Yet most schools do not have enough time to provide surface coverage of their entire curriculum, much less the time to allow students to get into the flow state necessary for content mastery (Marzano, 2003).

• *Students can hear the teacher well, above all the other random classroom noises.* Yet 80 percent of classrooms have substandard acoustics (Feth, 1999).

• *Students get enough sleep and avoid drugs or alcohol.* Yet more than 50 percent of students over age 13 are sleep deprived (Dexter, Bijwadia, Schilling, & Applebaugh, 2003).

• *Students do not have attention deficit or central auditory processing disorders.* Yet between 5 and 17 percent of students may have these complications (Cacace & McFarland, 1998; Castellanos & Tannock, 2002).

Add to this mix of attentional challenges the physical environment of the typical classroom—substandard lighting, poorly regulated temperatures, constant walk-in distractions, unergonomic "party rental" chair designs—and you're left with "Mission Impossible." Under these conditions, classroom attention is likely a statistical improbability.

There are a number of brain-related factors that can impede attention significantly; among the most significant are glucose levels, the threat response, and the process of meaning making. Let's take a closer look at each.

Glucose levels. Attention, learning, and memory tasks are an enormous drain on the glucose in the brain. The old dogma was that the brain would maintain glucose levels at almost all costs. New research shows glucose drops precariously and specifically based on the task we are doing (McNay, McCarty, & Gold, 2001). Students who show up in class with low blood sugar are likely to be tired, listless, and inattentive. In addition, an increasing number of students have early-onset diabetes—an issue because difficulty regulating glucose impairs the speed of cognitive and motor performance (Cox, Gonder-Frederick, Schroeder, Cryer, & Clarke, 1993). More and more schools are realizing that there's an advantage to making sure students have the proper fuel for thought. In a positive trend, they are wisely revising policies to allow students to bring snacks or gum to class, along with water for hydration.

The threat response. Students pay attention to content only when it is "safe" to do so. Many do not feel safe enough to ignore teasing classmates and bullies. To student brains, that outside influence is a potential predator, like a saber-toothed tiger. Some teachers call on an unprepared learner just to embarrass the student. In this risky environment, some learners cannot focus on content processing. Many schools ignore student safety issues, yet act surprised that students can't seem to focus in class.

The process of meaning making. Either you can have your learners' attention *or* they can be making meaning, but never both at the same time. Meaning is generated internally, and it takes time. External input (more content) conflicts with the processing of prior content and thoughtful reflection. Students rarely get training in how to be calm, thoughtful, or reflective, and they are given little time to practice these skills in class.

Practical Suggestions

Educators can take many approaches to solving these tricky issues. One is to constantly demand attention, but students habituate quickly to that. Changing the physical environment can also better support classroom attention. Some teachers have improved the situation simply by rearranging chairs—into a semicircle, for example. If you occasionally struggle with attentional issues, here are some other options.

Brevity. Cut the length of focused attention time expected or required. Remember that the human brain is poor at nonstop attention. It needs time for processing and rest after learning. Use the guidelines in Figure 3.2 to determine the appropriate amount of time to spend on direct instruction.

Compelling, relevant tasks. Video games force students to pay close attention or lose status (or money) *really fast.* In the same way, you can set up classroom activities that virtually compel learners to focus more attention on the task. First, goal setting is always a good idea. Encourage students to set their own goals, share them with others, and talk about why they chose them. Ask students to put some stakes in the goals: "What will happen when you reach your goal, and what will you experience?" When students realize they may experience, for example, increased satisfaction, this discovery creates emotional hooks to the goals. If the hooks are strong, attentional resources get a boost.

In the book *Classroom Instruction That Works* (2001), Marzano, Pickering, and Pollack advocate effective strategies such as comparing and contrasting the material learned. Other meaning-building activities that garner strong attentional resources include grouping and regrouping the material, critiquing and analyzing it, resequencing the content, using graphic organizers, and summarizing and retelling the material from another point of view. The strategies vary greatly in effectiveness, depending more on the skill level and experience of the teacher than on the specific nuances embedded in the activity. Each strategy improves learning by almost forcing the brain's attentional biases to focus on a task. The use of pairs and teams and cooperative groups can also heighten attention levels.

Attentional devices. Many teachers rely on old standbys such as a hand signal, a whistle, or a bell. But few things work forever. The moment your students habituate to any of these options, it's time to do something different. The brain's natural tendency is to learn from experience and to slowly lessen the response. Use other devices such as a different tone of voice, vocal pauses, change of location,

Figure 3.2

GUIDELINES FOR DIRECT INSTRUCTION OF NEW CONTENT

Grade Level	Appropriate Amount of Direct Instruction
K–2	5–8 minutes
Grades 3–5	8–12 minutes
Grades 6–8	12–15 minutes
Grades 9–12	12–15 minutes
Adult learners	15–18 minutes

props, purposeful changes in emotion, changes in group or team leadership, surprises, or content "cliff-hangers." Try using class rituals that create a strong attentional bias. For example, on cue, your students might do two stomps and a single clap, then focus their attention to the front of the classroom.

Amine activation. Another strategy is to tap into one of the brain's primary fuels for the attentional system: amines. Amines are the brain's "uppers." Levels of amines typically ebb and flow during the day. During a low time, you can raise amine levels with simple activities characterized by change, movement, small learning risks, artificial urgency, or excitement. Research suggests that activities that include movement, such as going for brisk walks, will elicit a state of aroused attention (Saklofske & Kelly, 1992). Here are some other suggestions:

- Ask students to stand for a moment.
- Switch to an active game or energizer.
- Take the class outside.
- Give an assignment that involves walking with a partner.
- Lead stretching, dancing, or marching activities.

Competitive activities and relay-type activities also work. And recess and physical education obviously can play a role. Teachers who include these kinds of activities arouse their students' attentional systems naturally. Teachers who avoid active learning run the risk of having bored, fatigued learners.

The sum of these practical suggestions calls for balance in approaches to learning. Figure 3.3 illustrates the need for a combination of active learning, passive learning, and settling time.

Repetition

We've all heard that repetition is valuable. This notion is not outdated, and it belongs in every child's upbringing. Students simply must memorize the alphabet, multiplication tables, names, addresses, phone numbers, and many other things. The simple fact is that repetition strengthens connections in the brain. As we learned in Chapter 1, researchers have discovered that synapses are *not* static; they constantly adapt in response to activity (Atwood & Karunannithi, 2002), thus creating an ever-changing set of memories about what was learned. On the one hand, the more we use an idea correctly, the more we activate a skill or complete the same process,

Figure 3.3

BALANCE IN LEARNING

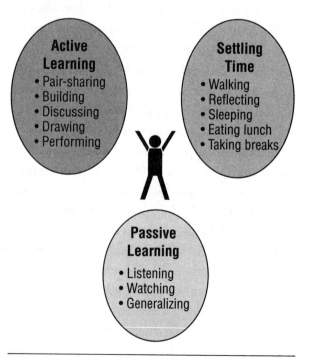

the smoother, faster, and more accurate we get at it. On the other hand, too much of the same thing can be boring to the learner. Excessive practice of a skill can become monotonous, so the repetition has to be interesting. The solution can be to use the principle of repetition, but under the guise of completely different approaches with varied timing. Figure 3.4 introduces several of these approaches—pre-exposure, previewing, priming, reviewing, and revising—and includes guidelines for when to use them.

Pre-Exposure

Pre-exposure is the process of covertly preparing students for future learning of content or skills days, weeks, months, or even years before they are accountable for knowledge. Although many teachers lament students' lack of content background in a particular subject, the more savvy teachers are creating pieces of background knowledge through pre-exposure. This undertaking can be extremely valuable for teachers who often get a "Huh?"

Figure 3.4

VARIATIONS ON REPETITION

Activity	When To Do It
Pre-exposure	Days, weeks, months, years ahead (covert)
Previewing	Minutes, hours ahead (overt coming attractions)
Priming	Seconds, minutes (covert exposure)
Reviewing	Minutes after learning (overt)
Revision	Hours, days, weeks later (overt)

response from students when presenting new information. Pre-exposure may be based on skill acquisition (as when we prepared ourselves to eventually drive a car by driving a tractor, a go-cart, or a bumper car as a kid). It may also be based on semantic processes such as vocabulary acquisition (as when we learned words as a kid that we were allowed to use only when we were more "mature").

In a well-planned curriculum, students are getting pre-exposure every month and every year. For example, 4th graders can be pre-exposed to algebra by working with symbols in basic problem solving. They can be pre-exposed to geometry by building models that include points, lines, planes, angles, solids, and the concept of volume. If you know the key ideas that your learners will need to know in a week or a month, create a summary and put it on a poster. Use vocabulary words before students need to know them. Show short DVD clips; use props or advance organizers. In literature, this kind of approach is often referred to as foreshadowing.

Previewing

Previewing is typically more overt and explicit than pre-exposure. It involves "setting up" the content minutes or hours, not days or weeks, before presenting it formally. Previewing is, in fact, a form of long-term priming. But it's blunt, often done as an overview of the topic. Previewing is typically done at the start of a lesson and may last for 30 seconds to 3 minutes. It allows the learners to become comfortable, to access prior knowledge, and to prepare for the material coming later. It can take the form of a handout, a simple explanation, a set of student-generated questions or brainstorming activities, a detailed teacher- or student-led overview, or a "heads up."

Priming

Priming is typically done minutes or even seconds before exposure to a learning event. It accelerates the understanding of concepts and gives the brain information to build into a more complex semantic structure or hierarchy later on. It also improves the efficiency with which a learner can name a word, an object, or a concept, or even perform a skill (Martin & Van Turenout, 2002). Semantic priming has been shown to have effects up to a year later (Cave, 1997). Figure 3.5 shows the positive effect of priming on verbal fluency.

Priming is so easy and quick to do that students often have no idea they are being introduced to new material. Its subtlety makes it both an efficient and a painless way to prepare learners for new content. To get *some* value out of priming merely requires some exposure to the intended target information (Martin & Van Turenout, 2002). Students need simply to see or hear the relevant words. To get the *maximum* value out of priming, students need to name or use the primed word. Although experiments have shown a wide time range for effectiveness, priming will work whether you use it a few minutes before the formal lesson or several weeks in advance. For example, if you ask your 4th grade students to name 10 animals from the African Serengeti, they might respond with only 3 or 4. But if you introduce the names of many animals as part of the weekly vocabulary words in the weeks before, they might average seven or eight correct responses.

Reviewing

Reviewing can be a strict rote process or a more creative activity. The review process implies "going over" what students have already learned. There is nothing brain-antagonistic about repetition; as the expression goes, "Neurons that fire together, wire together." When neural connections are stimulated repeatedly, they strengthen significantly. Make sure the repeated information is accurate. If the initial learning involved a simple word, phrase, or fact (such as state capitals), expect direct, accurate recall from students. To make review activities more meaningful, involve the students by allowing them to develop their own simple ways to review the learning.

Revising

Revising differs slightly from the other processes. It involves *reconstructing* the learning that was achieved hours, days, or weeks in the past, and

Figure 3.5

THE EFFECT OF PRIMING ON VERBAL FLUENCY

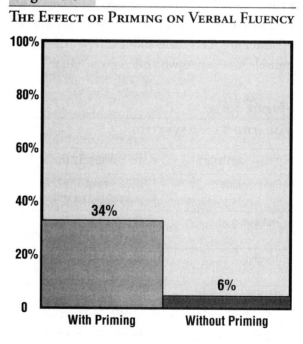

Source: Based on data from Mack & Rock (1998)

it's critical to student performance (Collie, Maruff, Darby, & McStephen, 2003). We use the word *revise* or *reconstruct* (not "review") for a reason. Our ability to recall complex learning is much more iffy than researchers once thought. A host of factors can lead to significant losses, confusion, confabulation, distortion, or simple erosion in memory (Schacter, 2001). It makes more sense to call the revisiting of the learning an update, a renewed version, or a revision. Why? The information that is recalled with each effort may be corrupted. If repeated, the corrupted version becomes as real as the original memory over time. But the reality is that most retrieving of old information is a revision, not a duplicate of the original. Allow students time to continually revise and refresh their learning. What is reviewed is remembered.

Practical Suggestions

Remember, there's a big difference between being familiar with something and truly knowing it. Don't get discouraged when students want to shrug off a repetition or revision activity. All that tells you is that you need to be a bit more creative. Here are some suggestions for each of the approaches to repetition. You'll quickly be able to generate your own.

For pre-exposure, priming, and previewing:

• Use vocabulary words as a way to prepare and prime. Either introduce them formally (presenting a new word every day), use them in discussions (pointing them out), or post them before the scheduled learning.

• Show a video well in advance of a topic.

• Take students on a field trip with a connection to the upcoming topic.

• Introduce incidental material such as works of art, names of famous people in the field, or related music or events.

• Display key concepts in a wall poster.

• Give a quiz in advance of the material and then repeat the quiz at the end of the lesson or unit. The questions will serve as a primer for later knowledge gained.

• Do fill-in-the-blank exercises with your students. Give them a set-up sentence and then prompt them with one or two letters of the word to fill in. For example, "We've been learning about a tool for increasing learning that starts with PR and it's called _____" (priming).

• Have students separate into small groups of three to four. Each student should come up with a different key point from the unit. The group then creates a question or a fill-in-the-blank sentence and writes it in big letters on a placard. These placards can then be used for whole-class review.

• Do simple whole-group choral-response activities. You give the first half of a phrase or concept; your students give the second half. For example, using the title of this chapter, we'd say it's called "The rules we _____" (learn by).

For revising and reviewing:

• Have students create a written quiz. Variations include having small groups each contribute three to five questions for a larger quiz, having a small group create a quiz to trade with another small group, or having every student contribute two questions to the whole class's effort.

• Ask students to summarize their learning in a paragraph, then to pair-share.

- Show students how to create a graphic organizer. Variations include students working on their own, students working with partners using flipchart paper, or students creating a mind map and passing it around for additions from others.

- Ask students in groups of three or four to summarize a key point in a rhyming one-line review. You might even ask them to add a little choreography and to present it to the class.

Input Quantity

Educators are under considerable pressure to teach more and more content during the school year. However, expanding content through increased exposure benefits only one subject—language acquisition. To learn a new language, one ought to listen, speak, and read it as much as possible. Such processes as "superlearning" and "accelerated learning" work well for exposure to language. Reading more often is better than reading less often. But in every other subject, more is not necessarily better. In the face of mandates from legislators and policymakers who add more to teachers' plates each year, somebody needs to stand up and say, "You can teach more and faster, but students will simply forget more and faster."

In-depth (as opposed to superficial) learning requires time for organizing, integrating, and storing new information. Even visual images require rest time for processing (Stickgold, James, & Hobson, 2000). It's clear that although humans have an enormous lifetime capacity for learning, on a daily or "per task" basis, that capacity is limited by the processing time that brain systems require. And furthermore, the brain has several systems and structures, such as the hippocampus (see Figure 3.6),

that actually *inhibit* higher speeds of processing. Learning involves multiple stages of processing via these structures and systems, and each one serves as a "gating" device. Considered as a whole, these structures act as a "surge protector" for the brain. Let's look at how the activities in some of these structures affect learning.

Frontal lobes (short-term memory limitations). The frontal lobes are where much of our short-term visual memory is located. Researchers have found that we can take in only three to seven chunks of information before we simply overload and begin to miss new incoming data (Linden et al., 2003).

Figure 3.6

THE HIPPOCAMPUS AS "SURGE PROTECTOR"

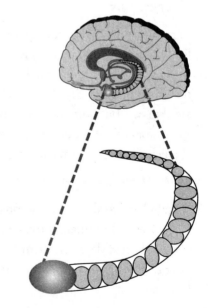

The hippocampus is a small C-shaped structure buried deep in the temporal lobes (we have one on each side). It learns fast, but has limited capacity.

Synaptic gap (formation time at each neuron). The physical process of building connections for explicit learning begins within 15 minutes of exposure to new information, and the synaptic connections continue to strengthen during the next hour. It takes up to six hours to complete formation of the synaptic connection for implicit learning (Goda & Davis, 2003). The new learning must "imprint." As McGill University's Peter Milner, one of the giants in the study of learning and memory, has observed, if the synapse is disturbed before it can be set in this way, the memory is lost (1999). (See Figure 3.7.)

Neurons (protein recycling time). The brain must recycle proteins in the neurons that are crucial to long-term memory formation. To help accomplish this, an incubation or settling time is necessary after new learning takes place (Schroth, 1992). This means that learning improves with short sessions and rest intervals versus constant exposure to new material. It is also dependent on frequent sleep for recycling of the learning (Bodizs, Bekesy, Szucs, Barsi, & Halasz, 2002).

Hippocampus (capacity and consolidation limitations). The hippocampus learns fast but has a very small memory capacity (Kelso, 1997). The organization and distribution of memory in the hippocampus takes time, and much of this work occurs while we sleep (Piegneux, Laureys, Delbeuck, & Maquet, 2001). The process of turning electrical and chemical input into a memory is known as *consolidation*. This physical process also requires time. It's just one more limitation on the speed of the learning process.

Given what the research shows, it should be apparent that presenting more content per minute, or moving from one piece of learning to the next too rapidly, virtually guarantees that little will be learned or retained. In fact, many teachers who complain of having to do so much "reteaching" are the same ones trying to cram too much content into too little time. The brain is not built for continuous focused input (Mednick et al., 2002). Learning can be far more effective when external stimuli are shut down and the brain can pause to link new information to earlier associations, uses, and procedures. "This association and consolidation process can only occur during down time," says Allan Hobson of Harvard University (1994, p. 115). One study conducted with medical students (Russell, Hendricson, & Herbert, 1984) showed that those

Figure 3.7

Time Schedule for Complex Learning

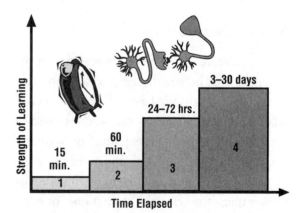

Time Elapsed

1. Initial connection is made. Synapses are formed or modified within first 15 minutes.

2. Most explicit learning is held for evaluation by the hippocampus. Synaptic adhesion strengthens.

3. At night, new learning is organized and codified. The hippocampus distributes it to the cortex through neural repetition for long-term storage.

4. Integration into related networks may occur with appropriate stimulation.

Source: Based on data from Goda & Davis (2003) and Sejnowski (2002).

who encountered the fewest new concepts or the least amount of additional detail per lecture retained more of the basic information than those who encountered more new concepts and more detail. The bottom line is that learning connections require time and maintenance (Sanes & Lichtman, 2001). Remember: *Less is more. Too much, too fast, it won't last.*

Many schools have a curriculum that is too wide and too shallow. We need to make some hard choices about what to offer, and policymakers and others need to stop their endless demands to add more content. If anything, a more brain-based approach would focus on critical-thinking skills, strategic decision making, learn-to-learn skills, cooperative alliance making, and strengthening of emotional intelligence.

Practical Suggestions

I asked world-renowned neuroscientist Terry Sejnowski what he would suggest for an approach to learning. His advice? "Learn, discuss, then take a walk." The essential point is that teachers must encourage "personal processing time" or "settling time" after new learning so that material can solidify. Students can be taught how to do this. Parents who are uncomfortable with the notion—or mistakenly see it as "loafing"—need some background information about it. Personally, I believe the phrase "settling time" better reflects what's needed by the brain than the word "rest," which implies the brain is doing nothing. As we have learned, those synapses take time to form!

Here are some suggestions for students at various levels:

• *K–2.* Use a nap, lunch, or rest period as settling time.

• *Grades 1–12.* Assign classroom chores or use recess, a walk, paired time, reflection, lunch, listening to quiet instrumental music, or quiet "choice time" lasting 5 to 10 minutes as ways to get students to wind down.

• *Adults.* Organize the presentation so that students get occasional breaks.

Keep in mind that writing in journals or discussing new learning in small groups is a great way to elaborate on learning, but is *not* settling time for the brain. The primary ingredient in settling time is "no new learning." If a teacher uses this time for seatwork or deadline-centered projects, the brain is not resting.

How *much* settling time is required depends on two variables: the material and the learner. If the material is both complex and novel, it requires much more elaboration and settling time. If the background of the learner is high and the content is familiar, much less settling time is needed. Teaching heavy, new content to novice learners may require 2 to 5 minutes of processing for every 10 to 15 minutes of instruction. But a review of familiar material to well-rehearsed learners should require less settling time. The learners will tell you what they can take. Consider the complexity of the content or skill, its novelty to the learners, and their emotional state.

Coherence

For simple learning (realizing that a stove is hot after putting your hand on it, or learning the definition of a single word), no "strategic content packaging" may be needed. There's no complexity to baffle the senses, nor is there a need for a particular order. Accurate learning occurs almost every time. However, most other learning is different. It does matter to the learner how things are "packaged," and there are countless variations, including the following:

- Global versus sequential.
- Emotional versus bland.
- Abstract versus concrete.
- Reflective versus active.
- In text versus in context (field-dependent).
- Novel versus familiar.
- Examples versus generalizations (rules).

There are data that support each of those choices under *certain* conditions and with *certain* subjects. Many of these variables, such as a sequence, we adjust to automatically while learning, if we are motivated to do so (Nissen & Bullemer, 1987). But we still have individual preferences. In other words, brain research does not offer guidance in creating a specific teaching template. Still, research does tell us that content is *more likely* to get our attention if it is

- Emotional (not bland).
- Specific (not general).
- Novel (not familiar).

The next time you're in the supermarket, look at the headlines of the tabloids. They follow that formula relentlessly. Furthermore, brain research supports the conclusion that content is more likely to *become meaningful* to us if we can

- Relate it to familiar, prior information.
- Be both active and reflective with it.
- Learn it in context.

Because many of these characteristics are covered elsewhere either in this book or in other books, I'm going to focus on just two of the more important elements that contribute to meaning making and coherence. Both are powerful brain concepts that are driven by the activation of individual connections and the power of neural networks. Each supports our ability to teach the understanding of difficult material. These concepts often go together, and the best teachers use them successfully. The first is the power of activating the familiar before the unfamiliar—the value of prior knowledge. The second is the power of examples and the extrapolation of mental rules or models.

The Value of Prior Knowledge

Have you ever done a word association? If I say a word—let's pick a random one, like "brain"—what other words come to mind? Every word you choose is an example of your prior knowledge. Now imagine this: *every other word, picture, or sound in your brain has some knowledge (detailed or scattered) attached to it.* We've all heard of the importance of prior knowledge, but I'd like you to elevate its importance. Whatever you thought about its value before, multiply that by 10. Here are some considerations:

- All students will have some prior knowledge, even if it's just random or unconscious learning.
- Prior knowledge is not a mythical concoction. It consists of real, physical brain matter (synapses, neurons, and related, connected networks).
- Prior knowledge fundamentally influences whether and how a student will gain an accurate or deep understanding of the topic.
- Prior knowledge is personal, complex, and *highly resistant* to change.
- The best way to teach is to understand, respect, and build on the student's prior knowledge.

One way to think about the prior knowledge that students have is to visualize a tumbleweed—those spherical brown weeds, often two to three feet in diameter. An ant can crawl from any part of this weed to any other part of the weed; some paths are just quicker than others. Inside our brain, we have massive, bushy, tumbleweed-like clusters of neurons. They connect and overlap extensively but are separated by their functionality.

These clusters can also be thought of as "knowledge trees" made up of neurons connected through prior associations accumulated over time. Consider what the following words have in common: oatmeal, ballroom, ozone, Calcutta, space shuttle, and Inuit. In my mind, they aren't connected at all. The funny thing is, a creative mind *could* connect them all, either in a fabricated story or as a result of having a *very* adventurous life! In theory, any bit of prior knowledge can become connected to any other bit, so these clusters of neurons can become extraordinarily complex and messy. You can "hear" some of the best manifestations of neural connections in an improvisation by Robin Williams. You can "see" them in action when students write out what they know in graphic patterns called clusters, webs, or mind maps.

Prior knowledge fundamentally influences all learning (Altmann, 2002). One common reason—and there are many—that students might not understand a concept is that they have competing, conflicting, or unreliable prior knowledge that dooms their thinking. The knowledge trees are triggered each time a student thinks of just part of the tree. Each mental tree is firmly in place and will *not* be removed by what a teacher says. No *F* on a test, no disappointed look, and no gentle verbal correction will erase faulty, incomplete, or incoherent sets of prior connections. The greater the complexity of the idea, task, or association, the greater the number of connected neurons. A single association of prior knowledge may have as many as 10,000 connections. As you'll soon see, these connections are so stubborn, you have to work with what students have, not try to erase or fix them.

The Power of Mental Models

Mental models are coherent structures for understanding things. Lambert and Walker (1995) define a mental model as

> an individual's existing understanding and interpretation of a given concept, which is formed and reformed on the basis of experiences, beliefs, values, sociocultural histories, and prior perceptions. It typically refers to internalized representations of a device or idea held in the mind of one or more persons. (p. 1)

The term mental model has been applied to quite a wide range of representations, sometimes *functional models*—the conception of how something works—and other times, *structural models*—an understanding of where all the parts of something are and what is connected to what. Our mental models (or schemas) affect how we interpret new concepts and events. They play a powerful role in the learning of both children and adults.

The term is also a way of simplifying and understanding the relevant processes involved in a more detailed concept. From a physiological standpoint, mental models could be described as simplified neuronal networks (Zull, 2002). They can be created in an hour after a learning experience, or they may develop over years. When you require students to make their own models, you're helping them reach a deep understanding rarely achievable by more traditional lecture.

You may assume that either your students know something or they do not. But the understanding of how mental models function, supported by many cognitive scholars, suggests otherwise. The organization of prior learning can be contradictory, messy, or coherent. Redish (2004) provides an example of "messy" organization when he describes the fragmented nature of students' acquired scientific knowledge, noting that it consists of separate pieces of information that often cannot be inferred from one another or from other knowledge.

When we describe mental models as "coherent structures for understanding things," it's important to note that *coherent* to one learner does not mean *coherent* to another. Nor does coherent mean *accurate*. Most learners begin with highly naïve preexisting notions. They often build their prior knowledge into thinking models that may be both incorrect and inconsistent (Pine & Messer, 1998)—and remarkably resistant to change. Here are some examples of poorly formed models:

• "They were poor when they were young, so they didn't learn much."

• "Tornadoes form because it's the season when it gets really windy in this part of the country."

• "I can't learn that subject because I don't have any background in it."

• "If a metal ball falls off this table, it will fall faster than a plastic ball."

Any effective instruction must first deal with bogus mental models. Students need skills to properly interpret new relevant concepts and principles, as well as to describe and organize knowledge more effectively. In other words, they need to know how to *purposely, consciously* create their own models.

Frederick Reif is a professor at the Center for Innovation in Learning and the Departments of Physics and Psychology at Carnegie-Mellon University. His work explores how to design instruction so that students can better learn thinking skills and can acquire both flexible and usable scientific knowledge for complex domains like higher mathematics or science. Reif (1987) asserts mental models are fundamental to teaching. He has plenty of support, including from Howard Gardner (1991), who believes mental models are critical and just as important as, if not more important than, the theory of multiple intelligences.

Trying to organize a significant body of knowledge is a challenge. It is reasonably easy to learn something that matches or extends an existing mental model, but if it does not match, learning is very difficult. Finding out what students already know and asking them to make connections to another, more accurate model is how the real learning process begins. Even complex, higher-level science and math courses can be effectively taught to novices with the use of developed mental models (McLachlan, 2003).

One study involving 6-year-old children looked at whether providing them with diverse information—information about more than one element of a mental model—could promote change in their mental models about the shape of the earth. The study randomly allocated 132 children to a control group or to one of two training groups. Some children received instruction that challenged their beliefs concerning (1) why the earth appears flat and (2) the role of gravity. Others received instruction that repeatedly challenged only one of these beliefs (Coley, Hayes, Lawson, & Moloney, 2004). The researchers interviewed the children before and after instruction to determine the children's mental models of the earth. They found that both instruction methods resulted in increases in factual knowledge, but only children receiving instruction about two core beliefs showed an increased rate of acceptance of a spherical earth model. The findings show that instruction that challenges diverse aspects of children's naïve scientific beliefs is more likely to produce conceptual change (Hayes, Goodhew, Heit, & Gillan, 2003). In short, instead of avoiding what students know and what they construct in their mental models, be proactive. The odds are in your favor.

Practical Suggestions

Presenting knowledge in well-organized form is useful, but it's also inadequate. It's far more important—and a requirement for good teaching—to ensure that the knowledge *in the student's brain* is well organized. Students are pretty good at understanding a simple example, but without support, they may not form an effective mental model. Once you discover false beliefs, it's also important to challenge them. Here are some strategies to help you accomplish this:

- Start with what students know. Let them write it out before they share it with others.

- Allow students to roughly cluster the information. Then insist they structure it more formally according to the way they think they understand it.

- Allow individual students to voluntarily explain what they know to the whole class. Learn from as many of your students as possible. It's often good to ask them privately to volunteer and get permission to call on them.

- Help students learn by teaching them how to organize information in a hierarchical (tree-shaped) form.

- Link new learning to students' prior knowledge. Make frequent use of analogies.

- Recognize that students will learn better by doing than by only watching something being done.

- Allow time for students to physically create written mental models on paper or to build them, if appropriate (typically in science and math).

- Practice, practice, practice. Students must actively practice using well-organized knowledge. Give them opportunities to exploit their personal organization to help them remember and retrieve pertinent information.

- Let students test their models to find out if these models work well for new information. If not, give them time to revise. Students can then accurately learn how to analyze problems, construct solutions, and check their solutions for consistency against known facts.

Timing

The brain and body have many different rhythms—patterns they fall into on a daily, monthly, and seasonal basis. You've probably noticed that you have periods of high and low energy throughout the day, and these shifts seem to either heighten or decrease your attention, interest, and learning. These fluctuations are known as ultradian rhythms, one of the brain's many different cycles. They last about 90 to 110 minutes, so there are about 12 to 16 cycles over a 24-hour period (see Figure 3.8). If you have a peak at 9 a.m., your low will occur about 45 minutes later. Your next peak of energy will occur at about 10:50 to 11:00 a.m. Keep in mind that many things can override these high-low cycles, such as exercise, novelty, caffeine, or emergencies. But the timing of the schedule is stable in our brain, shifting a little each day to keep pace with the daily changes in summer to winter lighting or changes in time zones. The brain's rhythms play a key role in understanding and influencing cognitive performance, memory processes, visual perception, levels of arousal, performance, mood, and behavior (both individual and even social).

It's odd that although we are familiar with and accept the notion of "light" and "deep" sleep, we rarely connect this with typical high- and low-arousal cycles during the day. These periods of alternating efficiency correlate with a known body rhythm, "the basic rest–activity cycle." Some students who are consistently drowsy in your class may simply be at the bottom of their attentional cycle. The daily low, or "down," parts of the 90- to 110-minute cycle reflect a "take it easy" message from the brain. These low-energy times strongly affect adolescent moods (Barber, Jacobson, Miller, & Petersen, 1998).

Ultradian Rhythms and Cognition

Moods and energy levels are not the only things affected by ultradian rhythms. The brain also shifts its cognitive abilities on those high and low cycles. There's literally a change in blood flow and breathing that affects learning (Shannahoff-Khalsa, 1993). The brain becomes alternately more efficient in processing either verbal or spatial information. One study (Gordon, Stoffer, & Lee, 1995) tested subjects' performance on cognitive tasks over a period of eight hours. The verbal task of written word production cycled at 80 minutes; the spatial task of locating points in space cycled at 96 minutes. Remember, these are just averages; individuals' cycles will vary. These ultradian rhythms of the right and left brain also affect tactile learning. For example, the sensory pathways from each hand terminates in the contralateral (opposite) hemisphere of the brain. There's an increase in the skill of the right or left hand during every two-to-three-hour shift as our brain's chemicals change throughout the day (Meier-Koll, 1999).

Hormones and Cognition

Hormones play a key role in the brain's rhythms. It is not a myth; hormones can and do alter how we learn. Various hormones are associated with various kinds of learning tasks, and the hormones fluctuate according to different cycles.

Figure 3.8

HIGH AND LOW DAILY ENERGY CYCLES

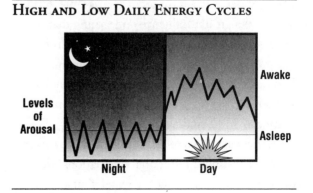

Although you have little direct control over your own hormones, you have some options in how you handle the hormonal variations in your students.

We know that the brain hemispheres are not the same. As we learned in Chapter 1, the left hemisphere is generally associated with verbal skills, and the right hemisphere with spatial skills. We also know that males and females tend to differ in their ability to perform certain skills—so-called "sexually dimorphic" skills, such as fine-motor coordination, verbal fluency, and the ability to mentally "rotate" shapes. Studies have found that the hemispheres function at different levels of efficiency that change systematically across both the menstrual cycle and the male's testosterone cycle. Research also indicates that left-hemisphere performance increases as testosterone levels decline, whereas right-hemisphere performance increases as estrogen levels decline (Sanders, Sjodin, & de Chastelaine, 2002). These findings suggest that as the levels of these hormones shift and affect the performance in each hemisphere, skills related to language and spatial tasks also fluctuate. Figure 3.9 shows variations in task performance related to testosterone levels in both males and females.

A growing body of research suggests that hormones (such as insulin, estrogen, and testosterone) and peptides (such as oxytocin and vasopressin) may have a greater influence on learning than was once believed. This discovery has gender-difference researchers scrambling to design experiments to find out whether the differences between males and females are perceptual, cognitive, emotional, or motor. Some findings are now emerging. The differences across same-sex populations are moderate and consistent. Hormonal fluctuations within the menstrual cycle influence females' brain activity. Findings suggest that higher estrogen may facilitate the automatic activation of verbal representations in memory (Maki, Rich, & Rosenbaum, 2002). Studies have also found that the menstrual cycle affects performance of spatial, verbal, and even mental arithmetic tasks (Kasamatsu et al., 2002). In males, low to moderate levels of testosterone result in better performance on spatial tasks; high levels undermine task performance (Neave, Menaged, & Weightman, 1999). Females also have testosterone, but what are considered "high" levels in a female are actually about the same as "low" levels in a male. Women with high testosterone scored higher on these same measures of spatial ability than women with low testosterone did. However, the results depend on the specific task, which suggests that other learning variables may be involved (Gouchie & Kimura, 1991).

Practical Suggestions

The most challenging aspect of these phenomena is that each learner has a different brain, different hormones, and a unique body clock. Some educators may simply throw their arms up in the air and say, "So we're all different; what's new?" But there's more to it than that. At any given time, nearly half your class will be experiencing a "low" in energy, but a hundred minutes later, that half will likely have higher energy. At any given point, some will be better at spatial tasks, others stronger at verbal tasks. Instead of being frustrated by these variations, now you know why they occur. So it's up to you either to develop a curriculum that takes account of the low-energy times or to take charge (without judgment) and meet it head on with some of the ideas below.

Tolerance. Expect students to vary in performance. Expect them to get frustrated occasionally because they can't do what they'd like to do. You can simply tell younger children that some days we're better at some things than other days. With older students, remind them that bodies and brains have varying levels of chemicals that can lead to varying levels of performance. Do not offer these explanations as an excuse, but rather as one more factor that we all have to either accommodate or adjust to daily.

Activity shifts. Although most classroom activities use both hemispheres rather than being hemisphere-dominant, some are more specifically verbal or spatial. Reading, for example, is verbal and sequential. Some students who struggle with it

will do better when their brain is processing in a way that uses more left-hemisphere activations. If you teach reading at 10:00 a.m. every day, start alternating the times. Teach reading at 10:00 a.m. three days a week and at 11:40 a.m. two days a week. You'll find that some students will do better, because changing the time of instruction opens the window of "cognitive efficiency" wider. Approach math the same way.

Movement. Physical movement such as standing, stretching, walking, or marching can increase brain amine levels, which can help improve attentional focus. As a general policy, if students feel drowsy, they should be allowed to stand at the back of the room for up to two minutes and stretch on their own, provided they do so without attracting attention to themselves. Cross-lateral movements (crossing over a right arm or leg to your left side and vice versa) are especially helpful in activating contralateral blood flow in both hemispheres. (For more about the importance of movement, see Chapter 4.)

Scheduling. Brain cycles make a good case for the use of block scheduling at the secondary level. With a longer block of time, the teacher can include break activities without feeling pressured to teach content every minute. Teachers can also offer different types of activities to reach different learners with varied internal clocks. Physical and mental breaks may be especially helpful for students who get too little sleep at home. Several breaks, from 5 to 20 minutes each, several times a day will increase productivity.

Testing. The oscillation in brain activity suggests that certain students will get lower scores on tests if we test them at the wrong time—a particularly troubling situation if grades are based largely on

Figure 3.9

EFFECT OF TESTOSTERONE ON TASK PERFORMANCE

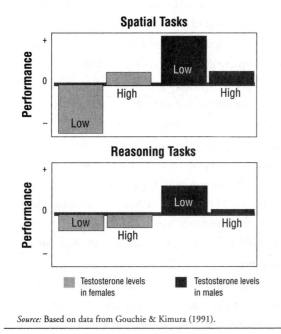

Source: Based on data from Gouchie & Kimura (1991).

the results of one or two tests. This understanding makes a case for allowing students some choice in the assessment process. Portfolios, which are compiled over time, are more inclusive and accurate than a "snapshot" test, because they may account for students' "highs" and "lows" better, producing a more reliable average indicator of performance.

Error Correction

As we know, learning comes in many forms. Stimulus–response learning and classical conditioning are quite simple. Do a task, hear a bell, and we associate one variable with another. The two get "paired" in the brain. (Does the name Pavlov ring a bell?) This is also the "hand on the hot stove" effect. But for the most part, we're interested in deeper, more complex learning, and nervous systems facing complex environments have to balance two serious requirements. First, they must quickly and reliably extract and use salient features from sensory inputs. Second, they must generate coherent perceptual and cognitive action states, which are fast moving and task specific. In other words, our nervous system must figure out what's going on and then do something about it.

The rule of error correction, or trial-and-error learning, is based on two simple truths about the brain: (1) the brain rarely gets it right the first time, and (2) making mistakes is key to developing intelligence. The exceptions to the first truism would occur in cases of very simple learning and exposure to trauma. Because we don't get complex learning right the first time, trial-and-error learning is needed to sort out those mistakes. But why do we have a brain that doesn't get it right the first time? Here are three reasons:

• We get a massive amount of sensory exposure every day. Typically, we don't pay much attention to new material. Because we're not yet sold on its importance, we let it go.

• Often the new material exceeds our short-term memory capacity, so it fades quickly.

• Our capacity to process information is often overloaded in the hippocampus. After an hour-long lecture in a college classroom, students are lucky to remember the title of it, much less any of the 10,000 to 15,000 words that were spoken so eloquently.

The rule that "trial and error is ideal" does not mean that teachers should forgo direct instruction entirely. Direct instruction is appropriate for certain knowledge bases, particularly when students must learn core, rules-based strategies under a time limit. According to Carnegie Mellon psychologist David Klahr, direct instruction may be the best way to teach young children about science, because teachers don't have the time to elicit all the possibilities through discovery learning. What's more, there is no guarantee that the students will uncover the complete picture or gain an accurate understanding through trial and error alone. Many cognitive process skills must be taught directly; they're not something that most children acquire naturally, even if they have a lot of exposure to discovery learning experiences (Chen & Klahr, 1999). Klahr suggests using specific, concrete examples and plenty of hands-on tasks. This guidance helps ensure that students will grasp the underlying logic and will be able to apply the new principle in a broad way.

Note that this science-based methodology contrasts with the traditional concept of direct instruction model: tell students what you are going to tell them, then tell them, and then tell them what you told them. I don't mean to suggest that all lecture is bad. But if you lecture, you must remember that you have no idea whether your students have acquired the information correctly until you use another strategy to check their understanding. Here's where we see the value of group discussions, case studies, self-scoring, game simulations, writing assignments, student rubrics, and a host of other high-feedback activities. They are what trial-and-error learning is all about.

Trial-and-error learning is also valuable because it's intuitively simple. And mistakes, not correct answers, make us smarter. While we could never memorize all the right answers needed to thrive in the future, we can eliminate some of the more costly mistakes (by learning, for example, to "look both ways before crossing"). Of course, most exposure to new learning comes at us so fast that we rarely get a chance to try it out and make mistakes with it. The brain has a specific structure that is automatically activated when there's a discrepancy between what was expected and what actually happened. It's located in the upper, front middle of the brain and known as the anterior cingulate. This area seems to be designed by nature to help us take advantage of trial-and-error learning (Kopp & Wolff, 2000).

Inside the brain, neural networks become more efficient when a learner tries out several possible options and eliminates the ones that don't work. Feedback-driven learning makes more accurate and complex connections. It's no different from trying out several routes in the drive home from work; after a while, you find the most expedient route and stick with it. The neural connections are made *more efficient* by feedback-driven learning. They are made

stronger by usage. Combine the two and you get a smarter learner (see Figure 3.10).

As you might have surmised by now, nature prefers trial-and-error learning. When we say, "That kid hasn't got a drop of common sense in him," we are usually referring to someone who hasn't learned from his mistakes. Why all of us don't learn from our mistakes is a bit complex, but three reasons are most common. First, often the neural structures have been misguided, impaired, or damaged. This problem is common with cases of fetal alcohol exposure, brain injury, and autism. Second, our own prior learning and mental models

Figure 3.10

THE VALUE OF TRIAL-AND-ERROR LEARNING

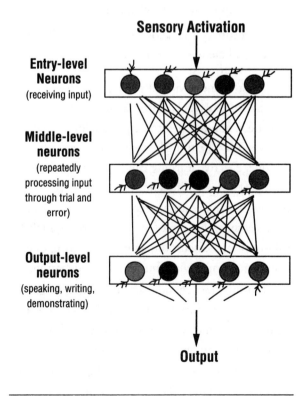

of what we think and know are surprisingly resistant to change. And third, there may have been no reflection or debriefing to create a clear understanding or mental model of what just happened so corrections could be made.

Now for the caveat: we must make mistakes *and* get enough appropriate feedback from them to learn. Let's say a student makes a mistake and then covers it up when no one's looking. If the student gets away with it, the feedback is that mistakes are fine as long as you can hide the negative results. Obviously, trial and error alone is not enough. The following closely related components are also required:

- Consistent activities in which students can test hypotheses and make mistakes.

- Opportunities to make mistakes that they can get immediate feedback about.

- Feedback that allows students to evaluate, reflect, and change their behavior.

Most learners will tell you they'd rather be active than passive. Unfortunately, many students have been conditioned to be passive for so many years that by the time they're in secondary school or college, active learning can feel strange. In one sense, the biggest difference between the two is that with active learning, feedback may be built in to the activity. Examples of active learning include call–response, discussion, games, answering questions, problem solving, building, and debating.

On the practical side, active learning might involve opportunities to make mistakes and learn from them, which can eliminate wrong choices faster. If students are building a model instead of reading about how to build it, they'll get feedback on the success or failure of the steps quickly—which

leads to quicker learning. Active learning gives teachers the opportunity to more quickly find out what students know and don't know. Active learning also makes the learning more fun for the students and helps the class time go by faster.

On the biological side, active learning has some additional advantages. First, because it involves motion, it requires and brings more neural resources to the moment. This means an increase in attention, focus, and thinking skills. Second, human beings are designed to recall better what we do actively than what we do passively. Active learning may involve more senses, motor learning, or varied spatial locations. Also, active learning allows us to have a greater variety of unique mental, emotional, and physical states, which are essential to learning (Sporns, Tononi, & Edelman, 2000). Each of these states mobilizes additional neurons in far different, more lasting, and more complex ways than semantic (word-based) learning.

Finally, learning from trial and error activates more emotional structures in the brain, both positive and negative. The area of the brain involved with error correction and doing the right thing is the anterior cingulate. It's in the top back of the frontal lobe near the corpus callosum. (Curiously, this structure is also activated by pain.) Neural activity across the whole brain arises from the specific predictions that we make, which are culled from prior learning and our expectations about future learning (Schultz & Dickinson, 2000). In other words, prediction—and subsequent feeling—is driving the learning process. Trial-and-error activities also activate more of the pleasure structures in the brain than do simple memorization tasks (Poldrack et al., 2001), increasing their appeal and the odds of learners' continued engagement. In short, it's not just what we think; it's where, when, with whom, and *how we feel* about it that matters.

Practical Suggestions

Thousands of studies support the role of feedback in the learning process. Getting enough good-quality, accurate feedback may be the single greatest variable for improving learning (Hattie, 1992). The feedback must be corrective and positive enough to tell the student what the desired change must be. It also must be timely. For most students, "timely" means immediately following the learning or testing (Bangert-Downs, Kulick, Kulick, & Morgan, 1991), but for students with high reactivity or with chronic anxiety and stress, it's often preferable to provide additional time between the learning event and the feedback on their performance. The element of choice is also key. When learners can choose the type and timing of the feedback, they are more likely to internalize and act on that feedback and improve their subsequent performance.

Students tend to make more mistakes in the early stages of any new learning. Prompt feedback at this time is essential to prevent them from getting too far off course. As students' experience deepens, their error rate drops, and feedback can be more measured, infrequent, and deliberate. But how do you offer good, timely feedback in a busy, differentiated classroom? The answer is feedback-driven activities that involve less of the teacher and more of the student. Most of these activities are simple, quick, and easy to do. Most of them you've either participated in or actually used with students. And finally, they are activities you could use at least once in every class you teach, every single day. Here are some examples:

- Model building.
- Peer editing.
- Doing a gallery walk.
- Pair-sharing.
- Using spell-check functions.
- Conducting student presentations with audience feedback.
- Playing competitive games.
- Using a video, audiotape, or mirror.
- Doing author's chair or fishbowl processes.
- Using a checklist or rubric to evaluate performance.

Your first reaction to these activities might be "How simple! I already do these things in my classroom." If so, that's great. Still, take some time to reflect on the qualities of each of the activities listed. Notice that they all allow learners to make mistakes and to *get feedback* that will allow them to learn from those mistakes. And remember that active learning does not necessarily include feedback. As an example, a student doing a writing assignment is engaged in active learning, but something like peer editing at the first-draft stage would be necessary to add the valuable feedback element otherwise missing. What doesn't make sense is constant one-way learning. Our brain is designed to learn from mistakes. We need to give it a chance to do just that!

Emotional States

Learning happens in many complex layers. Retrieval of some learning seems to require specific physiological states, suggesting the role of emotions in memory. In fact, emotion turns out to be one of the most important regulators of learning and memory. The more intense the emotional state, the more likely we are to remember the event (see Figure 3.11). Whether we get scared out of our wits or experience an ecstatic love fest, nature wants us to remember the incident that caused that reaction. We explore emotion in depth in Chapter 5. Here, we'll consider just some of what research has uncovered about learning and emotions.

Negative Emotions

Negative emotions are well known for influencing brain function. We know, for example, that a stressful event leads to the secretion of glucocorticoid hormones, including cortisol, which influence cognitive performance (Roozendaal, 2003). Researchers have found that, in general, moderate (not high) levels of cortisol are an ally in encoding learning, *but not in retrieving it* (Cahill, Gorski, & Le, 2003; Van

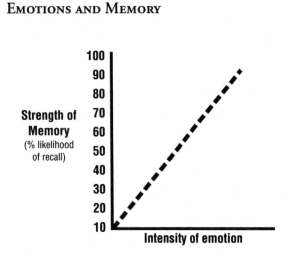

Figure 3.11

EMOTIONS AND MEMORY

Correlation is .90 between how vivid the memory is and how emotional the original event was.

Honk et al., 2003). Other studies have concluded that heightened cortisol levels seem to enhance memory for material with an emotional aspect (Abercrombie, Kalin, Thurow, Rosenkranz, & Davidson, 2003).

The relationship among stress, glucocorticoids, and memory is complex (Sauro, Jorgensen, & Pedlow, 2003). As an example, researchers have found that males show higher cortisol levels than females in response to stress. With too much cortisol, semantic memory is impaired. But adding just the right amount of norepinephrine results in a *stronger* memory (Cahill, Prins, Weber, & McGaugh, 1994). Negative emotional events, as you might expect, weigh heavily on the brain. They seem to "drag down" more of the brain's other circuits (Ito, Larsen, Smith, & Cacioppo, 2001). We recall negative emotional events longer, and they affect more brain circuits.

Fear has been studied more than any other negative emotion because it is relatively easy to produce and measure in a controlled environment. How does the brain deal with fear? It goes through a three-stage process of recognition, priming, and action. First, the brain recognizes what's urgent, risky, exciting, scary, or uncertain and immediately gives it preferential processing treatment. The input senses (visual, auditory, tactile, olfactory) send the messages to the thalamus, an oval-shaped processing structure in the center of the brain. Emotions are initiated by a series of mid- and lower-brain structures. Simultaneously, the combined emotional valence and significance are evaluated by a circuit below the cortex that involves the amygdala (see Figure 3.12). As we learned earlier, the amygdala (there are actually two, one in each temporal lobe) is the brain's "uncertainty detector." With any hint of change in conditions, fears, threats, or danger, it wins the competition for access to selective attention and subsequent reaction. This initial recognition of uncertainty causes the amygdala to send a message to the hypothalamus to begin the chemical message to release glucocorticoids (like cortisol). The peripheral nerve endings' amines (like noradrenaline) then prepare you for the event, and the frontal lobes monitor the event (Kilpatrick & Cahill, 2003).

Now the amygdala is primed for other new stimuli. We are in a better learning state because of this priming effect. The brain is alert, sensitive, and hypertuned to the most subtle environmental cue for further potential action. This process involves bottom-up inputs from the amygdala, as well as top-down influences from frontal-lobe regions involved in goal setting and maintaining representations in working memory (Compton, 2003).

Finally, a class of chemicals known as neuromodulators modulates activity at the synapses, where they can enhance the formation of memory. These neuromodulators may be hormones, peptides, neurotransmitters, or combinations of all three. Hormones include the stress-related glucocorticoids (cortisol is the best known) and the sex hormones known as androgens. Peptides may include oxytocin or vasopressin, both known to be closely related to stress and sex hormones. Neurotransmitters may include epinephrine and norepinephrine. Cortisol affects multiple cognitive domains including attention, perception, memory, and emotional processing.

Positive Emotions

Positive emotional events also get priority for memory. But how they do it is a bit more complex than with negative emotions, and human variations make it difficult to gauge the brain's mechanisms for recalling positive events. Dopamine is a neurotransmitter that is linked to pleasure and our perception of positive experiences. It plays a role in the brain's "reward system," which controls our ability to predict and enjoy perceived rewards (Schultz, 2000).

Other evidence links dopamine to positive cognitive functioning, suggesting that it may enhance attentional systems to improve event or semantic memory (Denenberg, Kim, & Palmiter, 2004; Tanaka, 2002). Dopamine also controls fundamental operations related to spatial memory. Pleasurable events enhance the production of

---

Figure 3.12

THE AMYGDALA

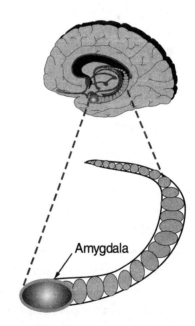

Amygdala

Recessed deep in the temporal lobe, at the base of the hippocampus, this structure mediates uncertainty, danger, and intense emotions.

dopamine. Positive smells can work, too. Do you have a favorite? It might be freshly baked bread or chocolate chip cookies, or the fragrance of a favorite flower. Neurobiological evidence indicates that the emotional experience of odor-evoked memory also activates the amygdala during recall and influences the organization of memory (Herz, Eliassen, Beland, & Souza, 2004).

Do males and females experience emotions differently? It appears that they do. The right-side amygdala modulates right-hemispheric processing of global or central aspects of a situation, and this effect is more pronounced in males. In contrast, the left-side amygdala modulates left-hemispheric processing of more local or fine-detail aspects of a situation, and this effect is more pronounced in females. Females' emotionally influenced memories are more detailed, whereas those of males are more global or general (Cahill et al., 2003). This finding supports the hypothesis that the left and right amygdalae serve different functions in emotion processing: the left may respond to a specific stimulus, whereas the right may respond to any stimulus (Glascher & Adolphs, 2003).

Practical Suggestions

Do you have any influence over the chemicals that can strengthen your students' memory capabilities? It turns out that you do have some influence. As we have learned, the brain chemicals that support improved memory include cortisol, norepinephrine, and dopamine. These are produced and released in the brain under reasonably predictable conditions, including risk, excitement, urgency, and pleasure. In the past, you may have created activities that purposely evoke emotions. Now you have one more good reason to do those activities—they enhance memory.

Risk. Many situations involve risk. They include activities that involve a potential loss of social status among peers or even perceived danger. But what's risky for one may be blah to another. Suggestions for activities with an element of risk include public speaking, pair-sharing, having to role-model something, or meeting new people.

Excitement. For most students, excitement is halfway between something that's fun and something that's scary. So any activity you use in this category may be exciting for 80 percent of your students, but either so-so or scary for the other 20 percent. This does not mean that you should avoid these activities. But it does mean you should monitor them closely, use plenty of variation, and avoid overusing them. Activities that create excitement include a public performance, a science fair, a debate, a field trip, or a series of relay races.

Urgency. This one seems straightforward, but it's a bit tricky. To evoke the stress hormones, an activity needs more than a deadline. The students need to (1) perceive that the task or goal is worth accomplishing, (2) have the resources to make it happen, and (3) have a reasonable deadline. Otherwise, you risk what is known as "learned helplessness." One strategy is to start the activity with less time than is needed and add "bonus minutes" if necessary.

Pleasure. When we think of pleasure, we might fixate on hot fudge sundaes, pampering massages, or time with our loved ones. But life is filled with pleasures that students can look forward to in class. Examples include finishing on time, getting less than the expected amount of homework, taking home something built in class, being able to sit with a friend, or having other privileges. Pleasure can be found in the simple things.

Summary

Although it's clear that these rules for learning are built into our natural learning systems, experience also affects how they play out in the brain. Part of the theme of this chapter was that you have much, much more to do with how your students turn out than you previously thought. But a corollary to that theme is just as powerful: You've already been influencing your students by using the rules without necessarily knowing them. Now you can be far more purposeful about *how* you use them. The chapters to come will explore other principles and strategies. For now, though, let's take a break (interval learning is best) before heading on to the next chapter.

Movement and Learning

I t's truly astonishing that the dominant model for formal learning is still "sit and git." It's not just astonishing; it's embarrassing. Why do we persist when the evidence that lecture alone does not cut it is so strong (Dolcourt, 2000; Slavin, 1994)?

The reason for the dissonance between what we know and what we do may be traced back a hundred years. For decades, the educational and scientific communities seemed to believe that thinking was thinking and movement was movement, and each was as separate as could be. Maverick scientists envisioned links between thinking and movement, but their ideas gained little public support. Today we know better. This chapter discusses the strong connections between physical education, movement, breaks, recess, energizing activities, and improved cognition. It demonstrates that movement can be an effective cognitive strategy to (1) strengthen learning, (2) improve memory and retrieval, and (3) enhance learner motivation and morale.

In times of diminishing financial resources, educators must make hard choices. Do dance,

KEY CONCEPTS

▶ The mind–body link

▶ How exercise affects cognition

▶ The importance of play, recess, and physical education

theater, recess, and physical education belong in the curriculum? Can we afford to keep them in the budget? Are they frills or fundamentals? What does brain research tell us about the relationship between body and mind? If movement and learning are connected, we should expect evidence to support the idea. In fact, there is plenty of evidence.

Why is all this important? One of the fundamental tenets of this book is that we have to teach *with the brain in mind.* Because movement is a natural part of the school day, that movement *will influence* the brains of students. It is essential that we explore the ways we are shaping students' brains. To do so, let's look at some anatomical, imaging, cognitive, and functional studies that suggest we ought to be supporting more movement in the learning process, not less.

Evidence of Mind–Body Links

The first evidence of a linkage between mind and body was scattered in various proposals over the past century (Schmahmann, 1997). Today, the evidence has become a groundswell, and most neuroscientists agree that movement and cognition are powerfully connected.

Anatomical Evidence

The area of the brain most associated with motor control is the cerebellum. It's located in the back of the brain, just under the occipital lobe, and is about the size of a small fist. The cerebellum takes up just one-tenth of the brain by volume, but it contains *nearly half* of all its neurons (Ivry & Fiez, 2000). This structure, densely packed with neurons, may be the most complex part of the brain. In fact, it has some 40 million nerve fibers—40 times more than even the highly complex optical tract. Those fibers feed information from the cortex to the cerebellum, and they feed data back to the cortex. In fact, most of the neural circuits from the cerebellum are "outbound," influencing the rest of the brain (Middleton & Strick, 1994). Peter Strick at the Veteran Affairs Medical Center of Syracuse, New York, has documented another link. His staff has traced a pathway from the cerebellum back to parts of the brain involved in memory, attention, and spatial perception. Amazingly, the part of the brain that processes movement is the same part of the brain that processes learning (see Figure 4.1).

Figure 4.1

LINKS BETWEEN THE CEREBELLUM AND OTHER PARTS OF THE BRAIN

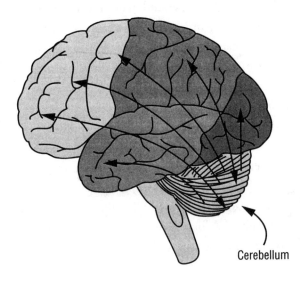

Cerebellum

Information travels to and from the cerebellum, the brain's center of motor control, and other parts of the brain involved in learning, but most of the neural circuits are outbound.

Evidence from Imaging Techniques

New data, primarily from studies using functional magnetic resonance imaging (fMRI), have provided support for parallel roles of cognitive structures and movement structures such as the cerebellum. We learn to predict (think about) our movements before we execute them (move) so that we control them better (Flanagan, Vetter, Johansson, & Wolpert, 2003). This ability suggests that all motor activity is preceded by quick thought processes that set goals, analyze variables, predict outcomes, and execute movements. Pulling this off requires widespread connections to all sensory areas.

Various studies support the relationship between movement and the visual system (Shulman et al., 1997), movement and the language systems (Kim, Ugirbil, & Strick, 1994), movement and memory (Desmond, Gabrielli, Wagner, Ginier, & Glover, 1997), and movement and attention (Courchesne & Allen, 1997). These studies do not suggest that there is movement in those functions. But they suggest a relationship with the cerebellum in such mental processes as predicting, sequencing, ordering, timing, and practicing or rehearsing a task before carrying it out. The cerebellum can make predictive and corrective actions regardless of whether it's dealing with a gross-motor task sequence or a mentally rehearsed task sequence. In fact, the harder the task you ask of students, the greater the cerebellar activity (Ivry, 1997). Taken as a whole, a solid body of evidence shows a strong relationship between motor and cognitive processes.

Cognitive Evidence

Just how important is movement to learning? The vestibular (inner ear) and cerebellar (motor activity) system is the first sensory system to mature. In this system, the inner ear's semicircular canals and the vestibular nuclei are an information-gathering and feedback source for movements. Impulses travel through nerve tracts back and forth from the cerebellum to the rest of the brain, including the visual system and the sensory cortex. The vestibular nuclei are closely modulated by the cerebellum and also activate the reticular activating system, near the top of the brain stem. This area is critical to our attentional system, because it regulates incoming sensory data. This interaction helps us keep our balance, turn thoughts into actions, and coordinate movements. That's why there's value in playground activities that stimulate inner-ear motion, like swinging, rolling, and jumping. A complete routine might include spinning, crawling, rolling, rocking, tumbling, and pointing. As noted in Chapter 2, Lyelle Palmer of Winona State University has documented significant gains in attention and reading from these stimulating activities (Palmer, 2003).

Functional Evidence

Currently, the MEDLINE database shows more than 33,000 scientific articles on the topic of exercise, and the vast majority of them confirm its value. One study showed that people who exercise have far more cortical mass than those who don't (Anderson, Eckburg, & Relucio, 2002). Simple biology supports an obvious link between movement and learning. Oxygen is essential for brain function, and enhanced blood flow increases the amount of oxygen transported to the brain. Physical activity is a reliable way to increase blood flow, and hence oxygen, to the brain.

In William Greenough's experiments at the University of Illinois, rats that exercised in enriched environments had a greater number of connections among neurons than those that didn't. They also had more capillaries around the brain's neurons than sedentary rats (Greenough & Anderson, 1991). Solid evidence suggests that even going for brisk walks can elicit this state of arousal—meaning an increase in heart rate, EEG activity, and more excitatory active brain chemicals (Saklofske & Kelly, 1992). In fact, if you haven't yet taken a break from reading this riveting chapter, you might stand and stretch for a moment. Why? Standing can raise heart rate (hence, blood flow) by as much as 5 to 8 percent in just seconds (Krock & Hartung, 1992). And finally, here's a powerful research finding: evidence from animal studies indicates that voluntary exercise influences gene expression to improve learning and memory (Tong, Shen, Perreau, Balazs, & Cotman, 2001). This improved pattern of gene expression enhances many factors that support the encoding and transfer of data, synaptic structure, and the activity and plasticity of neurons. All of these processes facilitate learning.

School Applications

An astonishingly high 68 percent of high school students in the United States do not participate in a daily physical education program (Grunbaum et al., 2002). Why should we be concerned? Because in the same way that exercise shapes up the muscles, heart, lungs, and bones, it also strengthens the basal ganglia, cerebellum, and corpus callosum—all key areas of the brain. We know exercise fuels the brain with oxygen, but it also feeds it neurotropins (high-nutrient chemical "packages") to increase the number of connections between neurons. Most astonishingly, exercise is known to increase the baseline of new neuron growth. Rats grow more brain cells when they exercise than when they don't exercise (Van Praag et al., 1999). In addition, studies link this increased neurogenesis to increased cognition, better memory, and reduced likelihood of depression (Kempermann, 2002).

Imagine that: Exercise may grow a better brain! It suggests both a huge opportunity and the liability suffered by students who don't get enough exercise. We may not be overstating the case to say that it's educational malpractice when only about a third of K–12 students take part in a daily physical education class.

Support for Recess, Play, and Physical Education

Researcher Terrence Dwyer is one of many who have conducted multiple studies suggesting that exercise supports success in school. His research found that exercise improves classroom behavior and academic performance (Dwyer, Sallis, Blizzard, Lazarus, & Dean, 2001) and that even when an experimental group got four times more exercise per week than a control group of their peers (375 minutes versus 90 minutes), their "loss" in studying time did not translate into lower academic scores (Dwyer, Blizzard, & Dean, 1996). His research further revealed that social skills improved in the groups who exercised more. Other research (Donevan & Andrew, 1986) has found that students who are engaged in daily physical education programs consistently show not just superior motor fitness, but better academic performance and a better attitude toward school than their students who do not participate in daily P.E.

Human play has been studied quite rigorously. Some studies suggest that students will boost academic learning from games and other so-called "play" activities (Silverman, 1993). There are several theories about why all mammals (including humans) play. But there is no controversy around the notion that we do play, and that it is generally good for us. Many early cognitive researchers ignored play, assuming it had nothing to do with intellectual growth. They were dead wrong. Many play-oriented movements have the capacity to improve cognition, including the following:

• Exercise play (aerobics, running, chasing, dance routines).
• Rough-and-tumble play (soccer, football, wrestling).
• Solitary play (doing puzzles, object manipulation).
• Outdoor learning activities (digging, observing insects).
• Stand and stretch activities (tai chi, Simon Says).
• Group or team competitive games and activities (relays, cheerleading).
• Constructive play (building with blocks, model building).
• Exploratory play (hide and seek, scavenger hunts, make-believe).
• Functional play (purposeful play, such as practicing a new skill).
• Group noncompetitive games (earth ball).
• Individual competitive games (marbles, track and field, hopscotch).
• Adventure or confidence play (ropes courses, trust walks).
• Group noncompetitive activities (dance, drama).
• Walking excursions (outdoors, indoors).

Play, recess, and physical education are essential for many brain-based (biological) reasons. Here are just some of the benefits of exercise:

• It allows learners to make mistakes without "lethal" consequences (with far less embarrassment and more fun than in a traditional classroom situation).
• It enhances learning (Fordyce & Wehner, 1993).
• It improves the ability to handle stress by "training" the body to recover faster from the quick surges of adrenaline associated with demanding physical activity . . . and classroom environments.
• It triggers the release of BDNF, brain-derived neurotrophic factor (Kesslak, Patrick, So, Cotman, & Gomez-Pinilla, 1998). This natural substance enhances cognition by boosting the neurons' ability to communicate with one another.
• It can enhance social skills, emotional intelligence, and conflict resolution ability.
• Exercise may increase catecholamines (brain chemicals such as norepinephrine and dopamine), which typically serve to energize and elevate mood (Chaouloff, 1989).

The case for children doing something physical every day is growing. Jenny Seham of the National Dance Institute (NDI) in New York City says she has observed for years the measurable academic and social results of schoolchildren who study dance. She notes the positive changes in self-discipline, grades, and sense of purpose in life that her students demonstrate. She's now in the process of quantifying the results of more than 1,500 kids who dance weekly at NDI.

Although many educators know about the connection between learning and movement, nearly as many dismiss the connection once children get beyond 1st or 2nd grade. Yet the relationship between movement and learning is so strong that it pervades all of life—and emotions are intertwined into the mix as well. Educators generally consign movement, emotion, and thinking to separate "compartments." Students may feel awkward if they want to express emotions or move around when teachers want them to be still and think. *Boys especially* Teachers need to realize that what the students are experiencing is simply a healthy integration of mind and body (see Figure 4.2).

Additional Benefits for Special-Needs Learners

Many teachers have found that programs that include movement help learners with special needs. Several hypotheses may explain this phenomenon. Many special-needs learners are stuck in counterproductive mental states, and movement is a quick way to change them. Second, movements, such as those involved in playing active games, will activate the brain across a wide variety of areas. It may be the stimulation of those neural networks that helps trigger some learning. For other students, it may be the rise in energy, the increased blood flow, and the amines that put them in a better mood to think and recall. Some routines that call for slower movement can do the reverse, calming down students who are overactive, hence supporting a state of concentration.

A study by Reynolds and colleagues (2003) found that children with dyslexia were helped by a

movement program. Those in the intervention group showed significantly greater improvement in dexterity, reading, verbal fluency, and semantic fluency than did the control group. The exercising group also made substantial gains on national standardized tests of reading, writing, and comprehension in comparison with students in the previous year.

Figure 4.2

OLD AND NEW UNDERSTANDINGS OF THE MIND-BODY RELATIONSHIP

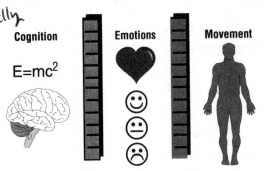

Old, Compartmentalized Paradigm

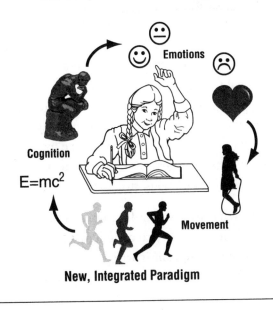

New, Integrated Paradigm

Practical Suggestions

Some of the smartest things teachers can do are the simplest. When we keep students active, we keep their energy levels up and provide their brains with the oxygen-rich blood needed for highest performance. Teachers who insist that students remain seated during the entire class period are not promoting optimal conditions for learning.

Educators should purposefully integrate movement activities into everyday learning: not just hands-on classroom activities, but also daily stretching, walks, dance, drama, seat-changing, energizers, and physical education. The whole notion of using only logical thinking in, for example, a mathematics class flies in the face of current brain research. In fact, Larry Abraham in the Department of Kinesiology at the University of Texas–Austin says, "Classroom teachers should have kids move for the same reason that P.E. teachers have had kids count" (personal communication, 1997).

Brain-compatible learning means that educators should weave math, geography, social skills, role-play, science, and physical education together, along with movement, drama, and the arts. Don't wait for a special event. Here are examples of easy-to-use strategies.

Goal setting on the move. Start class with an activity in which everyone pairs up. Students can mime their goals or convey them by playing charades with a partner, or the pairs can go for a short walk while setting goals. Ask students to answer three focusing questions, such as these:

- What are my goals for today and this year?
- What do I need to do today and this week in this class to reach my goals?
- Why is it important for me to reach my goals today?

You can invent other questions or ask students to create some of their own.

Drama and role-plays. Get your class used to daily or at least weekly role-plays. Have students play charades to review main ideas. Students can do an extemporaneous pantomime to dramatize a key point. Do one-minute commercials adapted from television to advertise upcoming content or to review past content.

Energizers. Energizer activities can (1) raise blood pressure and epinephrine levels among drowsy learners, (2) reduce restlessness among antsy learners, and (3) reinforce content. Use the body to measure things around the room and report the results. For example, "This cabinet is 99 knuckles long." Play a Simon Says game with built-in content: "Simon says point to the south. Simon says point to five different sources of information in this room." Do team jigsaw puzzles with huge, poster-sized mind maps. Have young students get up and move around the room, touching seven colors on seven different objects in a particular order. Teach a move-around system using memory cue words. For example, "Stand in the place in the room where we first learned about . . ."

Quick games. Use ball-toss games for review, vocabulary building, storytelling, or self-disclosure. Have students rewrite lyrics to familiar songs in pairs or as a team. The new words to the song can provide a content review. Then have the students perform the song with choreography. Get physical in other ways, too. Play a tug-of-war game in which everyone chooses a partner and a topic from a list of topics that every student has been learning about. Each person forms an opinion about his or her topic. The goal is for each student to convince a partner in 30 seconds why his or her topic is more important. After the verbal debate, the pairs form two teams for a giant tug of war for a physical challenge. All partners are on opposite sides.

Cross-laterals. Learn and use arm and leg crossover activities that can force both brain hemispheres to "talk" to each other better. "Pat your head and rub your belly" is an example of a crossover activity. Other examples include marching in place while patting opposite knees, patting yourself on the opposite shoulder, and touching opposite elbows or heels. Several books highlight these activities, including *Sensorcises* by Laurie Glazner and *Smart Moves* and *The Dominance Factor* by Carla Hannaford.

Stretching. To open class, or anytime that you and your students need more oxygen, get everyone up to do some slow stretching. Ask students to lead the whole group, or let teams do their own stretching. Allow learners more mobility in the classroom during specific times. Give them errands to do, make a jump rope available, or simply let them walk around the back of the classroom as long as they do not disturb other students.

Physical education and recess. Budget cuts often target physical education as "a frill." That's a shame, because, as we have seen, good evidence indicates that these activities make school interesting to many students, and they can help boost academic performance. We're not talking about going overboard with exercises. Thirty minutes a day, three to five days a week will do the job (Tomporowski, 2003). Any school that has problems at recess or with physical education should fix the problems, not throw out an important asset.

Teachers should also ensure that breaks include some movement—no standing around at recess

time! Breaks can include fast walking, running, or high-energy play (McNaughten & Gabbard, 1993). The breaks must last for 30 or 40 minutes to maximize the cognitive effects (Gabbard & Shea, 1979). For breaks of that length, it may make sense to alternate highly challenging activities with more relaxing ones. A short recess arouses students and may leave them "hyper" and less able to concentrate. A longer break engages high energy, but it cannot be sustained. Thus, a more calm, restful state of relaxation should follow. This pattern allows the students to focus better on the task at hand. Breaks at midday and early afternoon provide a greater benefit to the students than an early morning recess (McNaughten & Gabbard, 1993). Because longer breaks are more valuable than shorter ones, timing may dictate that the midday break also be used for lunch.

Summary

Strong evidence supports the connection between movement and learning. Evidence from imaging sources, anatomical studies, and clinical data shows that moderate exercise enhances cognitive processing. It also increases the number of brain cells. And as a bonus, it can reduce childhood obesity. Schools that do not implement a solid physical activity program are shortchanging student brains and their potential for academic performance. Movement activities should become as important as so-called "book work." We need to better allocate resources to harness the hidden power of movement, activities, and sports. This attitude has become more and more prevalent among scientists who study the brain. It's time for educators to catch on.

Emotional States

Where do we put this "slippery variable"—emotional states—in the discussion about learning and teaching? How do we talk about something that is pervasive but so tough to categorize, understand, and compete with? Other chapters in this book have touched on the role of emotions in learning, but now it's time to focus more closely on the topic.

For much of educational history, critics have dismissed the role of emotions in learning. The stable, dependable, so-called "scientific" path has been that of reason and logic. But our current understanding of the brain shows that these critics are out of step with reality.

Today's neuroscientists are breaking new ground in helping us understand why emotion is an important learning variable, and how the affective side of learning is the critical interplay between how we feel, act, and think. Mind and emotions are not separate; emotions, thinking, and learning are all linked. What we feel *is* what's real—even if only to us and no one else. Emotions organize and create our reality.

The classroom and the school provide opportunities for endless emotional experiences, and students' brains will be altered by

KEY CONCEPTS

▶ **Why emotions are now "mainstream"**

▶ **How emotions are processed in the brain**

▶ **The power of emotional states**

▶ **How to influence emotional states**

those experiences. This chapter makes the case that emotions have an important and rightful place in learning and in schools.

It addresses three major topics:

- *Distribution.* Emotions involve many brain areas, including areas also involved in cognitive functions.
- *Potency.* Emotional states influence all life functions.
- *Opportunity.* We can influence emotional states in learners.

Before we explore these three ideas further, let's look at the context for the study of emotions.

Emotions Go Mainstream

For a long time, brain researchers avoided the study of emotion. It was considered professional suicide. In recent years, though, several highly respected neuroscientists—among them Joseph LeDoux of New York University, Candace Pert of Georgetown University Medical Center, Jerome Kagan of Harvard Univeristy, and Antonio Damasio and Hanna Damasio of the University of Iowa—have emerged with important research that has helped change the way we think about emotions. Emotions are now on the cognitive map—something to be taken seriously. The publication of *The Cognitive Neuroscience of Emotion* (Lane & Nadel, 2000) formalized this burgeoning field and showed how chemistry influences our emotions.

Here's what we know: Emotions drive attention, create meaning, and have their own memory pathways (LeDoux, 1994). They regulate behaviors, and they help us organize the world around us (Damasio, 1994). You can't get more related to

learning than that! Child development expert Jerome Kagan says, "The rationalists who are convinced that feelings interfere with the most adaptive choices have the matter completely backwards. A reliance on logic alone, without the capacity to feel . . . would lead most people to do many, many more foolish things" (1994, p. 39). The old way of thinking about the brain envisions a separateness of mind, body, and emotions. That idea is history. Antonio Damasio reminds us: "The body may constitute the indispensable frame of reference for . . . the mind" (1994, p. xvi); in fact, "reduction in emotion may constitute an equally important source of irrational behavior" (p. 53). We can now safely say that emotions

- Constitute the passion for learning.
- Help orchestrate our attentional priorities.
- Support either persistence or retreat.
- Are sources of information about the outside world.
- Evoke necessary empathy, support, or fear.
- Associate our learning with either pain or pleasure.
- Help us make meaning out of our learning, work, and lives.
- Push the pursuit of rewarded behavior.
- Improve social problem solving.
- Provide incentives for desired social behavior.
- Allow us to enjoy and even celebrate our learning success.

The popularity of Daniel Goleman's bestselling book *Emotional Intelligence* (1995) clearly tapped into the strong intuitive understanding many people have of emotions. Some are now calling the study of emotions an entirely new discipline in neuroscience (Davidson & Sutton, 1995). You never would have found this kind of scientific support for the role of emotions 10 years ago.

Today, when we say emotions are present, we have a vast array of highly specific and scientific ways to measure precisely what is happening. Changes can be measured in skin responses, heart rate, blood pressure, and EEG activity. In addition, we know emotions have "occurred" by charting differences in neurochemistry, stress levels, motility, immune systems, somatic markers, muscle patterns, expressive language, reflex modulation, and direct actions (Bradley & Lang, 2000). In short, one cannot claim that emotions are either ethereal or simply not happening. Emotions are real.

Neuroscientists often separate the "built-in" biologically based emotions—joy, fear, surprise, disgust, anger, and sadness—from the more casual, fleeting, second by second, life experience called "states." All states are not emotional, but all emotions are states. For example, we experience physical states: soreness, fatigue, and pain. We also experience feeling states: curiosity, craziness, supportiveness, love, or optimism. And then there are "emotional states," which are our *experience* of joy, fear, surprise, disgust, anger, and sadness (Izard, 1998)—emotions that are generated from universal, cross-cultural, biological pathways. States in general help prepare an organism to deal with important events. In some way, all states can be linked to survival. We feel disgust when something is poisonous, gross, or socially unacceptable; when we express it, the message conveyed may prevent another person from doing something unsafe.

The Distribution of Emotion

Emotions are not located in a single "emotion center," but are instead distributed throughout the brain (Heilman, 2000; Kolb & Taylor, 2000). For example, the frustration or pain of getting negative feedback activates the anterior cingulate, the pleasure of a drug-induced high activates the nucleus accumbens, and the terror of fear activates the amygdala. The amygdala then becomes part of the decision-making process (Bechara, Damasio, & Damasio, 2003). The processing of emotive facial cues may activate the orbitofrontal cortex. But none of these areas functions independently. As a generalization, emotions, feelings, and sensations have an effect on many areas of the brain, even if they originate in only one area (see Figure 5.1). What makes this issue even more complex is the presence not of the highways, but of the "messengers" on the highways.

Although it's true we have a blood–brain barrier that many chemicals cannot cross, the brain's overall exposure to chemicals is amazing (Damasio, 1999).

Figure 5.1

AREAS OF THE BRAIN ACTIVATED BY BOTH EMOTIONS AND LEARNING

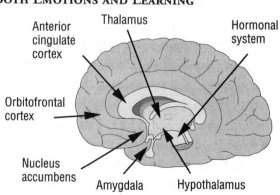

Brain chemicals not only are transmitted from the commonly cited axon–synapse–dendrite reaction but also are dispersed to wide areas of the brain. The person who is depressed is often treated with Prozac, a medication that modulates serotonin levels. Caffeine boosts amine levels, which increase alertness. When you experience a "gut feeling," it's because the same peptides that are released in your brain are also lining your gastrointestinal tract. Memory is regulated by levels of acetylcholine, adrenaline, and serotonin. These active chemicals are pushed out from areas such as the medulla and the pons (located in the brain stem), the kidneys, and the adrenal glands (located on top of the kidneys). These chemicals of emotion influence most of our behaviors. They linger in and often dominate our system. Figure 5.2 shows the variety of chemicals that influence our emotional states, and Figure 5.3 (see page 72) shows the functions of four of them.

This widespread dispersal of chemicals helps explain why, once an emotion occurs, it is hard for the cortex to simply shut it off. The old paradigm was that our brain was managed by the physical connections made at the site of the synapse. But the newer, emerging understanding is that the messenger molecules known as peptides not only are distributed throughout the brain and body, but also exert a far greater influence on our behaviors than previously thought. Miles Herkenham of the National Institute of Mental Health says that 98 percent of all communication within the brain may be through these peptide messengers (Pert, 1997). This view implies a far greater role for the understanding and integration of emotions in learning. Emotional states are powerful because they are produced and modulated throughout the body. Every cell (we have over a trillion) has

countless receptor sites on it for receiving information from other areas of the body. In fact, the bloodstream is the body's second nervous system! Ligands (the peptide messenger molecules) fit into receptor sites, transfer their information, and a new cell behavior begins. Multiply that by millions of cells, and a person simply feels different overall.

The Potency of Emotional States

All emotional events receive preferential processing in the brain (Christianson, 1992), and the brain is typically overstimulated when strong emotions are present. Because emotions give us a more activated and chemically stimulated brain, they help us recall things better and form more explicit memories. The more intense the arousal of the amygdala, the stronger the memory imprint (Cahill et al., 1994).

Figure 5.2

CHEMICALS THAT INFLUENCE EMOTIONS

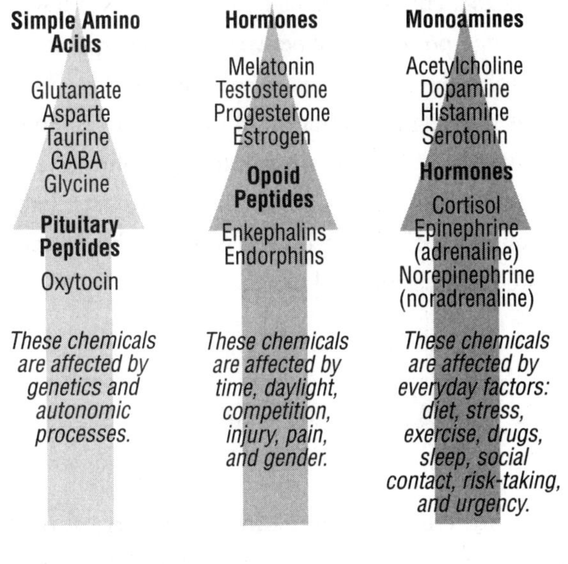

Figure 5.3

MAJOR EMOTION CHEMICALS AND THEIR FUNCTIONS

Name	Type	Function	How to Remember It (Semantic Memory Tool)
Cortisol	Hormone	Supplies energy	"Uh-Oh . . ."
Dopamine	Neurotransmitter	Produces pleasure	"Yahoo!"
Serotonin	Neurotransmitter	Induces calm	"Ahhhh . . ."
Epinephrine	Hormone	Alerts all systems	"Yikes!"

There's a reason nature helps us remember arousing events, good or bad: These are the events that are more likely to have future value for us. An encounter with a playground bully (or predator) and the rejection of a classmate (or future mate) are highly salient to our survival instincts.

As teachers, we see and hear the effect of students' emotions. It's common for students to remember the death of a friend, a field trip, or a hands-on science experiment far longer than they remember most lectures. Good learning does not avoid emotions; it embraces them, recognizing emotional states as fast-changing, specific neural networks that incorporate multiple areas of the brain (see Figure 5.4).

A thorough exploration of the potency of emotions in the learner's brain would take volumes. Here we'll focus on just four emotional states. Each is likely to occur in a typical classroom, though not all are recommended. They are

- Fear/threat.
- Joy/pleasure.
- Sadness/disappointment.
- Anticipation/curiosity.

Each of these is a combination of two very similar but distinctive emotional states. I bundle them together more for the sake of simplicity, convenience, and practicality than for neurological accuracy. Let's explore each of these in typical learning situations.

Fear/Threat

Fear usually arises from some sort of threat perception. The brain has three choices when confronted with overwhelming threat: We can fight, try to escape, or freeze. In nature, animals will freeze when confronted if (1) they perceive there is no escape, or (2) they are unlikely to win a fight. It's no different in the classroom. Students who feel threatened will fight back if they feel they can get away with it. Or they might just sit there and "take it" while stewing about it. Generally, they don't feel they can escape. But make no mistake; if there's a threat, the student's brain is going in high gear.

In an emergency, prolonged evaluation may cost you your life. Any life-or-death situation needs immediate resources, not reflection and contemplation. Although some feeling-states travel a circuitous, slower route throughout the body, threats always take the brain's "superhighway" (see Figure 5.5, page 74). In the midbrain area, there is a bundle of

Figure 5.4

Brain Areas Involved in the Regulation of States

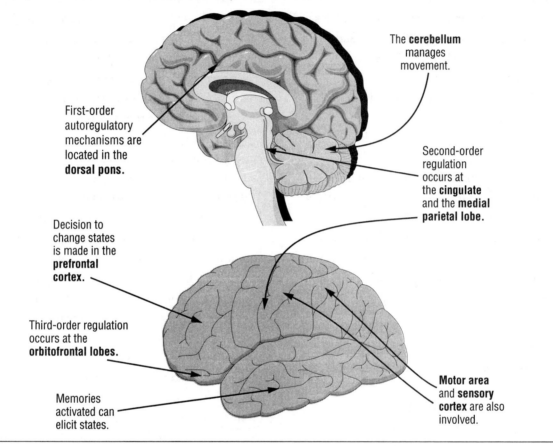

The **cerebellum** manages movement.

First-order autoregulatory mechanisms are located in the **dorsal pons.**

Second-order regulation occurs at the **cingulate** and the **medial parietal lobe.**

Decision to change states is made in the **prefrontal cortex.**

Third-order regulation occurs at the **orbitofrontal lobes.**

Memories activated can elicit states.

Motor area and **sensory cortex** are also involved.

neurons that lead directly from the thalamus to the amygdala, which is designed to respond to threat (Armony & LeDoux, 2000). The amygdala exerts a tremendous influence on the cortex: More inputs travel *from* the amygdala into the cortex than the reverse. Any experience that evokes threat activates specific neurons that respond *only* to these events. But information does flow both ways. The design of these feedback circuits ensures that the effect of emotions will usually be greater than that of other kinds of input. Emotion adds weight to all our thoughts, biases, ideas, and arguments.

Researchers at Arne Ohman's lab at the Karolinska Institute in Stockholm, Sweden, showed that certain threat stimuli—namely, facial displays—are highly effective in engaging attention (Ohman, Flykt, & Lundqvist, 2000). Consider this classroom example. A student who's getting threatening looks from another student may strike back at the perceived threat before even thinking about it. The teacher's "behavior improvement lecture" after the event usually does little to change the next "automatic" occurrence of hitting. For some students, the perceived threat needs to be dealt with as a survival issue. Common "threat"-linked experiences that students encounter in school include peer pressure; serious deadlines with significant consequences if they are missed; and being forced to stay after school, make reparations, or give public apologies.

Violence adds another, powerful dimension to threat. Recent studies suggest that the threat of violence in the learning environment, whether real or perceived, can have a negative impact on learning. Under violently threatening circumstances, blood flow decreases in various parts of the brain that are linked to cognition (Fischer, Andersson, Furmark, & Fredrikson, 2000). In animal studies, it's clear that threat impairs the hippocampus and derails new learning (Diamond, Park, Hemen, & Rose, 1999). There's no question that school stress associated with

Result of ↗

violence affects test scores, absenteeism, tardiness, and attention span (Hoffman, 1996). In a study of 4th and 5th graders, Nettles, Mucherah, and Jones (2000) found that students who perceived their environment to be violent performed significantly lower on standardized exams of reading and mathematics compared with students who did not have a perceived exposure to violence.

A corollary of fear is stress. Occasional or moderate stress is, for the most part, a healthy state. In fact, many studies (Shors, Weiss, & Thompson, 1992) show that a brief period of stress enhances hippocampal learning (the source of our explicit memories). In addition, children exposed to consistent moderate stressors over which they have some control usually turn out to be highly resilient. However, very high levels of stress over time—typically called *distress*—are damaging and can impair cognition (see Figure 5.6).

To be labeled distress, an emotional state must include the following three factors: (1) heightened excitability or arousal, (2) the perception of the event as aversive, and (3) the loss of controllability (Kim & Diamond, 2002). Distress has been shown to kill brain cells (Sapolsky, 1992), to reduce the number of new brain cells produced (Gould, McEwen, Tanapat, Galea, & Fuchs, 1997), and to damage the hippocampus. It is also linked with mood disorders (Brown, Rush, & McEwen, 1999). At Rockefeller University, neuroscientists have shown that chronic exposure to stress can cause atrophy of the dendrites—certainly a negative factor for cognition (Sousa, Lukoyanov, Madeira, Almeida, & Paula-Barbosa, 2000). Chronic stress also impairs a student's ability to sort out what's important and what's not (Gazzaniga, 1988). Corticosteroids—one of the many kinds of chemicals

punishment ↗

Figure 5.5

How the Brain Responds to Threat

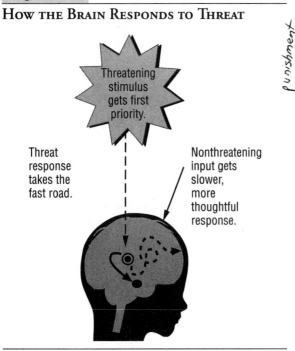

Threatening stimulus gets first priority.

Threat response takes the fast road.

Nonthreatening input gets slower, more thoughtful response.

involved in stress situations—reduce blood flow in the top of the frontal lobes, an area activated in "on your feet" thinking. As a result, although stress is less likely to impair long-term memories, it does impair verbal and working memory (Lupien, Gillin, & Hauger, 1999) and episodic memory (Sapolsky, 1990). Figure 5.7 (see page 76) illustrates how the body reacts to stress.

Our baseline level for stress—what we would call a normal degree of stress—is not set for life. It's a myth that once an intensely stressful episode is over, we return to "the way we were." Life experiences can and do reset our brain's "stress thermostat" at a higher level, so that we may see chronically higher levels of stress reactivity if we've been exposed to repeated stressors within a short time frame or have undergone a particularly traumatic experience. Unfortunately, both scenarios seem to be more common than ever, suggesting that we'll continue to see students who are in chronic states of helplessness and alarm.

But students are only part of the equation. What about the teachers? Under stress, females (who make up the majority of elementary teachers) tend to increase nurturing behavior, whereas males (who are more likely to work at the secondary level) show withdrawal and sarcasm (Repetti & Wood, 1997). Staff stress is likely to increase as accountability rises, control and resources diminish, and the school year proceeds. Schools would do well to support stress-reduction programs for all staff members because teachers' stress levels will clearly affect students.

Joy/Pleasure

The joy and pleasure areas of the brain actually form a pathway from an area near the brain stem

known as the ventral tegmental area. From there the "pleasure chemical" dopamine pushes outward toward the front of the brain and concentrates in the nucleus accumbens. This state is absolutely essential for all learning. On the one hand, if students experience fear, hopelessness, distress, chaos, and disappointment during their learning, the association is made. Their brains will pair up negative emotions with each new learning experience. In a short time, the student may simply quit; it's too painful! On the other hand (or perhaps I should say "the other hemisphere," as positive emotions are typically left-hemisphere activations), positive emotions during the learning experience create a great association in the brain.

A positive emotional state is valuable for several reasons. First, an increased positive affect leads to improved flexibility in behavior and judgment (Ashby, Isen, & Turken, 1999). Furthermore, high levels of dopamine are associated with greater flexibility in the brain's executive attentional system

Figure 5.6

STRESS AND COGNITION

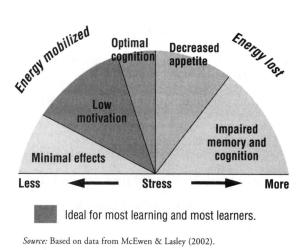

Ideal for most learning and most learners.

Source: Based on data from McEwen & Lasley (2002).

Figure 5.7

THE BODY'S RESPONSE TO STRESS

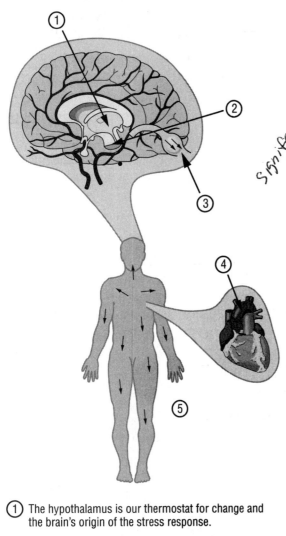

① The hypothalamus is our thermostat for change and the brain's origin of the stress response.

② It sends CRF (corticotropin releasing factor) to the pituitary gland.

③ The aroused pituitary now releases ACTH (adrenocorticotropic hormone) to the bloodstream.

④ Within seconds, ACTH arrives at the adrenal glands.

⑤ The adrenal glands secrete glucocorticoids such as cortisol into the bloodstream.

(Aspinwall & Richter, 1999). This frontal lobe system contributes heavily to school success, because it is associated with working memory, decision making, and judgment functions. In many students, too much internal focus can promote feelings of negativity; however, dopamine promotes an external focus (Sedikides, 1992) that encourages greater feature recognition. This recognition capacity enables students not only to recognize the salient physical features (say, the aspects of an overhead presentation that are relevant to their learning goals), but also to suppress other features that are irrelevant at the moment (everything else in the cluttered classroom). And finally, from a practical point of view, students who experience positive feelings at school will associate these positive feelings with learning, teachers, and school in general. That may help strengthen attendance and, ultimately, boost graduation rates.

Sadness/Disappointment

Generally, feelings of sadness are experienced in the lower half of the brain. This system is mediated by our stress hormones (like cortisol and norepinephrine) and originates in the temporal lobes, specifically in the amygdaloid complex (McGaugh, Roozendaal, & Cahill, 2000). This state sounds negative, and for the most part, it is. For some biological reason, our brain systems are set up to experience pain and sadness longer than joy. Biologically, sadness may be more instructive for the long haul. Researchers investigated and contrasted the effects of laughing and weeping on humans. The study subjects experienced each emotion via watching comedy and tragedy videos while their own mood was monitored. The results suggest that

not long lasting

laughing has strong but transient effects on the autonomic nervous system, whereas weeping or feeling sad has more moderate but sustained effects on it (Sakuragi, Sugiyama, & Takeuchi, 2002).

However, there is good news about this state. We are more likely to remember an experience with a negative bias than one with a positive bias (Ito et al., 2001). If we remember it better, we may be less likely to repeat the behaviors or actions that contributed to the experience. So it's okay for students to know they've disappointed you or themselves. It's okay for them to be sad about a poor effort *if* they can become mobilized by the emotion. Michael Jordan has hinted more than once that getting cut from the high school basketball team was a huge emotional crush for him. But, as Jordan's case illustrates, negative events have a tendency to result in greater mobilization of a system's resources (Taylor, 1991). Jordan never wanted to feel that bad again (being left out or feeling like a loser), and he used his feelings as a motivation to excel.

Anticipation/Curiosity

Anticipation and curiosity create a positive state of hope and vigilance. This state causes increases in the activity of the attentional areas of the brain, including the frontal lobes, the thalamus, the reticular activating system, and the pulvinar nucleus. Visual attentional prompts activate the sensory areas of the occipital cortex, the entire visual system, and the lateral geniculate nucleus, which is the brain's visual "switchboard." Auditory stimuli trigger extra activity in the auditory cortex.

Curiosity and anticipation are known as "appetitive" states because they stimulate the mental appetite. They are highly motivating states that drive hungry organisms toward their goals; in this case, the goal is to feed their hunger by learning more (Bradley & Lang, 2000). Strong evidence shows that positive expectancy robustly and consistently influences the formation of new knowledge. That is to say, when we anticipate and are curious about a subject matter, our learner response goes up (Kirsch, 1999). Good teachers capitalize on this state often. They know that it's the anticipation of positive events that drives up the pleasure in the brain even more than the reward itself (Schultz, Dayan, & Montague, 2002).

The Opportunity: How to Influence Emotional States

Emotions affect student behavior because they create distinct mind–body states. A state is a moment composed of a specific posture, breathing rate, and chemical balance in the body. The presence or absence of norepinephrine, vasopressin, testosterone, serotonin, progesterone, dopamine, and dozens of other chemicals dramatically alters a person's frame of mind and body. Teachers who help their students feel good about learning through classroom success, friendships, and celebrations are doing the very things the student brain craves. Here are the most important things every educator should know about emotional states:

• *They are ubiquitous.* Emotional states run our lives, including how we think, feel, remember, act, and dream. Everything we do is state dependent.

• *They are connected.* All behaviors must come from an appropriate emotional state, and we each have a "pool" of states that dictates our possible behaviors. For example, when I'm depressed, I won't be celebrating anything soon. This means that if a student is not in an appropriate state for the behavior you want, the behavior won't happen until the state is changed. A student who is not in a state to read won't read.

• *They are not who we are.* Emotional states are something we experience; we are not our states, although if you're in a certain state too often, others may generalize and label you ("She's a lot of fun" or "She's a downer"). There is no such thing as an unmotivated student, but there are students in unmotivated states. Never label a student unless it's a positive label.

• *They are transient.* All emotional states are mobile, in process. It takes considerable skill or unusual circumstances to maintain the same state for long. States typically lead to other states. Students need help in managing this flow.

• *Stable emotional states can be a problem.* Anyone in a particular state for too long, too often runs the risk of stabilizing that state in the nervous system. A student who shows up in a state of defiance is not a problem. What is a problem is your allowing that state to persist. The longer it persists, the more familiar and comfortable that state becomes to the nervous system of that student. It becomes "home," and the student will seek that state out of comfort. Do not allow negative student states to persist. They only get harder to change over time.

By now you're sold (I hope!) on the idea that emotional states have a pervasive influence on student learning. And by now you may have already asked yourself the million-dollar question,

"Can I influence these states?" The answer is a resounding yes. And you already *have* influenced them. Although almost anything can change a student's emotional state (chocolate, for example), some strategies are more reliable than others.

Practical Suggestions

Triggering emotions randomly is counterproductive. In addition, extremes of emotion are generally counterproductive to school goals, and a lack of emotion is just as dangerous as uncontrollable emotion. The old adage was, "First, get control of the student; then do the teaching." Today, neuroscientists might recommend engaging emotions as a part of the learning, not as an add-on. There are many appropriate ways to include emotions in the classroom.

Compelling questions. If the questions you ask students do not change their state from reflective to eager, change the questions. Here's an example of a weak question: "What do you think about Winston Churchill's role in military intelligence during World War II?" Try this instead: "If you were the leader of Britain during the war, and you knew one of your cities was going to get bombed that night (this actually happened), under what circumstances would you not warn the citizens in advance?" (Churchill knew and did not warn the citizens—for a very good reason.)

Role-modeling. Teachers should model the love of learning, and they should show enthusiasm about their job. Build suspense, smile, tell a true emotional story, show off a new CD, read a book, or bring an animal to class. Get involved in community work, whether it's for a holiday, disaster relief, or ongoing service. Let students know what excites you. We've all heard of infectious enthusiasm; it works!

Celebrations. Smart schools have pep rallies, guest speakers, poetry readings, community service efforts, storytelling sessions, debates, club activities, sports, and dramatic performances. Teachers use acknowledgments, parties, high-fives, food, music, and fun. A celebration can show off student work in different ways. For example, when students are finished mind-mapping something, ask them to get up and show their poster-sized mind map to eight other pairs of students. The goal is to gather at least two favorable comments about a specific element of the mind map. Playing celebratory music can help everyone have a good time. Ideally, celebrations will become "institutional," so students will celebrate without a teacher prompt every time.

Physical activity. You may have already used music, games, drama, or storytelling to engage emotions. Our body releases dopamine and norepinephrine during movement and fun activities, as we learned in Chapter 4. Human studies show that these chemicals enhance long-term memory when administered either before or after learning (Soetens, Caesar, D'Hoodge, & Hueting, 1995). Create some positive emotions! It's better to have students remember the positives from school than the negatives. Use more standing than sitting, more walking than standing, and more organized activities than walking.

Engineered controversy. Setting up a controversy could involve a debate, a dialogue, or an argument. Any time you've got two sides, a vested interest, and the means to express opinions, you'll get action! Have students prioritize a list by consensus, and you'll get emotions. Afterward, split up

sides for a tug of war outside. As mentioned earlier, research indicates that when emotions are engaged right after a learning experience, the memories are much more likely to be recalled and accuracy goes up (Cahill et al., 1994). The debate could be among pairs of students, or it could be turned into an academic decathlon or game show. Theater and drama can create strong emotions: the bigger the production and the higher the stakes, the more the emotions are engaged. For example, having your class volunteer to put on a play for the entire school involves stress, fun, anxiety, anticipation, suspense, excitement, and relief.

Purposeful physical rituals. Rituals in your class can instantly engage learners. Examples include clapping patterns, cheers, chants, movements, or a song. Use these to announce arrival, departure, a celebration, and getting started on a project. Make the ritual fun and quick, and change it weekly to prevent boredom. Each time teams complete their tasks, they could give a team cheer. Or they could have a special cheer for each member upon arrival and another for the close of the day. Obviously, rituals should be age appropriate.

Getting personal. The use of journals, discussion, sharing, stories, and reflection about things, people, and issues engages students personally. If there is a disaster in the news, ask students to write or talk about it. Current events or personal dramas work well too. If appropriate, students can share their thoughts with neighbors or peer groups. Help students make personal connections to the work they do in class. For example, if students are writing journals, have them read the letters to the editor in the local newspaper and then discuss or even critique them. Students can choose an issue they are passionate about and submit letters to be printed.

Summary

Although all of us acknowledge that we have emotions, few of us realize that they are not the cards at the game table but the table itself. Everything we experience has an emotional tone to it, from calm to rage, from pain to pleasure, and from relaxation to a state of feeling threatened. And because emotions mediate meaning, our emotions are, in fact, the framework for our day. Even if you use a logic-driven rubric to evaluate every student's project, *emotions still rule.* On a bad day, your feelings about certain students or particular rating criteria will lead you to rate one project as more creative, another as less organized. We remember that which is most emotionally laden.

Students need to be taught emotional intelligence skills in a repetitive way that makes positive behaviors as automatic as negative ones. This point is particularly important because although today's students have no saber-toothed tigers to fight off, they have equivalent threats: fear of embarrassment, fear of failing in front of their peers, fear of getting bullied in the hallway. Their brains have adapted to treat those emotional, psychological, and physical threats as if they are life-threatening.

Good learning engages feelings. Far from an add-on, emotions are a form of learning. They are the genetically refined result of lifetimes of wisdom. We have learned what to love, when and how to care, and whom to trust. We have felt the pain of losing esteem, the exhilaration of success, the joy of discovery, and the fear of failure. This learning is just as critical as any other part of education. Research supports the value of engaging appropriate emotions. They are an integral and invaluable part of every child's education.

Physical Environments for Learning

How important are the effects of physical environments on students? You may be surprised at how seriously neuroscientists are taking this issue. At a recent national convention for 18,000 members of the American Institute of Architects in San Diego, California, the keynote speaker was not an architect. He was internationally known, award-winning *neuroscientist* Fred Gage, from the Salk Institute of Biological Studies in La Jolla, California. Gage provoked the audience with this statement and question: "Our environments are having an effect on our brains. To what extent are architects taking this into consideration when they design buildings?" Out of this intellectual ground breaking, a new academy, the Academy of Neuroscience for Architecture, was launched. "We're looking at this *as a whole new discipline,*" says academy founder John Eberhard (Whitelaw, 2003, p. 4).

Was the creation of the academy an anomaly or the wave of the future? The scene shifts from San Diego to Woods Hole, Massachusetts. Recently the National Academy of Sciences held a workshop on Neuroscience and

KEY CONCEPTS

▶ Neuroscience's new interest in physical environments

▶ How seating, temperature, lighting, noise, and building design affect learning

▶ Factors to consider when designing smarter schools

Health Care Facilities Design. The speaker at the opening session called for architects and neuro-scientists to begin using "evidence-based design." Another speaker, Terry Sejnowski, also of the Salk Institute, said *we now have enough evidence* to show how environments affect brain function.

Sejnowski's and Gage's workplace, the Salk Institute, is one of the most admired buildings in the United States. Not coincidentally, the productivity of its staff is legendary, with Salk ranking among the top scientific research facilities in the world, according to the number of times other scientists cited works published by Salk faculty over a two-decade period ("Twenty years of citation superstars," 2003). Co-created by architect Louis Kahn and Nobel laureate Jonas Salk, the Salk Institute's building was literally designed with the brain in mind. Some of the issues considered in the design were stress, safety, privacy, mobility, lighting, humidity, temperature, convenience, aromas, collegiality, and productivity. In London, a recent symposium titled "Building Bridges of Knowledge" brought together architects, climatologists, information technology experts, and neuroscientists to understand how these variables interact. A new discipline is beginning, linking neuro-science with the design and building industries.

One of the first things students do when they walk onto a school campus is look around. They also listen, breathe in the air, and form judgments about the environment. Students then decide whether their surroundings feel familiar, safe, and friendly—or not. This automatic filtering of environmental cues is an ongoing process that occurs every minute of every waking hour. It is so much a part of being human that most of us don't give it a second thought. But in the research about learning and the physical environment, three points stand out:

- Physical environments influence how we feel, hear, and see. Those factors, in turn, influence cognitive and affective performance.

- Some variables exert a much greater influence on student achievement than others.

- Better awareness, smarter planning, and simple changes can be made in every environment to improve learning.

Because the environment is a variable that can be easily enhanced, it makes good sense for teachers to do what they can to make it most conducive to learning. It's the ethical thing to do. In this chapter, we focus on five variables in the physical environment that have the greatest effect on academic success: seating, temperature, lighting, noise, and building design.

Seating

Student seating can affect student success in several ways. First, the location of students' seating within a classroom influences stress levels. Students care about whom they sit next to (friends? enemies?) and where in the room they are (up front, near the teacher? "safely" positioned in third or fourth row?). The stress that students may feel as a result of where they sit influences their cognition. Second, seating location influences access to resources—materials, lighting, teachers, music, heat, bathrooms, and quiet. These, too, can affect student stress levels.

The actual design of students' desks and chairs also plays a role in their cognition. For example, tilted desks provide a better angle for reading, according to Galen Cranz, a professor of architecture at the University of California–Berkeley.

Cranz (1998) calls for a more pragmatic and posture-friendly approach to the way we design and use chairs. The traditional classroom chair (part of an attached desk-and-chair combination) pushes the sitter's weight straight down, increasing pressure on the lower back and forcing the student to sit *on* the chair rather than *in* it. Warning against equating cushiness with comfort, Cranz proposes that a good classroom chair should keep the shoulders back and the chin up, as well as provide arm rests to minimize strain on the upper body. It should be as adjustable as possible and easy to modify. The seat should not be so long that it digs into the back of the student's legs, nor should it be so high that the student's feet don't touch the floor.

Research suggests that a well-designed chair can be a crucial factor in preventing health and cognitive problems. Conversely, chairs that don't provide good support can hamper blood supply to the nervous system and the disks in the vertebral area, causing fatigue and eventually back pain or discomfort, both which impede cognition (Linton, Hellsing, Halme, & Akerstedt, 1994). Linton's 1994 study involving three classes of 4th graders found that the introduction of ergonomically designed school furniture resulted in a significant reduction in musculoskeletal symptoms among students.

Finally, how students' seating is arranged can matter, too. Although group seating can foster important social and peer interaction among students, such arrangements often lead to an increase in chatting and other disturbances that discourage deep concentration (Bennett & Blundell, 1983). Conversely, row seating provides a more structured setting, allowing students to focus more on the task at hand rather than on one another. This does not imply that group- or table-seating arrangements should be avoided in the classroom, researchers emphasize. On the contrary, the *integration* of group activities with traditional learning tasks has been found to have *a significant positive effect* on learning.

Previous research by Hastings (1995) produced similar findings: group seating around tables with four or more makes learning more difficult for the most distractible pupils. One portion of the study found that on-task time dramatically increased when row seating was instituted, but group seating was more conducive to genuinely cooperative learning. The impact of group seating on team learning was also borne out in a study by Marx, Fuhrer, and Hartig (1999), who found that 4th graders tended to ask more questions when seated in a semicircle than in rows. This finding supports earlier studies and bears out the benefit of cluster seating for group discussions and interactive learning tasks. The key, therefore, is to match the appropriate seating arrangement to the activity—for example, use a cluster arrangement when collaboration is the goal or row seating when concentrated independent learning is the goal.

Practical Suggestions

Here are some practical ways to apply research findings related to student seating:

- *Provide unattached chairs and movable desks.* These are best for maximum comfort and flexibility.
- *Allow students to position themselves in different ways.* For example, allow them to lean up against a wall or sit on the floor while reading. Or let them find a friend to "pair-share" with while walking (roller-derby style) around the room.

• *Ask students to stand occasionally for brief learning periods.* For example, you might have students stand while you conduct a review or facilitate a partner exchange.

• *Encourage learners to avoid incorrect posture while sitting.* Slumping overstretches the muscles and ligaments and puts stress on the back. In addition, poor posture shifts the body out of balance and forces a few muscles and joints to do all the work.

• *Provide an inflatable exercise ball as alternative seating for certain students.* Those with sensory disorders or attention deficit or your highly kinesthetic learners may find the inflatable balls easier to sit on than a chair.

• *Group carefully.* If you routinely use group seating for all types of class work, place no more than two or three students together at a table and avoid placing friends in the same group. This arrangement may help reduce the incidence of idle chitchat and distractions.

Temperature

We know that the human brain is extremely temperature sensitive and that temperature is a factor that significantly affects cognition. In U.S. Defense Department studies, Taylor and Orlansky (1993) reported that heat stress dramatically lowered scores on both intellectual and physical tasks. Jeffrey Lackney (1994) at the University of Wisconsin–Madison, has shown that reading comprehension declines when room temperature rises above 74 degrees Fahrenheit and that math skills decline when it rises above 77 degrees Fahrenheit.

Up to a point, the cooler your brain is, the more relaxed, receptive, and cognitively sharp you are. In general, cooler (but not cold) is better than warmer (or hot). Our body, for example, can more easily adjust to a room that is a few degrees too cold than one that is a few degrees too hot. However, classrooms kept between 68 and 72 degrees Fahrenheit are most comfortable for the majority of students (Harner, 1974). Harner also reports that a room temperature of approximately 70 degrees is ideal for most learning situations, particularly those involving reading and mathematics, which require optimal focus and concentration.

Researchers report that higher temperatures can influence levels of neurotransmitters, especially norepinephrine and serotonin, two chemicals associated with moods ranging from depression to relaxation (Donovan, Halperin, Newcorn, & Sharma, 1999; Howard, 1994; Izard, Kagan, & Zajonc, 1984). Excess levels of neurotransmitters can lead to aggressive behavior—a persistent obstacle to learning. This basic insight sheds light on the important role that temperature plays in the learning environment and how it can affect our behavior, thoughts, and emotions.

Practical Suggestions

Here are some practical ways to apply research findings related to temperature:

• *Keep temperature within the comfort zone.* This is generally between 68 and 72 degrees Fahrenheit.

• *Know temperature control alternatives.* If you don't have a temperature control device in your classroom, try some of these options: (1) use fans; (2) keep windows or doors open; (3) point fans across a tray of water to humidify or cool the room; (4) if your room gets direct sunlight, allow students to move around to cooler or shaded areas; (5) incorporate colors that create cooling effects, such as blues and greens; (6) encourage students to layer clothing for more flexibility; and (7) ensure that students drink water often.

• *Attach a ribbon next to a window or air conditioner.* This allows students to tell at a glance if the air is circulating.

• *Be mindful that very warm temperatures can increase anxiety and aggressiveness.* This is especially important if you have students with panic disorder or attention-deficit hyperactivity disorder. In others, it induces lethargy

Lighting

Budget constraints, apathy, and a lack of awareness continues to allow the underuse of natural lighting in the classroom and the overuse or misuse of artificial light. In fact, some children spend six continuous hours or more in school facilities illuminated by artificial light. But is this really a problem? Research suggests that it is.

Over the past 100 years, the amount of outdoor light we are generally exposed to has declined (Lieberman, 1991). Ultraviolet light, present only outdoors, activates the synthesis of vitamin D, which aids in the absorption of essential minerals such as calcium (MacLaughlin, Anderson, & Holic, 1982). And insufficient mineral intake has been shown to be a contributing factor in nonverbal cognitive deficiency (Benton & Roberts, 1988).

An older, but quite large, blind study (Harmon, 1951) examined the effect of environmental factors on learning problems and reported that more than 50 percent of children developed academic or health

deficiencies as a result of insufficient light at school. The study, which evaluated 160,000 school children, also reported that when lighting was improved, various problems were dramatically reduced. Visual difficulties declined by 65 percent, nutritional deficits by 48 percent, chronic infections by 43 percent, postural problems by 26 percent, and chronic fatigue by 56 percent.

A 1999 study conducted by the Heschong Mahone Consulting Group in Fair Oaks, California, involved 21,000 students from three districts in three states. After reviewing school facilities, architectural plans, aerial photographs, and maintenance plans, the researchers assigned each classroom a code indicating the amount of sunlight it received during particular times of the day and year. Controlling for variables, the study found that students with the most sunlight in their classrooms progressed 20 percent faster on math tests and 26 percent faster on reading tests compared with students exposed to the least lighting. These gains are astonishing, especially considering how hard school districts try to raise reading and math scores.

In a follow-up study (2003), the Heschong Mahone Group found that sources of glare have a negative effect on learning. Students in classrooms exposed to morning sun that is unfiltered by blinds or tinted windows will underperform compared with students in classrooms where the windows face north. In subjects that require more vision, such as math, students did better when whiteboards were used (versus overheads) because the lighting was better.

Because many bodily functions and hormones are regulated by daily dark-light cycles, it's not surprising that researchers have established a link between seasonal mood changes and the amount of light present during the day (Brennen, Martinussen,

Hansen, & Hjemdal, 1999; Leppämäki, Partonen, & Lönnqvist, 2002). Scientists know that limited exposure to sunlight for extended periods suppresses the production of melatonin, a neurotransmitter that plays a key role in setting the body's time clock, or circadian rhythm. They also know that too little sunlight also decreases the production of serotonin, which at reduced levels causes depression. Ultimately, mood, alertness, and cognitive performance are compromised (Antoniadis, Ko, Ralph, & McDonald, 2000).

Chronic and intense mood changes that include depression during winter months may be a sign of seasonal affective disorder (SAD). Researchers estimate that 5 percent of school-age children are depressed. But exposure to bright lighting for extended periods can reduce the symptoms (Yamada, Martin-Iverson, Daimon, Tsujimoto, & Takahashi, 1995). Other studies (Schwartz, Rosenthal, & Wehr, 1998) confirm the key roles that melatonin and serotonin play in SAD. As you might guess, there's evidence suggesting that reflected sunlight enhances mood (Harmatz et al., 2000; Michalon, Eskes, & Mate-Kole, 1997), and when we feel better, we usually perform better. Assuming that the outdoors presents no serious noise problems, open windows should be an option for teachers; when teachers do not have control of their windows, student performance is negatively affected (Heschong Mahone Group, 2003).

Many studies have explored the effects of varying amounts of artificial light. Students in brightly lit classrooms perform better in school compared with students in dimly lit classrooms (London, 1988). Sustained exposure to bright light reduces eye fatigue during activities involving close work, making it easier to read and to solve complex problems. Some research suggests that students exposed to long periods of dim light—the kind that is typical in a darkened lecture hall—are more likely to be lethargic, sleepy, and less motivated in class (Aoki, Yamada, Ozeki, Yamane, & Kato, 1998). And a study involving two simulated eight-hour night shifts (Campbell & Dawson, 1990) also found that young adults maintained significantly higher levels of alertness and wakefulness when exposed to brighter ambient lighting rather than dim ambient lighting.

Not all bright lighting is created equal, however. Ordinary fluorescent lights have a flickering quality and emit a barely audible hum. These properties can increase cortisol levels in some, which can suppress the immune system. In addition, the humming noise emitted by fluorescent lights has a detrimental effect on student performance, especially in reading. Statistically, its negative impact on reading scores exceeded that of construction noise, socioeconomic status, and musty or moldy classroom air (Heschong Mahone Group, 2003).

Considering the overall findings from the various studies on lighting, we can conclude that indirect, natural sunlight is probably best for learning. However, many schools confronted with the need for cost savings have introduced "low-light days" to save on electrical bills. As the research clearly indicates, this approach is a mistake. Students enrolled in schools with above-average lighting had higher attendance and their students had higher physical growth rates (averaging 10 millimeters), increased concentration, and better academic performance (Lemasters, 1997). Given schools' large electricity requirements, installing skylights and even solar panels could realize real cost savings. Overall, school systems would do well to factor in research on lighting and student performance when considering building designs and operations (see Figure 6.1). The goal should be to keep the classrooms bright and find other ways to cut costs.

Practical Suggestions

Here are some practical ways to apply research findings related to lighting:

• *Maintain a constant, adequate level of bright lighting in your classroom.* Bright lighting helps reduce drowsiness by suppressing the production of melatonin in the brain.

• *Limit student exposure to darkened lecture halls and similar environments.* When such exposure is necessary, include low-level background lighting from a hallway or a window.

• *Maximize student exposure to daylight.* Make sure students are exposed to as much natural light as possible, especially during fall and winter months. Open classroom blinds and skylights. Take students on field trips and brisk walks, when possible, and hold P.E. classes outdoors rather than in a gym.

• *Hold class outside on occasion.* Not only will students be exposed to more sunlight and fresh air, their brains will be stimulated by the novelty of learning in a new and different environment.

• *Watch for signs of trouble.* If a student appears depressed during fall and winter months, encourage the parents to consult with their child's physician about the possibility of SAD.

Noise

In poorly designed classrooms that fail to address and reduce ambient noise, echo effects,

reverberation, and other acoustical problems, student attention decreases and off-task behaviors and discipline problems increase (Berg, Blair, & Benson, 1996); obviously, these issues take a serious toll on learning.

Our amazing brain typically processes up to 20,000 bits of auditory stimuli every second, which means that nearly every sound in the range of 20 to 15,000 cycles per second is fair game for processing. Getting students to hear what we want them to hear in the classroom, therefore, can be a problem. As an example, the most significant

Figure 6.1

LIGHTING AND LEARNING

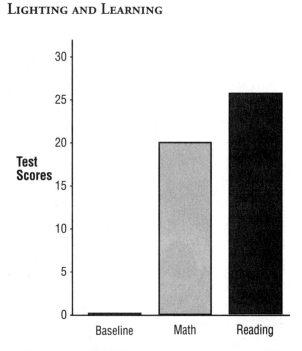

One firm grouped 2,000 classrooms into a range of six lighting conditions. Compared to students in the darkest rooms, students in the brightest rooms progressed 20 percent faster on standardized math tests and 26 percent faster on reading tests.

Source: Based on data from Heschong & Heschong Mahone Consulting Group (1999).

variable in predicting reading performance (even greater than being identified as a gifted student) comes from a factor mentioned earlier—the loud "ballast hum" from flourescent lighting. It has a - 19 percent influence compared to a +16 percent effect of being a gifted student (Heschong Mahone Group, 2003). "Situations that compromise student focus on the lessons at hand, such as reverberant spaces, annoying equipment sounds or excessive noise from outside the classroom have discernable negative effects on learning rates" (Heschong Mahone Group, 2003, p. 17).

Lawrence Feth, professor of speech and hearing science at Ohio State University, conducted an extensive acoustical study of classrooms. He found that many classrooms are acoustically unsound, which makes listening and learning difficult (Feth, 1999). In fact, the study found that of the 32 primary school classrooms studied, only 2 met the acoustical standards recommended by the American Speech-Language-Hearing Association (ASHA). The majority of classrooms in the study had enough background noise and echoes present to hamper the learning of children with even mild hearing problems.

Noise may have physiological implications in addition to cognitive ones. For example, one study (Evans, Lercher, Meis, Ising, & Kofler, 2001) found that children in noisier areas had higher blood pressure and heart rates, plus elevated stress levels—factors that aren't conducive to learning.

Children for whom English is a second language and children with hearing or learning deficits have an especially hard time attending to the teacher in a noisy classroom. Smaldino and Crandell (2000) note that both hearing-impaired and at-risk children have difficulty separating the

teacher's message from background noise. These learners may require support technology, ranging from headphones to earplugs to well-placed supplemental speakers. Moreover, research strongly suggests poor acoustical conditions can lead to stress, impaired learning, and frustration for students with normal hearing (Nelson & Soli, 2000; Smaldino & Crandell, 2000).

Although scientists have known for some time that chronic noise can have a negative effect on academic performance, they are now considering the possibility that noise may actually prevent children from acquiring speech recognition skills. Evans and Maxwell (1997) compared children in a noisy school (in the flight path of a New York international airport) with similar children in a quiet school. Unlike subjects in other noise studies, both groups of children were tested in quiet conditions. This method allowed the researchers to eliminate an important variable. By testing subjects in a quiet room, they demonstrated that decreased reading scores are due to *chronic* noise exposure— not noisy *episodes* that might have occurred during the testing sessions. Results indicated children chronically exposed to aircraft noise had significant deficits in reading. The researchers believe that noise-induced reading problems may be partly due to deficits in language acquisition, because the chronically exposed children also suffered from impaired speech perception.

Feth (1999) reported that the most prominent sources of background noise in classrooms (both new and old) are the heating and cooling systems. Many schools still opt for individual units instead of the more quiet central air systems. In addition, a typical classroom's uncarpeted floors and hard-surfaced walls make it highly conducive to sound reverberation that can interfere with speech recognition and understanding. The echo-y effect can be mitigated by a building design that angles walls at least five degrees out of their original parallel plane or by positioning hard surfaces (window glass, blackboards, or whiteboards) opposite textured, uneven surfaces like doors, hanging fabrics, or counters. Carpeted floors and acoustical ceilings also reduce reverberation. Solid walls or walls with sound insulation prevent exterior noise transfer. Any movable classroom walls should extend from floor to ceiling. And if windows or doors must be opened for ventilation, a low-frequency sound device (a "white noise" machine) can help mask ambient sounds.

Excessive environmental noise—including traffic sounds, aircraft noise, machinery, beepers, and even casual conversation—can reduce comprehension and work performance, especially in the early stages of learning a new task (Berglund, Hassmen, & Job, 1996; Gomes, Martinho, Pimenta, & Castelo Branco, 1999). The Environmental Protection Agency recommends that noise levels generally not exceed an average of 45 decibels in the daytime and 35 decibels at night. Unfortunately, ambient or environmental noise in many urban areas often reaches 70 decibels during the day and more than 60 decibels at night. In comparison, a whisper is approximately 20 decibels and a stereo at full blast is about 120 decibels.

Researchers have reported dramatic improvement in students' speech discrimination after classrooms were refitted with sound-absorbing material that reduced ambient noise (Pekkarinen & Wiljanen, 1990). Acoustical experts know that children are especially sensitive to overly noisy classrooms because they are still learning language

and need to clearly hear new speech sounds for effective acquisition. In comparison, adults have a larger vocabulary, which helps them mentally compensate when they can't hear clearly. Beyond causing an immediate stress response in the nervous system and the voluntary muscular reflex system (including the release of such neurotransmitters as epinephrine, norepinephrine, and cortisol), loud noise also increases heart rate, grimacing, and sudden muscle flexion. Together, these stress responses impair learning over time.

Practical Suggestions

Here are some practical ways to apply research findings related to noise:

• *Take stock of the noise level in your classroom.* Do you notice students straining to hear you or their classmates? Do you have hearing-impaired students or students who speak English as a second language? These students may find it especially difficult to understand speech in a noisy classroom.

• *Do what you can to soften the noise level in your classroom.* Try hanging egg cartons, fabric, or tapestries on the walls, which will absorb some of the sound waves.

• *Take official action if noise is a serious problem.* If your classroom has a significant problem with ambient noise, consult your school administration or an acoustical engineer on the most efficient way to eliminate the distractions. Allergy-sensitive carpeting, drapery, sound-absorbing panels, wall hangings, and commercially available sound amplification systems may be options to explore.

• *Make appropriate use of soothing "white noise" or music.* Some options for masking disturbing noise include fish tanks, desktop waterfalls, and classical or environmental music.

• *Schedule activities that require the most intense mental concentration when environmental noise levels are lowest.* It is especially important to maintain a quiet environment when learners are taking exams or doing other important mental tasks.

• *Spread the word.* Do your part to see that school planners and administrators know the research that suggests children who attend schools near noisy airports, major roads, and railways may not learn to read as well as children in quiet schools.

Other Environmental Considerations

Teachers often ask if the color of the classroom walls affects the brain, learning, and cognition. The studies are not absolutely clear on this issue, but findings do lean toward an answer of yes. Harry Wohlfarth, who has pioneered dozens of studies in this field, believes wall colors do matter. His research (Wohlfarth, 1984; Wohlfarth, 1985, Wohlfarth & Schultz, 1982) suggests the following recommendations to bring about the most consistent positive effects on behavior and cognition:

• Use a warm yellow on the three walls that students face (in regular education classes).

• Use a light blue color on the rear wall—the wall that the teacher faces.

• Use contrasting cool colors as accents around the front of the room.

• Use warmer colors (red and yellow) to stimulate students and cooler colors (light blue) to calm overactive students.

• Use a warm golden-gray on carpets.

A host of other variables influence the student learning environment. Many are concepts well supported and often used by classroom teachers. Although there may not be compelling data to support trumpeting them as "key variables," for the most part, they are good to do.

Room décor. Classroom walls do not need to look like the walls in students' homes. School is not like home, and furthermore, there are students for whom home is not necessarily a pleasant place. Walls and ceilings ought to be full, rich, and interesting, but not distractingly cluttered. Use the walls for affirmations, information, inspiration, or sneak previews of upcoming learning and reviews of prior learning. In such a positive setting, students unconsciously begin to acquire a foundation for "understanding" before they even know they know something—in fact, even before the teacher enters the room.

Opportunities for mobility. Students need privacy, reflection, and thinking time. We ask students to either suppress those needs or to reflect and think in workspaces that would strain our sensibilities. The key is reasoned flexibility in seating.

Aromas. These ought to be kept to a minimum. Many students have an allergic sensitivity to flowers, candles, room-freshener sprays, and even some natural aromas. Having said that, an occasional aroma of freshly baked cookies or bread rarely draws complaints!

Accommodating special needs. Many students, perhaps up to 6 percent depending on students' age and background, have hyperactivity or sensory integration disorders. Of those with sensory disorders, some have auditory sensitivities and may need exceptional quiet—perhaps achievable only through use of earplugs. Those with visual sensitivity may want to seek out a darker area of the room to avoid the flicker in the fluorescent lights. Those with tactile sensitivities may need to sit on the floor or on a large exercise ball. Some students may need extra mobility. In short, be prepared to accommodate those with special needs. It usually costs little or nothing, and it makes a world of difference to the student.

Overall School Facilities and Cognition

The whole of the school environment, the "gestalt," is another influence on student learning. Research indicates that well-planned learning environments stimulate learning and reduce discipline problems. When coupled with sound teaching strategies, brain-friendly learning environments strengthen neural connections and support long-term memory, planning, and motivation (Frank & Greenberg, 1994).

Ayers (1999) examined the relationship between high school facilities and student achievement. The researchers used the Design Appraisal Scale for High Schools (DASH-I) to measure the different design variables and to determine a total-quality score for each school in the study. Based upon the results of the analyses, school-design variables explained approximately 6 percent of the variance in English and social studies performance, 3 percent in science performance, and 2 percent in both mathematics and writing performance.

Schools with shattered windows, broken-down restrooms, leaky roofs, insufficient lighting, and overcrowding have a significantly negative impact on cognition. Such conditions are found in many U.S. schools, meaning far too many children, especially those in poor urban areas, are schooled in dilapidated, crowded facilities. According to a comprehensive study (Cash, Earthman, & Hines, 1997) covering 325 public schools in three school districts, the adverse effect that these conditions had on academic performance was significant. Cash found a positive relationship between poor building conditions and lowered academic performance, delinquent behavior, and absenteeism. His findings also suggest that quality facilities, coupled with strong academic programs, are conditions essential to optimum student learning.

Designing Smarter Schools

School-facility design has garnered much recent attention. With an increased interest in student performance as well as safety, the old bricks-and-mortar "cheapest is best" notion is dead and buried. "Innovative school design" no longer refers merely to creating facilities that have a splashy, interesting exterior. Today, it means schools that are socially smart, cognitively supportive, emotionally safe, and environmentally friendly. One of the leaders in this movement is Jeffrey Lackney, assistant professor at the University of Wisconsin–Madison. He's been an advocate for the research on "smarter" school design and for building learner-friendly educational environments. Lackney has often articulated that while we may not know all of the social and academic effects of school environments, we still have enough evidence to prompt us to take corrective action (2001).

Who is paying attention to the findings on school design and learning? Are the decision makers getting it? According to Scott Midler of SHW Group Architects in Dallas, Texas,

> More and more research is emerging that links building condition to student achievement. . . . Educators are under enormous pressure to be frugal in their spending . . . . Unfortunately it's short-term cost-cutting when they could design the environment to improve learning and amortize the costs over the life of the building. (S. Midler, personal communication, January 22, 2004)

SHW Group Architects is a firm specializing in sustainable and brain-friendly learning environments. Along with other innovators, the firm now designs schools with the whole community in mind, including such elements as safety, cognition, curiosity, economics, mood, attendance, ecology, and social factors. In fact, the award-winning SHW Group is nationally recognized for outstanding contributions to the design profession and has been named one of the top 20 design firms nationwide. Here is an overview of what the top design firms are now incorporating into school designs.

Acoustics. Building a sound system into the school from the start is much less costly than doing it later. There are no walls to tear down, and any wiring can be hidden. In addition, walls can be set at better angles, and carpeting can be used to reduce sound reverberation. Such factors are more than just functional; they raise or lower stress levels.

Daytime lighting. The trend is toward more natural lighting and better use of skylights. New vertical solar monitors can scoop up the natural light and provide 100 percent of daily classroom light. The sunlight is drawn into the light monitor and bounced off a series of baffles to provide soft, evenly distributed daylight throughout the facility.

Ecology. Many schools include ecology in their curriculum, but the school itself is commonly an ecological disaster. Why not model ways to effectively deal with the energy crisis? This is an area of knowledge sure to profoundly affect the work and lives of the next generation. Students can learn how to conserve electricity and manage it wisely, how to improve the environment, and how to sustain the earth for future generations.

Temperature, humidity, and ventilation. Issues include providing flexibility and individual classroom control so that teachers can maintain the appropriate comfort levels. Heating and cooling mechanisms should also be simple to operate and quiet.

Learning spaces. In the well-designed school, traditional classrooms give way to multipurpose "learning studios" or "zones"—places where children can engage in specialized, task-specific activities together. "Learning streets," atrium entranceways, and sitting areas replace nondescript, narrow corridors. Wider hallways without lockers reduce bullying, running, and discipline problems. Shorter, more socially compatible cubbyholes replace the standard maze of uniform lockers. A supervised atrium lobby allows students to de-stress and write, draw, or reflect in creative ways.

Optimal views. It's not just windows and sufficient lighting that can improve learning. The view also makes a difference! With more than 50 measured variables in school environments, from pets to moldy air and carpeting, you'd think having a view would rate low. But it doesn't. Students do better when they have a calming, distant view of vegetation, as opposed to a close-up view of people walking by (Heschong Mahone Group, 2003).

School size. Smaller overall facilities create a psychologically and emotionally better environment for growth. They are both ecologically sound and easier to integrate with the community. It is now possible to build and operate small campuses for 300 to 700 students for the same cost per student as schools that accommodate 500 to 1,400 students. If you can't do that, subdivide your school into smaller ones. To save space, students older than 16 could spend part of their time outside the classroom, involved in community service and school-to-work programs.

Although smaller is better in overall school size, students need adequate "elbow room" in classrooms and other learning spaces. Research from the School Design Lab in Georgia suggests that elementary schools with less than 100 square feet per student have lower overall scores on the Iowa Tests of Basic Skills (Zernike, 2001).

Staff areas. Teachers and staff need comfortable spaces where they can get away from the hustle and bustle to think, relax, plan, and reflect. Smart schools provide at least three places where teachers can get support: (1) a quiet reflective spot for power naps; (2) a learning center, library, or staff media center; and (3) a de-stressing area with a treadmill and a floor mat for stretching. Most businesses have an employee lounge, and many provide facilities that nurture good health and well-being. Teachers, on the other hand, despite having one of the most stressful jobs in our society, are lucky to have one small, crowded staff lounge per school.

Major components of a sustainable school include protecting the environment, channeling daylight into classrooms to minimize the use of artificial light, using recycled products and materials, and incorporating the school's design into the academic program. The slightly higher initial cost is offset by lower maintenance costs over the long haul. An example of this new breed of "brain-smart" schools is Roy Lee Walker Elementary in McKinney Independent School District in North Texas, a facility built as one of the nation's first "high-performance" schools. Designed in 2000 by the SHW Group, this school combines what's best for safety, aesthetics, function, and cognition.

Summary

Environments do matter! If new schools are being planned in your district, build alliances with key decision makers and design firms that are well versed in the research on the effects of school design, learning, stress, and cognition. Be proactive. Do what you can with what you have. If the only things you can modify are lighting, noise levels, and seating, begin there. Sometimes businesses are willing to pitch in and provide materials, supplies, or financial support for school- or classroom-improvement projects. If you don't have the funding, consider a partnership with a local corporation. Could the Home Depot sponsor a new vocational wing? Could Microsoft support a new block of rooms? Anything is possible once you set a goal and develop the attitude and the team to reach it.

For students to learn, grow, behave, and perform optimally, a smartly designed, high-performance environment is necessary. Take charge; do your best to support your students in being their best by orchestrating powerful learning environments.

Managing the
Social Brain

KEY CONCEPTS

▶ **How social interaction affects the brain and cognition**

▶ **The effect of stress, bonding, bias, and peer pressure**

▶ **How to make school a more positive social experience**

Humans are essentially social beings, and school is a complex social experience. It's true that in some classes, you'll see students sitting quietly in rows, working independently with little or no social contact. As an occasional strategy, this kind of independent learning makes sense. But what about our social brain? As we know, humans act very differently in social settings than they do individually. Now emerging evidence tells us those social experiences literally *change* the human brain. In fact, an entire new discipline has developed called social neuroscience. It's the study of brains in a social environment. Neuroscientists Stephen Quartz and Terry Sejnowski neatly summarize the interdependent nature of the brain and society: "Culture helps to shape your brain, which in turn creates culture, which acts again on the brain . . ." (2002, p. 59).

Significant social experiences take place in the classroom and the school, and we now know that students' brains *will be altered* by those experiences. To ignore the social influence on student brains is irresponsible. We must understand

94

and take responsibility for the ways we are shaping brains in the social environment of schools.

Student brains spend approximately 13,000 hours in the social environment of schools. Wouldn't you want to know—if it was your child—how that environment is changing his or her brain? How might schools change the brain for the worse? What could the most recent brain research lead us to do better or differently? This chapter considers what happens to learners in the social context that is relevant to educators and policymakers. We'll focus on three major themes:

- How social experiences affect the brain.
- The complex nature of the "social brain."
- How to enhance the social experience of school.

How Social Experience Affects the Brain

We've all used the phrase "people smarts" to refer to social skills. Social cognition is the processing of information that leads to the accurate processing of the dispositions and intentions of others (Brothers, 2000). It appears to have a plausible evolutionary basis, to be operationally distinct from other types of knowledge, to have a developmental pathway, and to have inborn selective absences (which show up in disorders such as autism at the lower end of the social skill spectrum and Williams syndrome at the higher end). These are some of the key premises for Howard Gardner's identification of social skills as one of the eight intelligences (1995).

Social neuroscience has revealed an astonishing array of influences that social contact has on the brain. And the influences are not random, isolated, or piecemeal. Environmental events *at one level* of an organism (chemical, cellular, tissue, organ, system, behavioral, social, and so on) can profoundly influence events at other levels (Cacioppo et al., 2001). For this reason, it makes sense to consider the connection between school social climates and the people within the schools. Schools are social places; as a result, they change students' brains.

It's a profound paradigm shift to suggest that the social environment of school is actually shaping students' physical brains. Data from multiple sources (social and behavioral studies using both physical data and functional neuroimaging) indicate that the development and influence of the social cognitive brain is not limited to just one area. The areas of the brain active in processing social events (the visual system, frontal lobes, sensory cortex, and emotional pathways) often process cognitive events as well (Frith & Frith, 1999). Their "double duty" nature helps explain why social events so strongly influence cognitive events.

It's becoming clear that social contact affects human physiology in a number of remarkable ways. Researchers have found stunning evidence of social influence on genetic expression (Suomi, 1999) and hints of change through genetic constitution (Wilson & Grim, 1991). Evidence suggests that an increase in social support lowers blood pressure in hypertensive subjects (Uchino, Cacioppo, & Kiecolt-Glaser, 1996). We've learned that social contact improves or hurts immune activity (Padgett, MacCallum, & Sheridan, 1998) and that social stress weakens immune systems (Padgett & Sheridan, 2002). Researchers have found that social isolation is just as devastating a health risk factor as is smoking or high blood pressure (House, Landis, & Umberson, 1988) and that social stress early in life can lead to lasting changes in the stress–response system (Rojas, Padgett, Sheridan, & Marucha, 2002). And Yeh and colleagues (1996) found that social status modified levels of serotonin in the brain, which is highly implicated in attention, memory, aggression, and the growth of neurons (see Figure 7.1).

Figure 7.1

How Social Contact Affects the Brain and Body

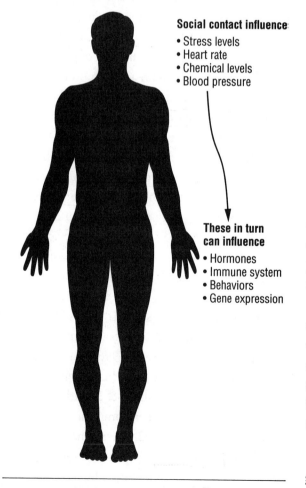

Social contact influences
• Stress levels
• Heart rate
• Chemical levels
• Blood pressure

These in turn can influence
• Hormones
• Immune system
• Behaviors
• Gene expression

The Complex Nature of the Social Brain

An important characteristic of healthy, social humans is their capacity and desire to detect the features of mental lives, both their own and others'. We want to know what we are thinking and feeling, and what everybody else is thinking and feeling too. When this feature is diminished, as is the case with autism, social skills are undermined. In short, a complex set of anatomical structures and chemicals mediate both social skills and cognition (see Figure 7.2).

What can we expect of our developing social brain? How does it respond to small or large social gatherings? How is our behavior when we are in a social setting different from our behavior when we are alone? Are there gender differences in the social brain? These are the kinds of questions we need to explore.

Cognition

The extent to which social conditions can influence cognition cannot be overestimated. Some of the key factors to consider within the learning environment are peer pressure, acceptance, disapproval and reinforcement, and the role of emotions in decision making.

Solid evidence supports the notion that working cooperatively can enhance learning. Cooperative work has helped civilizations survive for thousands of years, and it works in the classroom, too. The most important elements in good cooperative learning structures, according to Johnson and Johnson (1999), the leaders in the field, are the following:

• Face-to-face interactions that promote the group (smiling, helping, reinforcing).

• Positive interdependence (the idea that we are all in this together and must help each other).

• Both group and individual accountability (the belief that personal and group achievement goals matter).

• Small-group and interpersonal skills like listening, decision making, trust, and conflict resolution.

• Metaprocessing skills (the ability to reflect on whole-group effectiveness and to improve functionality).

Note that many of these require social skills—and that's the point! Without social cognition either already in place or being developed by the group interactions, the cooperative process is impaired. Yet social cognitive skills are not universal. The prefrontal cortex, the area of the brain that is critical for sophisticated social cognition, matures slowly and often does not reach complete maturity until we are well into our teens and 20s (Durston et al., 2001). This means that students are not even close to being born with social skills—it's something they have to be taught.

To help students develop social cognitive skills, it makes sense to allow them to spend some part of their learning time in groups. Options for grouping include pair-share, competitions, simulations, cooperative groups, and unstructured social time for discussions.

Social grouping comes with many caveats. First, most students do better when they are in groups with others who share their same approximate academic readiness level. Although low-ability students gain more from being in groups of higher ability, medium-ability students gain the most in a medium-ability group, and high-ability groups gain a small amount in a high-ability group. Second, smaller groups of three to four perform better than larger or smaller ones (Lou et al., 1996). Finally, relying too exclusively on social grouping may create excessive familiarity or dependence, not independent skills. Ideally, students should spend 5 to 20 percent of class time in social groupings, and grouping should be used purposefully and strategically. These principles also apply to various kinds of informal groups, such as pairs and impromptu groups.

As we learned in Chapter 4, social play also has a role in the classroom. Studies have shown that such play can help in the development of quick-thinking skills (Dugatkin, 2002). Quick, active play enhances the ability to handle unexpected events and regulate stress; fosters quick planning, decision-making, and evaluative judgments; boosts creativity; forges social bonds; and introduces emotional intelligence and codes of conduct.

Figure 7.2

SOCIAL BRAIN REGULATORS

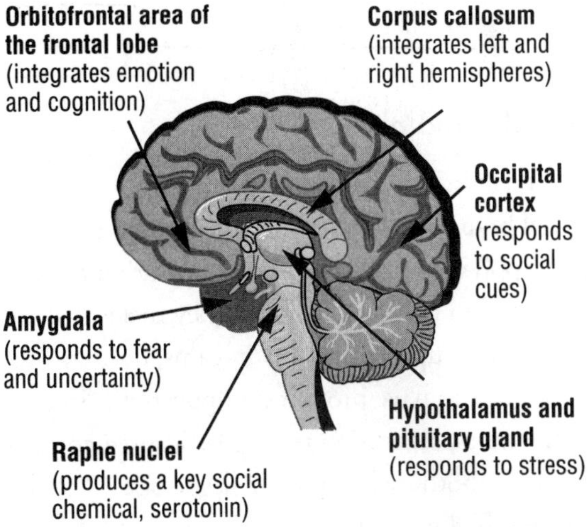

Orbitofrontal area of the frontal lobe (integrates emotion and cognition)

Corpus callosum (integrates left and right hemispheres)

Occipital cortex (responds to social cues)

Amygdala (responds to fear and uncertainty)

Hypothalamus and pituitary gland (responds to stress)

Raphe nuclei (produces a key social chemical, serotonin)

Social Stress

Stress plays a role in many social interactions, including so-called "flocking" behaviors in which adolescents or teens form groups for social comfort, camaraderie, or protection. At school, we see specific examples of the social brain acting under stress, and many of the behaviors show gender differences. For example, females are more likely to mobilize social support under stress than males are; females report more sources of social support than males do. This lack of social support can put males at greater risk for suicide. Males are more likely to affiliate with groups of people with similar status or power; females are more likely to affiliate by friendships or task needs (Baumeister & Sommer, 1997). And animal studies suggest that position within a social group may influence brain chemistry, which, in turn, affects behavior. In one study involving primates, monkeys that rose to top of the social hierarchy showed increased levels of dopamine (Czoty, Morgan, Shannon, Gage, & Nader, 2004), the "natural high" brain chemical. It does feel good to be right, to win, to come out on top. The anticipation of that "high" is partly what pushes students to do an activity.

Social Bonding

Preening is a common manifestation of the social brain. Students spend time grooming, posing, applying makeup—all in preparation for social contact and bonding. Choices they make at school to join a group, pair up, form teams, or leave others alone can have profound implications. In animal studies, separation from peers caused cortisol levels for both males and females to rise 18 to 87 percent higher than for those housed with friendly,

established social groups (Lyons & Levine, 1994). We also know that the loss or absence of a valued social companion is a robust risk factor for depression (Billings, Cronkite, & Moos, 1983). The increased risk of depression and suicide among teens makes obvious their need for more guidance, camaraderie, and support. These findings all reinforce the importance of social bonding with peers and others.

Social Bias

Racial differences can be a serious social issue. One of the more interesting studies on race focused on the question of built-in racial bias. Adolphs (1998) found that some students experience discomfort around members of a race other than their own. This typically happens when students have had few or no multicultural experiences or friendships during their upbringing. Is the brain biased against other races? No, racism is learned. But wariness about "different" others is built in. How you treat another after the initial wariness is the learned behavior.

Racial bias has absolutely no biological basis, but our brain does respond in a negative way to those different from ourselves if we have not been desensitized to those differences. As we learned earlier, the amygdala is the brain's "uncertainty activator." When we don't understand what is happening or we detect any uncertainty, this structure initiates either a fear or a stress response. Studies show that the response is indirect and implicit. The subjects claim no explicit bias, but various measures show a clear negative response (Phelps et al., 2000). These studies, along with others, show that we often choose friends on a subconscious basis (Greenwald & Banaji, 1995).

Peer Pressure

Although the young brain's priorities are focused more on pleasing others, developing self-concept, and making friends, things change somewhat with age. Adolescent and teen students are more interested in peer approval, autonomy, and discovery. These tendencies can be either a nightmare for a school or a delight, depending on how well they are managed. For example, many teens will not exercise unless their friends do (Winters, Petosa, & Charlton, 2003). Because social influence is a significant factor in an adolescent's decision to exercise, policymaking might focus on making previously unpopular activities (for example, high academic achievement or exercise) a group activity or a "cool" thing to do with peers.

Although some educators complain that school-age kids are too social, many other, more perceptive educators are taking advantage of this reality through the smart use of cooperative learning in the elementary classroom and the use of teams in the secondary classroom. It just makes sense to engage and structure social forces to help shape student behavior in a positive way instead of complaining that the social forces are out of control.

Social Difficulties

Research suggests that more than 10 percent of students may suffer some social impairment (Cicerone & Tanenbaum, 1997; Rilling et al., 2002). Sometimes social difficulty is a result of an "emotionally poor" upbringing—one characterized by neglect, abuse, or a lack of proper emotional modeling. Sometimes it has genetic causes or is the result of congenital factors, such as fetal alcohol syndrome. Sometimes, as with autism and Asperger's syndrome, there is a less clear-cut biological origin.

We have learned from neuroimaging that certain social impairments often involve the amygdala, the system deep in the temporal lobes of the brain that is critical to emotional processing (Bechara et al., 2003). The brains of people whose social skill deficits are associated with fetal alcohol syndrome, genetic disorders, or traumatic brain injury are more likely to show compromised function in the orbitofrontal lobes, the area linked to self-expression, problem solving, willpower, and planning.

When specific areas of the brain are damaged, social skills fail. A classic example is the story of Phineas Gage, a 19th-century railroad worker who suffered a terrible accident. A 13-pound tamping iron more than three feet long exploded and flew like a missile through Gage's left cheek. The metal pierced his frontal lobes and exited his head, landing a hundred feet away. Miraculously, Gage lived, but his personality was never the same and his social skills were ruined (Damasio, 1994).

Enhancing the Social Experience of School

Social contact has significant and broad-based effects. Because students spend so many hours of their lives in school, we must consider what we're doing to their brains during that time. Socially, we are influencing them a great deal. If we believe that school is about the "whole person," then the social side is worth understanding and addressing.

Practical Suggestions

There are many practical ways to apply research findings related to the social brain.

Information gathering. For starters, educators can do a better job in gathering information about students' social preferences. How much time do students want to spend alone, how much time in pairs, and how much time in groups or teams? To find out, simply ask them. Then watch and listen for changes in their preferences over time. Once you have a sense of what they prefer, you can plan accordingly. But don't forget, variety is always a good strategy.

Quick social grouping. Much of the social time students need can occur in informal groupings. Ask students to stand up, walk 10 steps, and find a partner. Students can then pair-share or interview each other, test a hypothesis, or review prior learning. They can switch from one pair to another to "jigsaw" their learning. Ask them to find a partner outside of class—perhaps a parent, a school employee, or a friend with whom they can discuss their classwork. Another option is to incorporate simple social greetings in class with the use of "turn-to's." When appropriate, you say, "Turn to your neighbor and say, 'Good morning.'" Or "Turn to your neighbor and say, 'Good job!'"

A balance of social and individual events. Mandated social events such as assemblies and team activities should be a part of school life; however, it's important to balance these with time spent on individual work. The goal is a good middle ground between social and individual experiences. To a certain extent, student choice should play a role, allowing individuals to go with their strengths and decide which mode will work best for them.

Cooperative learning. When done well, cooperative learning does teach social skills and its effects are strong (Johnson & Johnson, 1999). Research on students engaged in cooperative learning suggests that they achieve better learning when compared with students competing against each other individually (Walberg, 1999). Teams can work well, too—and are properly deployed for focused, goal-oriented work on a specific project (as contrasted with cooperative group learning, which is a more open-ended, long-term arrangement). The bottom line is this: social-bonding structures like either of these are important and valuable.

Social skills instruction. Most elementary teachers invest time in developing students' social skills, but the practice is far less common in middle and high school. When blended into the curriculum, teaching social skills takes little extra time. And you may get a significant payoff in terms of efficiency: fewer disruptions, more camaraderie, and better overall feelings about the learning.

Summary

The social experience is a brain-changing experience, and it can be either positive or negative, depending to a large degree on how schools and teachers orchestrate it. Classrooms that feature too little social contact between students raise long-term concerns, especially when you consider the clear evidence that face-to-face contact is a positive and powerful force in increasing cooperation (Dawes, McTavish, & Shaklee, 1977).

The negative effect of social isolation suggests troubling implications for two growing areas of education: online schooling (increasingly attractive to school systems looking to cut costs) and home schooling. Although both approaches have many virtues, one cannot help but wonder about important questions: What kind of social skills will these students have? What kind of world will we live in if millions of young children are raised in child care centers, educated online, and then expected to work in a social world? We have, at this time, more questions than answers. But the implications are sobering in a world that seems to have all too little cooperation as it is.

Motivation and Engagement

I s she or isn't she? Is he or isn't he? Within the first few days of meeting a student, teachers often want an answer to the compelling question: Is this student intrinsically motivated or not? And, if the student is not motivated, what approach should be taken to change this?

Researchers often refer to motivation as "arousal" and "drive." Arousal suggests orientation toward a goal, and drive is caring enough to do something about achieving the goal. Another way to think of motivation is that it consists of the willingness to be active (volition) combined with the actual behavior (meaningful participation). It's common knowledge that different students will have varying levels of these two motivational forces. But does our new understanding of the brain tell us anything about learner motivation? Is there really such a thing as an unmotivated learner? Why are some learners intrinsically motivated? And what does brain research tell us about using rewards? These are some of the questions we explore in this chapter. Here are the three main topics:

KEY CONCEPTS

▶ **Common causes of demotivation**

▶ **The brain's reaction to rewards**

▶ **The nature of intrinsic motivation**

▶ **Tools for motivation**

▶ **The SuperCamp model**

- Common sources of demotivation.
- Rewards and the brain—good or bad?
- Ways to motivate and engage students.

Clearly, motivation is an issue for many teachers. The story is the same, whether middle school teachers or college professors tell it: "Today's students just aren't as motivated as I was when I was in school." First, remember you are the person who survived and made it through school, so you're not exactly part of a random population sample. Second, many students who do not appear to be highly motivated in school turn out to do well in life. Finally, there is plenty that you can do to reduce the problem of low student motivation, which leads us to the theme for the chapter: *You have far more influence over the volition and engagement of your students than you may realize.*

Common Sources of Demotivation

The causes of reduced student motivation are virtually unlimited. They vary by student population, by time of year, and even by income level. In many ways, it would be productive to flush out all the potential causes at your school and eliminate them. Realistically, you can learn a lot just by talking to your students to find out what holds them back. Their reasons may be very different from what you think. Without some careful homework on your part, you might end up investing resources to solve a nonexistent problem.

Although causes of demotivation will vary from one student to another, certain causes are fairly universal. Here are some of the more common ones:

- *Lack of positive relationships.* A negative relationship with the teacher or even the lack of a best friend can be demotivating.

- *Learned helplessness.* This attitude is more common in middle and high school students than in elementary school students.

- *Awareness of disrespect toward one's culture or ethnicity.* Every culture carries a language, a set of values, a set of learning styles, and a work ethic.

- *Perception of threats.* These threats may be real or imagined, and may be related to something going on during the commute to school, in the hallways, or in the classroom.

- *Brain anomalies.* Abnormal brain function can result in delayed development, dyslexia, emotional distress, or attention deficits.

- *Drug use.* Marijuana use is strongly demotivating; chronic alcohol use reduces motivation, as do many over-the-counter medications.

- *Perception that class assignments or tasks are irrelevant.* Why work hard when what you're working on doesn't seem to matter?

The list is varied and interesting for a good reason: differences in the brain, which commonly result in differences in behavior. And remember that it goes the other way, too: differences in behavior usually lead to differences in the brain, which is why there are many "right" ways to motivate students. The brain is changed for the better by good parenting, tutoring, good friends, smart nutrition, healthy habits, perceptive teachers, or even drugs prescribed to treat a problem. The best and most lasting way to motivate students involves creating long-term internal motivation through good parenting *and* through effective schooling that offers meaningful choices and appropriate curriculum. (See Chapter 12 for more about this kind of schooling.) Here, I want to focus on two other ways to motivate and engage learners, both of which use instructional strategies to get the job done. The first is the simplest form of motivation: using direct rewards.

Rewards and the Brain: Good or Bad?

Teachers often use rewards as a motivational strategy. Rewards seem harmless and are often effective, which leads us to an important question: Are rewards good for the brain?

Biologically, human brains are designed to predict, process, enjoy, and remember rewards. This process has enormous survival value; consider behaviors related, for example, to such factors as food, safety, attracting a mate, and sex. When we think of rewards, we usually think about the positive functions they serve. For example, rewards can

- Induce pleasure.
- Increase the frequency of goal-seeking behaviors.
- Maintain learned behaviors.
- Increase social behaviors.
- Reinforce existing learning.
- Increase the success rate of new learning.

The brain's pathways for rewards are complex because they involve the tasks of prediction, detection, goal orientation, planning, pleasure, expectations, and memory (see Figure 8.1). The brain areas engaged include the hypothalamus, the orbitofrontal cortex, the prefrontal cortex, the amygdala, and other midbrain structures (Schultz, 2000). Keep in mind that there's an enormous difference in how the human brain responds to rewards for different kinds of accomplishments. Most brain-related research on rewards has focused

on simple tasks, and some evidence supports the targeted use of rewards for short-term tasks. Rewards can temporarily stimulate simple physical responses; however, more complex behaviors are usually impaired, not helped, by rewards (Kohn, 1993). So if you think giving rewards will help develop great minds, you're likely to be disappointed. Here's what one great mind, physicist and Nobel laureate Richard Feynman (1999), has to say about rewards:

> I don't see that it makes any point that someone in the Swedish Academy decides that this work is noble enough to receive a prize—I've already got the prize. The prize is the pleasure of finding the thing out, the kick in the discovery. (p. 12)

The brain makes its own rewards. They are called opiates, and they can produce a natural high similar to that produced by morphine, alcohol, nicotine, heroin, and cocaine. It probably does not matter to the brain whether the reward is concrete—like money or objects of value—or more cognitive—like privilege, status, recognition, attention, security, or fame. Working like a thermostat or a personal trainer, the brain's reward system ordinarily doles out good feelings on a daily basis, which suggests that the brain has a built-in bias to experience pleasurable causes and effects. But rewards are not as simple as a yes–no question. It turns out that the brain may have different types of reward signal systems (Fiorillo, Tobler, & Schultz, 2003). One of the systems includes codes for reward prediction, and the other, for error correction. The first system creates attentiveness (more if the reinforcer is random), and the second creates better learning.

Figure 8.1

The Biology of Rewards

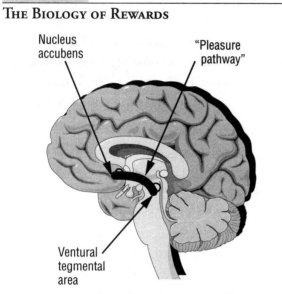

The "pleasure pathway" includes key structures that produce and distribute dopamine, the specific neurotransmitter that induces pleasure.

The reward–prediction system takes on the job of predicting upcoming pleasure. The prediction of a pleasurable outcome is enough to activate the pleasure network (Tremblay & Schultz, 2000), producing a burst of dopamine, the brain's reward neurotransmitter. Although you get pleasure from the anticipation of reward, your brain really goes crazy when the reward comes as a surprise, triggering a blissful release of dopamine. With this new-found pleasure, the brain then stores the reward condition as part of the memory, and reward–prediction may begin for next time. The catch is that although learners improve when they've received an initial reward, over time, the performance of many of them will actually drop as their actions are being rewarded. This pattern bears out research that dopamine is activated as much by the prediction of pleasure as by the pleasure itself (Berridge & Robinson, 2002).

Another problem, biologically speaking, is that the brain quickly habituates to rewards (Koob & LeMoal, 2001). Remember, we have an adaptive brain, a dynamic brain that changes in response to the environment, which means that what worked at one time may not work for long. We can quickly move from being satisfied with a dollar to wanting 10 dollars for the same task. In other words, rewards change the brain very rapidly, and what worked well before ceases to work (Koob & LeMoal, 1997). How does this relate to school? In 1st grade, a gold sticker may be a perfect reward. By 3rd grade, the child wants a cookie, and by 5th grade, only a pizza will do. (Note the escalation in value.) By 8th grade, pizzas are not quite so great, and the guys want a skateboard, PlayStation, Xbox, or Nintendo. By 11th grade, the girls want jewelry or a new car. Stickers have long since left the equation.

And, finally, what one student finds rewarding may not be rewarding to another. Most teachers have learned that two different students will react to the same external reward in different ways. The degree of pleasure that various students take in a reward is linked to the uniqueness of their brains, which makes rewards "unequal" from the start. A significant genetic susceptibility runs through the reward system, meaning that if you want to reward everyone fairly, all rewards must be individualized. In short, rewards are not without their down side. Where do these findings leave us in understanding the role of rewards? Perhaps we can conclude that rewards should be described in terms of "better" and "worse" instead of "good" and "bad."

Practical Suggestions

After all this, if you still want to use rewards for motivation in your classroom, here are some suggestions to keep in mind:

• *Use rewards judiciously.* Consider using rewards only for special populations, for short lengths of time, and for specific reasons. Remember, many students' performance will drop with the repeated use of rewards over time (Berridge & Robinson, 2002). It's the anticipation of pleasure that creates most of the good effects of rewards, not the reward itself.

• *Use low-cost, concrete rewards.* Choose economical items that are easy to give (such as tokens, M&Ms, and raisins), and plan to stop giving them after several weeks. Otherwise, your students will habituate to them, and you'll lose the effect. Get as much mileage as possible from the anticipation of a reward by reminding students how and when they will get it.

• *Use abstract rewards.* Rewards in the form of acknowledgments (certificates, thank-you notes, compliments) or celebrations with no monetary value (games, fun activities, privileges) are an effective alternative, especially when used unpredictably for task reinforcement. Rewards may seem to work in the short run, but, as you now know, over the long haul they can be demotivating (Kohn, 1993).

If you want to stop using rewards, keep in mind these suggestions:

• *Avoid going "cold turkey."* Don't dramatically stop giving rewards; phase them out gradually.

• *Begin to develop intrinsic motivation.* Allow students to make decisions, and let them learn to become responsible for the outcome of their choices. Be sure to celebrate successes.

• *Step up the abstract rewards.* These kinds of rewards include the acknowledgments and celebrations mentioned earlier (smiles, certificates, thank-you notes, games, fun activities, and privileges).

A useful guideline is that inappropriate (or "worse") rewards have two elements: predictability and market value. Let's say that your class puts on a play for the school and parents once a year. At the end of the play, the audience offers a standing ovation. The kids come off stage, and you proudly announce that you're taking everyone out for pizza. Is that a reward? No, it's a celebration. Had you said to the students right before the opening curtain, "Do well and you'll all get pizza," it would have been an inappropriate reward.

The predictability issue is legitimate because it becomes a racket over time. Students often begin to feel a sense of loss when they *don't* get a reward. Research suggests the absence of an expected reward is often interpreted as a kind of punishment (Schultz, Dayan, & Montague, 2002). Pizza, candy, stickers, and certificates all have market value. Research suggests that students will want them each time the behavior is required, they'll want an increasingly valuable reward, and rewards will provide little or no lasting pleasure.

Activating Intrinsic Motivation

Rewards may seem like a heck of a lot of work. Maybe you'd just rather activate a student's natural curiosity to learn. Making content more relevant by linking it to students' lives is always smart. There's no sense in the brain's making new connections if the task is already known well. But the task has to be *behaviorally relevant* to the learner (Ahissar et al., 1992), which is why the brain will not adapt to senseless tasks. Be sure to ask learners how they feel about a project up front—they'll tell you if they think it's stupid. Their feelings matter a great deal. Maybe a simple alteration in the project would make it worth doing. As the process proceeds, add feedback and debriefing sessions.

Whether you can activate intrinsic motivation easily or not depends on the student as well as your own skill level. Many factors contribute to motivation—only some of which you can control (see Figure 8.2). But your skills in orchestrating a good environment—one with low stress and high challenge—are critical. For many, intrinsic motivation is a state that is a bit difficult to access. There are, however, a few guidelines.

Practical Suggestions

Here are some ways to build students' intrinsic motivation.

• Make sure students have either a process model to follow or a strong end goal.
• Ensure they have the working tools they need.
• Provide plenty of encouragement, but not a direct reward.
• Allow students to exercise choice—for the little things as well as the big things.
• Role-model the joy of learning.
• Provide a variety of relevant experiences.
• Ensure that the content has high relevance.
• Allow students to be part of a successful team.
• Increase feedback to the learners.

• Allow more time for the "flow" state, when learners are so engrossed in their learning that they lose track of time.
• Set up apprentice programs.
• Invite past graduates to share success stories.

Alternatives to Rewards

You may recall that we discussed emotional states at length in Chapter 5. Another way to understand them is through the lens of motivation and engagement. Those positive states occur when we are in a particular mind-body-feeling state. A major revelation in the history of neuroscience was the discovery that all external behaviors somehow correlate to the brain's internal processes. Millions of neurons cooperate to

Figure 8.2

SOURCES OF MOTIVATION: THREE LAYERS

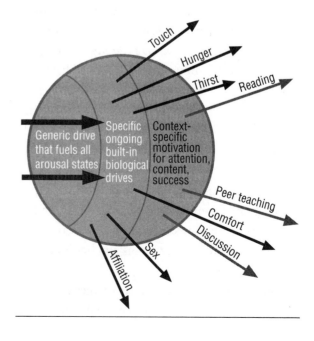

form complex, weblike signaling systems that represent the behaviors we call "states." This causation is similar to the way in which wind, sunshine, and moisture collectively form the complex atmospheric patterns we call "weather." States create "weather" conditions in our brains at every moment. You've probably observed that we all go through changes of states (unless we're in a coma). States change as our sensations (such as hunger, fatigue, itchiness), feelings (such as guilt, happiness, worry), and thoughts (such as optimism, gullibility, focus) combine and recombine simultaneously. But states are not intangible, as we once thought; instead, they are highly quantifiable, very real, and definitely cognitive (Damasio, 1994).

Now, what do states have to do with motivation and engagement? For one, states combine our emotional, cognitive, and physical interactions to allow us to make all our decisions. Evoking specific emotional states allows learners more freedom, not less, to make new discoveries. Once you learn to evoke a greater variety of learner states, you will begin to *uncouple the learner's rigidity.* You'll open up enormous flexibility because you will have artificially decoupled the stereotyped set of behaviors to which unmotivated students have become accustomed. These states are frequently activated, fast-changing, specific neural networks that typically incorporate multiple areas of the brain. Thousands, often millions, of neurons make up the integrated combination of mind, body, and feelings that are your states (see Figure 8.3). These systems inside our brains and bodies cannot be separated.

Surprisingly, states are moving targets, constantly fluctuating because of their high sensitivity

to both the internal and external environment. It makes sense to describe states as "emergent properties" of our self-organizing brains because they are *always* in a state of flux (Grigsby & Stevens, 2000). Even though you may experience your own state as stable at any particular moment, it is always in the process of strengthening, diminishing, or changing to another state. In fact, the majority of our states are more like background moods, occupying secondary positions we are hardly conscious of. Nonetheless, they are noticeable when we are able to stop, listen, and feel for them.

Now to the practical side. What does all this have to do with motivation and engagement? It has everything to do with it. All behaviors you want from students come from a pool of potential states. If I am being threatened with a gun, my life is in

Figure 8.3

BRAIN STATES

Our behaviors are limited by the mind–body state we're in.

One "pool" contains only our sillier, more wild and crazy behaviors.

A different "pool" contains only our more serious, intellectual, thoughtful behaviors.

States provide the "pool of choices" from which all behaviors emerge.

danger. I will not feel very romantic toward my wife in that state. Similarly, in a classroom, a student who is in a "You can't make me and I don't want to" state is unlikely to participate much. In a different state, that same student might be willing to participate in class. So now there's a new objective: Get students into the appropriate state first, into a better "pool" of potential behaviors. Then the change of behavior becomes more possible.

This approach suggests a very different take on this issue of motivation and engagement—that it's really an issue of state management (see Figure 8.4). How can you, as an educator, read and manage student states? Reading the states first is critical. If you see a student in a state of apathy, remember that he probably started out in another state, such as frustration. When a teacher does not deal with the frustration, the student could either get angry (enter an alternative state) or disconnect (enter a state of apathy). The point is that it's easier to make an effort to become aware of states like frustration than to have to deal with anger. Read your students' states constantly. They'll tell you what's going on if you pay attention.

Once you have read the state, you should ask yourself a question: Is the state I am seeing

Figure 8.4

SEVEN EASY STEPS FOR CHANGING STATES

1. Choose the target state for your audience.
2. Read present states.
3. Plan your strategy (Who? How? When?)
4. Create a back-up plan.
5. Set up the state change ("framing").
6. Begin the change of state.
7. Monitor and adjust during the process.

appropriate for the next action (target behavior) I want? If it's not, you have a potential solution: Change the state first, and then a change in behavior is easy. Here's an example. If you want to ask students to do an activity, first put them in an active state. Have them stretch or walk first, and then ask them to form groups while they are already standing. In a standing state, students are more likely to want to do something else similar to it.

Over the years, many educators have argued for the role of additional choice in the learning process. Clearly, choice matters more to older students than to younger ones, but we all like it. The critical feature is *choice must be perceived as choice* to be one. If you get to choose 10 things but not the 11th, you might take the first 10 for granted and grumble about the 11th. Many savvy teachers allow students to control aspects of their learning, but they also work to increase students' perception of that control. The teacher still quietly chooses which decisions are appropriate for the students to control, yet the students feel good that their opinions are valued. In other classrooms, students may play a larger role in decision making but still believe that the teacher is choosing for them. The secret? Point out choices whenever you can: "I have an idea! How about if I give you the choice over what to do next? Do you want to do choice A or choice B?"

More Tools for Motivation

Remember, in the ideal states, motivation and engagement are far easier to achieve than you could ever imagine. If you were going to receive a marriage proposal, certain states might lead you to say yes. But in other (nonromantic) states, you might easily say no. The point is this: States are the body's environment for making decisions. If you think you're going to get a negative response to the next activity you want your students to do, change their state first. Then ask them to do the activity while they're in a good state to say yes.

Practical Suggestions

Here are some practical ways to change student states:

- *Eliminate threat.* Use small-group discussions or an anonymous class survey to ask students what makes school uncomfortable and unpleasant and what would make learning more potent and enjoyable. Some of the likely sources of negativity are threatening comments, "score-keeping" discipline strategies, sarcasm, unannounced quizzes, a lack of resources, unforgiving deadlines, and cultural or language barriers.

- *Set daily goals that incorporate some student choice.* This strategy can provide a more focused attitude. Prepare students for a topic with "teasers" or personal stories to prime their interest, which will help ensure that the content is relevant to them.

- *Work to have a positive influence.* Do this in every way you can, symbolically and concretely. Don't forget students' beliefs about themselves and the learning. Exerting a positive influence includes the use of affirmations, acknowledging student successes, giving positive nonverbal signals, encouraging teamwork, and displaying positive posters.

- *Manage student emotions and teach them to do it too.* A good approach involves the productive use of rituals, drama, movement, and celebration. Use positive, structured conversations to manage

states. If students are in a negative state, give them a topic to talk about that allows them to express themselves and to direct their focus toward something more positive. Music and activities are excellent ways to influence or change the states of your students. But so are short walks, good stories, stretching, games, and going outside. In other words, use every tool at your disposal to influence student states.

- *Provide relevant curriculum and coherent activities.* Both are absolutely essential to maintaining motivation. When students are actively involved in something they care about, motivation is nearly automatic. Choice can and should be part of this strategy, too.

- *Give feedback.* It's one of the greatest sources of intrinsic motivation. Set up learning that students can do with built-in, self-managed feedback. A computer does this perfectly, but so do well-designed projects, group work, checklists, dramatic presentations, peer editing, and rubrics.

SuperCamp: A Motivation and Engagement Model

In 1981, two partners and I cofounded SuperCamp (www.supercamp.com), a 10-day residential academic immersion program for students ages 8 to 22 that incorporates many brain-compatible suggestions. Many students arrive at the program with a history of chronic demotivation. Yet after attending for just 10 days, students typically become insatiable learners who go on to improve their grades, their school participation, and their self-esteem. Many elements of the SuperCamp experience can be easily transferred to other settings.

The SuperCamp staff creates "emotional bridges" from students' worlds outside the classroom to the start of learning. To do this in your classroom, you need to assume (even though it won't always be true) that your students need transition time from their personal lives to their academic lives and from one teacher to the next. You never know what happens in the hallways. At the start of class, students could still be reeling from an insult, a breakup with a close friend, a fight, or the loss of something valuable. Using dependable activities that trigger specific, predictable states can be the perfect way to bridge into learning. Appropriate rituals keep the stress levels low and can even eliminate threat responses.

For example, each morning could start with "getting ready to learn" time. These predictable, safe rituals might include a morning walk with a partner, time with teammates to discuss personal problems, and a review of the previous day's learning. Such built-in transitions allow the brain to change to the right chemical state needed for learning. They also allow students to "synchronize" their clocks to the same learning time. During the day, high levels of novelty, movement, and choice will enrich a highly relevant curriculum. The end of the day can follow the same routine as the start, almost in reverse. Closure rituals help students put the day's learning in its new cognitive–emotional place.

You might consider arrival and beginning rituals that include a music fanfare, positive greetings, special handshakes, hugs, or sharing time. You can use certain songs to bring students back from a break and let them know it's time to start up. (Music sure beats a bell!) Group and organizational rituals also help, such as team names, cheers, gestures, and games. Successful situational rituals include applause when learners contribute, a song to close or end something, affirmations, discussion, journal writing, cheers, self-assessment, and gestures. These opportunities to influence the affective side of learning make a strong case for longer teaching blocks at the secondary level, so that a teacher can practice some of these strategies and still have adequate time for content.

The environment created at SuperCamp provides extensive opportunities for students to get personal and academic feedback. Typically, students get this feedback 10 to 20 times a day through the purposeful use of sharing time, goal setting, group work, question-and-answer time, observation of others, and journals. Teachers who follow the SuperCamp model and specifically design their teaching to include dozens of kinds of learner-generated feedback—not one or two—find that motivation soars.

Summary

As a whole, the collected research leads us to understand that part of the motivation problem is the way we treat students. They are not factory workers who need to be prodded, cajoled, and motivated by bribes, management, or threats. Instead of asking, "How can I motivate students?" ask, "In what ways is the brain naturally motivated from within?" Now you know: Rewards are natural to the brain, and states rule our motivations and behaviors. Start with meaningful, developmentally appropriate curriculum, and add learner choice and positive social groupings. Create the challenge, build a supportive environment with compelling biases, and get out of the way!

Critical Thinking Skills

Society in general and schools in particular place a high premium on thinking skills and intelligence. The reasons we value thinking skills and intelligence are obvious, but unfortunately, the path to develop them is not. In brief, thinking is the process; intelligence is the product. (The definition of intelligence can be debated, but that's a topic for another book.) We teach thinking skills so that learners will make decisions that are more intelligent. All of your students can and do think, and they use that facility to solve problems. What varies, of course, are the complexity, novelty, and quantity of that thinking.

All cognition is built from lower-order brain systems, including (1) sensory and motor systems, (2) auditory and language systems, (3) attention and executive functions, (4) social and emotional systems, (5) memory systems, and (6) behavioral and reward systems. We're not born with the "smart" package in place; these systems need to be "coaxed" into cross-modality or cross-platform functionality to perform at high levels.

To clarify how these systems work together, in this chapter, we'll explore the general brain-based principles that apply in

112

understanding limitations and opportunities. Then we'll consider the specifics of thinking skills. Although brain research does not tell us precisely what to do to develop thinking skills, we can gather some emerging principles that may have value for guiding our decision making. Some of the brain-based aspects that promote critical thinking of our intelligent brain include

- The unique brain.
- The problem-solving brain.
- The maturing brain.
- The adaptive brain.
- The emotional brain.

The Unique Brain

All humans are unique because of both prenatal differences and postnatal experiences. This uniqueness shows up as differences in the brain; although some parts of the brain show little variability from one person to another, other parts may vary considerably (see Figure 9.1). Even the same activity performed by two subjects may show up as very different activations in the cortex (Mills et al., 2000). The differences are attributable to many factors, including the following:

- Gender.
- Exposure to abuse or neglect.
- Specific disorders.
- Culture.
- Exposure to drugs, trauma, or toxins.

These realities suggest we consider approaches to teaching thinking that include a significant amount of variety and choice. As an example, students with fetal alcohol syndrome, prenatal

drug exposure, or head trauma may need far more repetition, explicit links, and hands-on learning than a student with a healthier brain. They'll often appreciate pictures that show clear relationships between cause and effect that a student without brain injury might infer naturally. A healthy student may need only to do some

Figure 9.1

DEGREES OF BRAIN VARIABILITY

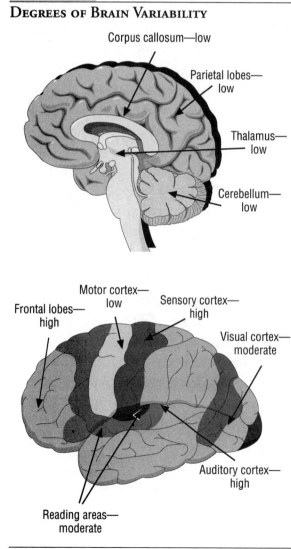

reflective thinking or brainstorming to come up with better-quality choices.

Gender Differences

Gender is an area of brain differentiation that is of considerable interest. For decades, it was politically incorrect to talk of biologically based gender differences. Then several reputable researchers began to publish studies that helped flesh out biological differences between the genders. Here's the bottom line: easily quantified, physical differences distinguish the brains of males and females. Top gender researcher Doreen Kimura asks, "Do systematic, meaningful, reliable differences exist in the problem-solving abilities of men and women? The answer is an unequivocal yes" (2000, p. 69).

Nobody with any credibility is denying that males and females are raised differently. And we also know that differences in experience change the brain. But the quantity, range, and quality of studies on physical, brain-based differences is staggering. Here are just five of the differences between males and females that researchers have found:

• Mean and median brain size varies, even when adjusted for body size (Ackney, 1992).

• Developmental schedules vary (Yurgelun-Todd, Killgore, & Young, 2002).

• Differences exist in cross-hemispheric connections (Allen & Gorski, 1991).

• Functional emotional processing differs (Killgore et al., 2001).

• Differences exist in language areas of the brain (Shaywitz et al., 1995).

Teachers know that 1st grade girls are typically more ready to read than are 1st grade boys. But there are other, lesser-known, maturational differences. For example, in one study of 30 boys and girls (Yurgelun-Todd et al., 2002), researchers used an MRI to track gender differences in cerebral tissue volume and both gray and white brain matter during adolescence. In the boys, greater white matter (more connective axons) was positively correlated with intelligence; information processing was faster and verbal abilities were higher. Surprisingly, the researchers found no significant correlations between cerebral tissue volume and stronger cognitive abilities in girls. This finding suggests that a slew of other compounding variables may be clouding our understanding of gender-specific brain differences. It's plausible that because male and female brain development is on such different time trajectories, we need to qualify any data emerging from studies where time is not considered as a factor. Still, these are the kinds of results that make it difficult to speak definitely about gender-based differences in the brain.

Researchers believe that biological differences do lead to functional variations in the brain, but they still don't know enough to make causal statements in this area. For example, in female brains, the anterior commissure, a bundle of nerves that functions much like the corpus callosum, is larger than it is in male brains. But can that difference—and the greater access it might provide females to "cross-hemispheric" (often called intuitive) knowledge—really be behind "women's intuition"? No one knows yet.

Here's some of what we do know about competencies and how the genders typically compare. Females recall words better, can label objects quicker, and have better verbal memory and better verbal fluency. But on overall tests of vocabulary or verbal reasoning, females and males show little difference. Females are better at remembering landmarks and people than they are at remembering distances and objects. Males throw and hit targets or objects more accurately. They do gross-motor tasks better and reason out math problems better. In higher-level math competitions, men outnumber women by 10 to 1. Women match pictures and letters with better perceptual speed, calculate quantities faster, and do fine-motor tasks better. Yes, it seems that males might be generally better hunters, and females might be better gatherers.

Practical Suggestions

Considering all of the differences in a typical classroom, one must be careful when making specific recommendations for a specific population. It makes more sense to use simple accommodations to support the learning than it does to make wholesale changes based on differences.

With this in mind, we can still make some healthy generalizations. Students with learning delays—regardless of cause—will need more time to master skills and understandings, more repetition, more explicit instruction, and more classroom support.

Males may act out and be more physical when frustrated or simply communicating a need. Females are typically more likely to use language and covert behaviors to meet their needs. In general, boys are more impulsive and quicker to get called on in class. In general, girls are more inclined to work cooperatively than boys, but they are also more inclined to socialize. Teachers might want to remember that and cut each gender some slack in different ways.

The Problem-Solving Brain

The human brain seems to be designed to solve problems. Usually the more compelling the need, the greater the resources, and the tighter the deadline, the greater the likelihood the problem will be solved. General problem solving requires many skills. In addition, specific expertise and talent are required to solve the "academic problem" (how to survive in school). Some of the more useful skills have been highlighted in other popular educational books, such as *Classroom Instruction That Works* (2001) by Marzano, Pickering, and Pollock. Here are some key thinking skills:

• Maintaining focus and attention (managing personal states).

• Having the ability to locate and prioritize resources.

• Making distinctions in relevance, similarities, order, and differences.

• Being able and willing to ask for help (social confidence).

• Reading and summarizing content.

• Being able to speak, draw, or build non-linguistic representations.

• Setting goals and using feedback.

• Having self-awareness of personal health and nutrition.

• Generating and testing hypotheses.

• Developing working-memory capacity.

• Being able to organize or map out ideas and information.

• Showing persistence and follow-through in the face of adversity.

It's critical to understand that healthy brains are born with the capacity to learn these skills, but there's nothing built-in or automatic about a student having them. They have to be taught as part of a well-thought-out curriculum. All the skills in the list (and there are certainly more of them), require the following:

- Motivation to use the skill.
- Role modeling (a visible, tactile, or audible model).
- Direct instruction or simply an opportunity to acquire the skills.
- Time for trial and error, practice, and debriefing.
- Time to use and strengthen the skill in multiple contexts.

Critical thinking skills take time to learn because you're asking the brain to make changes in both cortical organization and interregional connectivity. Learning new skills literally reorganizes brain mass. Yes, you're creating new connections at the synapse, but the brain will make changes, depending on the type, duration, and use of the skills. In Chapter 3, we explored some of the basic, built-in rules that govern learning in the brain. Although all of those rules apply to thinking skills, here are a few nuances for thinking skills in particular.

Intervals and Duration

A good rule is to limit the amount of training in new thinking skills. Although some researchers have found two hours to be the upper limit for skills training (Kilgard & Merzenich, 2002), clearly it depends on other variables, too. When you're planning your instructional time lines, be sure to consider the complexity of the skill building, how novel it will seem to the learner, and the learner's emotional state. Massed intervals (limited consecutive minutes, over many trials) may be optimal for thinking-skills training. For most of your students, the following guidelines may be appropriate:

- *Grades K–2:* Twenty to 30 minutes, two or three times per week.
- *Grades 3–5:* Up to 30 minutes, three times per week.
- *Grades 6–12:* Up to 60 minutes, three to five times per week.
- *Adult learners:* Forty-five to 90 minutes, three or four times per week.

Many improvements take weeks, even years to realize. It may be that essential neural scaffolding takes place early on, but that is conjecture at this point. It is also not clear whether there is a critical or sensitive period for these interventions. However, from a practical point of view, it is easier to get younger children (ages 2 to 8) to comply than older children (ages 8 to 16).

Context and the Learning Transfer Issues

Many things that we do are so highly embedded in a particular context that our learning drops dramatically in a new environment. In some cases, the new environment is distracting, uncomfortable, or just too novel. In other cases, the brain's memories are triggered only by the specific cues in the old situation. The most detailed minutiae may be stored as part of the original learning process. Finally, the skills or content learned may have prompted the formation of "rules" in the learning process. The learner may not have translated and applied these "rules" to the new environment, even if the rules applied perfectly.

> Neither context nor cognition can be understood in isolation; they form an integrated system in which the cognitive skill in question becomes part of the context. To try to assess them separately is akin to trying to assess the beauty of a smile separately from the face it is a part of. (Ceci & Roazzi, 1994, p. 98)

Here's a striking example of this phenomenon. The daily use of in-context mathematics by adolescent street vendors in Brazil is impressive, in the range of 98 to 99 percent accuracy. Yet in a laboratory setting, their accuracy *drops by half,* even on tasks that require the same skills (Carraher, Carraher, & Schliemann, 1985). This finding suggests that the skills are highly context dependent, not that the learners lack any general cognitive capacity. Unfortunately, most schools seem to have missed this concept. The evidence of the abysmal failure of students to transfer learning from school subjects to real life is legendary (Ceci & Roazzi, 1994) and cuts across age, IQ, and social status. The "street math" researchers conclude, "The performance of an individual in an experiment *is inherently grounded* [italics added] in the social situation of their performance" (Carraher et al., 1985, p. 21). One study at the University of Arizona showed that even students with a background in statistics, math, and science *do not transfer that learning* to novel contexts (Leshowitz, 1989). These data suggest that schools would do well to focus on much more real-world learning. Field trips, simulations, role-plays, and away-from-school activities that use school knowledge and

skills make much more sense than a focus on field-independent classroom learning.

Coherent, Challenging Learning

Typically, new learning creates new synapses, especially when the subject matter is challenging (Black, Isaacs, Anderson, Alcantara, & Greenough, 1990). This suggests that we should constantly manage the level of difficulty for our students. We can do that in three key ways:

• By varying the learning *resources* available (allowing students to work with friends, providing access to information or tools, varying the time allowed).

• By varying the learning *expectations* (asking for more or less quality, making the final output more public or more private).

• By varying the learning *context* (allowing students to work at home as well as in class to complete work over periods of days or weeks).

Practical Suggestions

In earlier chapters, we discussed other factors that support coherent learning and the development of thinking skills. These factors include relevance, activity, repetition, and specificity.

Relevance. As we discussed in Chapter 8, the brain will not adapt to senseless tasks. As a teacher, you have to constantly reaffirm the relevance, value, and meaning of the skills taught. Some of the better strategies related to relevance include the use of choice, real-world personal applications, and project-based learning.

Activity. Chapter 4 described in depth the importance of movement for "brain-friendly" learning. We learned, for example, that gross-motor activity may enhance the production of new cells known to be necessary for learning and memory (Van Praag et al., 1999) and that physical exercise can help some students who have difficulties learning to read (Reynolds et al., 2003). Allow and encourage your learners to be active through walks, recess, athletics, or personal workout routines.

Repetition. Neuroscientist Michael Kilgard has studied change in the brain extensively and found that repetition is a fundamental quality for learning new skills (Kilgard & Merzenich, 1998). It is also essential for supporting the brain reorganization that accompanies novel learning. Be sure to include repetition in your learning plans.

Specificity. Quality skill-learning programs can make a substantial difference, regardless of the intelligence level of the learner. The practice involved in learning a skill should move from the particular subskill (e.g., task analysis), to generalizing the subskill, to real-life experiences. Examples of good skill-building activities include tasks that require sorting, grouping, and rearranging. Others include building, organizing, or assembly. Art projects involving designing, building, and publishing are excellent. Dramatic arts including mime, theater, and role-plays are superb. And, finally, vocational or industrial arts all have built-in skills and subskills. No matter which kind of thinking-skills program you use, be sure to include feedback and debriefing in the process.

The Maturing Brain

One of the most remarkable bodies of recent brain-related research has shown us that environmental factors can influence brain maturation. Brain maturation is not a passive unfolding of nature's plan. Specific life experiences during the early years influence patterns of interactivity between brain areas. When youngsters are actively directed to orient and respond to certain stimuli, some brain systems will, in a sense, "tutor" the development of other brain areas (Johnson, 2001).

The tricky part is that *different areas* of the brain mature at *different rates* (see Figure 9.2). The peak of *synaptic* development in the prefrontal cortex happens between ages 1 and 2 (Huttenlocher & Dabholkar, 1997). However, the overall maturation of the frontal lobes is a slow process, not complete until as late as age 25 to 30. In fact, the brain changes so much that the same behaviors in infants and adults may be mediated by completely different brain structures (Mills et al., 2000). Clear changes in the thinking brain as we mature include the following:

- Theory of mind (ability to make inferences, perceive occluded objects, and so on).
- Perceptual functions.
- Social awareness.
- Working-memory capacity.
- Language and reading skills.
- Ability to infer cause and effect.
- Capacity for both concrete information and abstraction.

The process of brain maturation is clearly impaired in cases of prior diminution from neglect or poor nutrition. But it can also be enhanced, as we found earlier. One area worthy of special attention is the frontal lobes. Most of what we call "higher order" thinking skills incorporate a variety of subskills (e.g., attention and working memory), but they all engage the prefrontal cortex. This brain area is primarily responsible for planning, judgment, decision making, working memory, and most other critical-thinking skills. Life experiences will slowly prune and tune this critical brain area. Eventually, neurons in the frontal lobe orchestrate, encode, abstract, and form rules from a learned experience (Wallis, Anderson, & Miller, 2001).

Practical Suggestions

What we know about the maturing brain suggests that we can expect a wide range of student performance, and some of the inabilities students display may be merely a function of maturation. When you notice this, you can vary the type, as well as the complexity, of the assignment. For example, mental practice can improve actual performance (Driskell, Cooper, & Moran, 1994) but it requires visual thinking, which some students struggle with before ages 8 to 12. To develop frontal-lobe functions, include daily tasks that require delayed gratification, mental juggling, or persistence. Arts (music, performance, or drawing) are some of the best examples. Computer tasks, delicate experiments, or constructing something can work, too. Frontal-lobe function is uneven, fickle, and inconsistent while developing. In some cases, you might teach something five times and the fifth time might be the charm, especially if the brain is suddenly becoming ready for it. In other cases, you might simply plant the seeds for a task and let it go until next year.

The Adaptive Brain

The brain is exquisitely susceptible to postnatal experiences. To a large degree, it is the quality of the interaction with the environment that sculpts the thinking learner's brain. The developing brain engages in highly complex interactions that need stimulation, and these interactions, over time, prompt the brain to become increasingly specialized (Friston & Price, 2001). But what are the qualities of those experiences that sculpt more thoughtful, sophisticated, and complex thinking skills? Brain research can contribute only parts of the answer. Here are some of them.

Exploratory Learning and Play

Exploratory learning is what may allow infants to look "smart" long before parents have even

Figure 9.2

THE DEVELOPING BRAIN

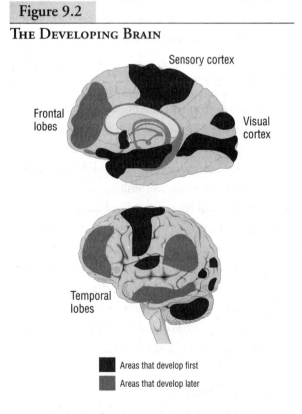

Source: Based on data from Gogtay et al. (2004); Paus et al. (1998); Sampaio & Truwit (2001); Sowell, Delis, Stiles, & Jernigan (2001).

noticed that the infant is using subtle trial-and-error learning. Parents who allow their children to play, who interact with them, and who provide them with early experiences that let them make mistakes are "doing it right." For the K–12 student, field trips, games, simulations, arts, and sports will fill the bill. Creative play is highly valuable. Students engaged in theater performance at school have higher SAT scores than their peers who are not involved in the arts, though the relationship is a correlation only (for more information, see the Web site of the National Association for Music Education at www.menc.org). When you include creative, exploratory play in the classroom, be sure to include discussion and feedback time at the end; otherwise, the activity may end up being only good fun (heaven forbid!).

Novel Circumstances

There's no need for the brain to adapt to change if what it must deal with is the same. Novelty creates a stronger opportunity for new learning and pathways in the brain. Often, children who grow up with exceptional thinking skills had something exceptional (either good or bad) in their upbringing. Examples include an unusually long walk or ride to and from school; opportunities and support for hobbies; and unusual mentors, teachers, or parents. Novelty is part of the foundation for gifted and talented programs nationwide. Provide something unusual and the support to go with it, and learning is off and running.

Nutritional Support

When it comes to nutrition, there's a wide range of what's considered acceptable. For poorer children, having anything to eat is better than having nothing. But if you're asking the brain to maintain sharp mental focus, respond to stress with poise, and encode and recall stored learning "on cue" in a classroom, then a diet of corn flakes, donuts, and soft drinks won't get it done. The evidence strongly supports the cognitive advantages of better nutrition among all school-age learners. Because we've explored this topic in more detail in Chapter 2, let's simply state that nutrition and learning are highly correlated.

Opportunities for Using Thinking Skills

Many students begin to develop specific thinking skills but then reach a plateau. This may happen because there was no adaptive advantage to fostering the skills. But when parents, peers, or teachers help provide ways to use the skills, they tend to develop. For example, if a student learns to play an instrument, being in a band is pretty important. If a student is good at spatial memory, then playing chess or football may support the related skills. The more opportunities we provide for students to develop talents and abilities, the more they are able to do so. This is as true for the development of thinking skills as it is for the development of other skill sets. This makes a good case for arts programs in schools (including music, dance, visual arts, vocational arts, and graphic arts). It also supports the value of clubs and other organizations, community outreach, and academic competitions.

The Emotional Brain

As we learned in Chapter 5, the ability to think critically is highly dependent on emotional states: complex patterns of spatiotemporal (space-time) brain activity that lasts for seconds or minutes. The patterns themselves are composed of cooperative neural clusters, activated by both chemical and electrical energy. Our emotional states are constantly fluctuating because of their high sensitivity to both the internal and external environment. Even though you may experience your own state as stable at any particular moment, it is always in the process of strengthening, diminishing, or changing to another state. You are feeling curious, then slightly blah, then a bit anxious, and then later, you're hungry. Because states are always in flux, it makes sense to describe them as "emergent properties" of our self-organizing brains (Grigsby & Stevens, 2000). These complex activities cannot be separated from cognition.

It's important for teachers to know that when students enter a state again and again (mischievousness, concentration, bullying, etc.), the neurons involved tend to coalesce into cooperative groups, self-organizing into collective behavior scientists call "stable states." The longer a person is a stable state, the more likely he or she is to re-enter that state at another time. Yes, this means that students who frequently get angry are able to reactivate that anger more quickly; however, it also means that when we teach students to focus, to concentrate, to be determined, and to think creatively, these too can become "stable states" for them—and priceless, lifelong skills. Anyone interested in improving students' thinking skills must understand the complex interplay between emotional states and cognition. For students to be able to think well, they absolutely must be able to manage their emotional states. This ability is not innate;

it must be taught. If the parents aren't doing it, someone has to jump in and get the job done.

Emotional states draws from three things: sensations (hungry, sunburned, bloated, cold, itchy, etc.), mental state (confident, calculating, scattered, etc.), and feelings (disappointed, joyful, disgusted, etc.). Although many things may be going on at the same time (we might be hungry, focused, and discouraged all at once), we can consciously experience *only one aspect of an emotional state at any given moment*. This finding is key, because good critical thinkers are able to downplay the "negative aspects" of a state (e.g. hungry, sad) and to consciously activate the state necessary to complete the task at hand, such as confidence or determination. This ability to "compartmentalize" is one of the most important for success in life. It allows you to focus on what you need to do to move ahead and set aside what stalls your progress.

Where do learners gain this facility—this marvelous ability to focus, to do what's necessary to succeed? Some students learn it at home, some learn it from sports, and others learn it from hobbies or through things like the Outward Bound program. In general, though, if students don't get it through school, they're not going to get it.

First, students need to become attuned to their emotional states. If they don't recognize their own states, they are powerless to influence them productively. In my visits to classrooms, I've seen a chart called "How am I feeling today?" that shows illustrations depicting 50 emotional states. This great tool helps students develop some awareness of their own states.

Second, students need to understand the direct links between how they feel and how they think. Emotional states are frequently activated, fast-changing, neural networks that typically incorporate multiple areas of the brain. Thousands, even millions, of neurons make up the integrated combination of mind, body, and feelings that are emotional states. These assemblies of neurons can be the difference between thinking clearly or not thinking at all. How can teachers support the development of these critical life skills? Give students a taste of what good emotional states are like! We can do it by carefully considering

- The questions we ask students.
- The postures, movement, and activities we use and incorporate in classroom activities.
- The personal encouragement we provide.
- The attitudes and opinions we hold of them.
- The respect and affirmation we give them.
- The hobbies and habits we encourage and support.
- The learning and successes they gain.

All these behaviors can elicit specific emotional states. Why is this so important? Again, the longer an individual remains in a state, the more easily he or she can reactivate that state. Over time and through continued activation and association with positive feedback (encouragement, smiles, etc.), the emotional states necessary for success can become a more reliable part of the student's everyday experience.

Finally, students must understand that *they can manage their own emotional states.* It's not an easy thing to do, however, and facility can be achieved only through practice. You might explain it this way: Our neurons may be busy all day doing many different tasks, but within a split second, they can arrange themselves into specialized clusters or "neural mobs" so that we can do or feel something: react to something hot, express pleasure at a

sudden turn of events, take a stand on an issue (or on a table!), and so on. Then, as quickly as these specialized clusters assemble, they collapse and other specialized clusters form. It's because our emotional states are so responsive and so susceptible to environmental influence that something as seemingly minor as moving from a slumped-over posture to sitting up straight can shift a state significantly.

When students realize the amazing power they have over their own cognition—a power they can grasp simply by changing their breathing or posture, or by consciously seizing on a new thought—it's typically a revelation. Teachers who help students understand and maintain useful productive emotional states that support thinking and living give their students a priceless gift.

Practical Suggestions

The reality of the emotional brain suggests that you can expect a wide range of student performance, depending on the states of the students. Doing one's best requires a person to get into and maintain the optimal emotional state to support thinking. The best learners "shift states" on their own; other students need to learn how. Begin by teaching the basic skills of emotional state recognition and management. There are countless activities that can help students' awareness of internal states, including the following:

- Drama, theater, and role-plays.
- Journaling about feelings.
- Identifying feelings from a list of options.
- Discussing emotional states with other students and adults.

• Discussing reading material that deals with the emotions of literary characters.

For pre-K through 3rd grade students, keep things simple. One idea is to use a set of standard signals to "trigger" and encourage certain emotional and physical states. For example, you might teach students that when you say, "Green light," they should proceed with active learning. When you say, "Yellow light," they should slow down, take a pause to think about what they're doing, or talk quietly. And when you say, "Red light," that's their signal to freeze and wait for directions or ask for help. It's important for young children to understand the process: You give them a cue, and then they exercise their power over their own behavior. These simple connections communicate the basic message that each of us has something to do with our own emotional states.

For older students, design simple activities so they can discover how things like food, romance, worry, excitement, despair, and anger influence their thinking. Then help them brainstorm ways to self-regulate their emotional states—ways other than sex and drugs and rock and roll (all of which work, but they do have side effects). For example, you might let them journal for two minutes each day. Ask them to write about what happened, how they felt about what happened, and what they did next to influence how they felt.

Finally, for all age groups, set up classes so that opening activities put students into receptive or curious states. Orchestrate the endings of lessons so that students are engaged in joyful states of celebration. If you can successfully influence students' emotional states, the behaviors you want will follow.

Summary

All children, adolescents, and adults can benefit from programs that develop thinking skills. All students, whether identified as academically "gifted" or "struggling," need education about thinking skills. The development of thinking requires constant layering and scaffolding. More exposure to this process is better than less because there's interplay between maturation and experience. The reasons are unclear, but it may be that early exposure to quality thinking skills creates the intercortical connections needed to develop much more sophisticated thinking skills as we mature.

Research into early childhood or school-based interventions for thinking and enrichment programs has been vigorous. Publicly funded early childhood programs have been divided into "flagship" (receiving much attention, involving small sample size, and gaining much publicity) and "fleet" programs (receiving less attention and offering broader public services, such as Head Start). As might be expected, the results of the flagship programs are superior (most likely because of the enhanced control over variables) to the results of the fleet programs (Ryan et al., 2002). Here's what we've learned about these programs:

• Language fluency, IQ, and other cognitive processes may improve in children in these programs when compared with children not in the programs.

• Quality programs can reduce discipline problems, tardiness, vandalism, theft, and academic failure in both elementary and high school.

• Children in quality early-childhood programs have better social and emotional intelligence than children who are not enrolled in early-childhood programs and, instead, stay at home with a parent.

• Children in these programs have fewer risk behaviors, less delinquency, fewer legal problems, improved graduation rates, and less welfare dependency.

An economically deprived or stressful home environment can "undo" the positive benefits of a thinking-skills program for some children. This finding suggests that we should adopt a "whole-child approach" and influence as many variables (such as home, community, nutrition, siblings, and after-school programs) as we can.

Whenever schools go through a budget-cutting frenzy, have you noticed what is cut and what gets preserved? What gets cut are the things that are most likely to be enriching experiences for building intelligence and thinking skills: field trips, vocational education, performance arts, after-school programs, lab classes, music instruction, competitions, visual arts, project-based learning, and a host of other positive programs. It's time to stand up for more of what's good and what's positive in school offerings. From a neurobiological standpoint, there is no longer a question as to whether we can change brains for the better. We can! And we have an ethical obligation to do so.

Memory and Recall

Memory and recall are critical elements in the learning process for very practical reasons. The only way we know that students have learned something is if they demonstrate recall of it. But why is it that just minutes or hours after learning something, many students seem to forget it? Why do they appear to experience a "faulty" memory?

In general, we have only three "chances" to help students in learning: (1) the original encoding, (2) the maintenance of that memory, and (3) the retrieval of the learning. Each stage gives us opportunities to influence the learning.

Taken as a whole, the latest discoveries about the brain provide a powerful framework for understanding and boosting memory and recall, and they reveal some good reasons underlying the near-universal phenomenon of forgetting. The biggest message of this chapter is straightforward: memories are malleable. Knowing that memories are malleable won't instantly give us all perfect recall, but it may illuminate some potential strategies for changing instructional approaches. In fact, children today probably learn a great deal more than they demonstrate, and the ways we ask for recall are part of the problem of "forgetful students."

Perspective

Before we discuss what current research tells us about memory and recall, it may be helpful to address a common misconception that emerged from the work of Canadian neurosurgeon Wilder Penfield in the 1930s and 1940s. Penfield reported that during surgery, an electrical stimulation of the temporal lobe produced episodes of recall, almost like seeing movie clips. Many concluded that the brain "videotaped" life, and to remember things, our memories simply needed to be prompted. But these episodes of recall occurred in less than 5 percent of Penfield's patients. In addition, these were seizure patients, not healthy, random individuals. Some psychologists have since dismissed the supposed recall he reported as "prompted" (Fisher, 1990), and the results have not been replicated by other surgeons. Still, somehow, the erroneous but popular concept of a brain that records or videotapes life like a CD or DVD player has persisted. But the reality is very different.

Current neuroscience describes memories as "dynamic" and not fixed. Among the many factors found to be important are background context, date of encoding, emotions, hormones, neurogenesis, and specific signaling stimuli (Nadel & Land, 2000). Using what we now know, we can define memory as the creation of a persistent change in the brain by a transient stimulus.

Survival-Based Memories

Because of occasional forgetfulness, many of us think our capabilities for memory are not good. But the situation is not as bad as we might think.

In fact, we are very good at certain types of memory. For instance, we tend to remember anything related to survival (see Figure 10.1). If you get food poisoning as a result of eating at a particular restaurant, do you remember to avoid that restaurant? Do you remember the names of your children, your parents, and your spouse? When was the last time you forgot your way home? Have you ever forgotten how to eat? When someone is rude to you, do you remember it? If someone did you a favor, do you remember him or her? These questions may seem laughable, but a second look at the kinds of things you consistently recall is quite revealing. We are very good at the following types of memories:

- Locations of food, housing, employment.
- How to cook, eat, walk, talk, drive, and work.
- Bad foods, strong aromas.
- The names and personal preferences of friends and family members.
- People who treat us well and people who have hurt our feelings.

Figure 10.1

MEMORY: ORGANIZED AROUND SURVIVAL

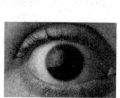

- **Locations** (of food, housing, social contacts)
- **How to do things** (locomotion, defense, tool making, child care)
- **Emotional events** (pain and pleasure)
- **Conditional response** (aroma, taste)

Locations. First, we remember *how to find* essential things. You are unlikely to forget where you live or where the grocery store and local hospital are. The brain has "where" pathways that constantly map locations that are important to us. We call this form of memory spatial or "episodic" memory. As you'll soon see, there are ways to take advantage of this unique type of storage.

Procedures. Second, we remember *how to do* essential things. Countless skills, including child care, eating, walking, driving, and putting on clothes are remembered effortlessly and are unlikely to ever be forgotten. And although these may not seem like notable feats, they involve a form of memory that is both reliable and lasting. This memory type has many practical classroom applications.

Emotional experiences. Third, we are very good at remembering events that affected us emotionally. Car accidents, robberies, or natural disasters—these are not things that we forget. We also do not forget significant life events, from getting married to having a baby to getting divorced. We remember well the people who are our parents, those who are good to us, and those who hurt us. We remember celebrations and reunions. These memories rarely need review and often last for a lifetime. In a school setting, the goal is to use more of these lasting pathways.

Conditioned responses. Finally, we are good at things that involve a *conditioned response,* that is, retaining certain patterns of behavior in response to specific stimuli. We may respond in a certain way to how our spouse says our name when he or she is angry (or seductive). We may respond in a predictable way to the offer of a particular food (chocolate, anyone?) or to a reprimand (how do you feel when your driving is

criticized?). In general, these memories get strengthened through repetition, and good teachers know that repetition—as long as it's sprinkled with novelty—is a good idea.

Did you notice what was *not* on the list? In general, we are not very good at recalling words, names, equations, or facts: *much of what's taught in school.* Of all the kinds of memories we could form, semantic or word-based memories are least related to survival. Do you really need to know the names of the world's seven longest rivers? Assuming you're not an international consultant on river hydrology or preparing for a College Bowl geography quiz, you probably don't. The message is simple: Some types of memories we are "automatically" good at and some we are not.

Understanding where our strengths are is critical to succeeding in the classroom. Let's start with a very fundamental question. How do we actually remember anything?

Making Memory

In the simplest terms, memories are the probability of a particular neural firing pattern in a network of cells (see Figure 10.2). Typically, thousands of neurons are activated to retrieve a memory. More complex memories require the activation of specific networks involving millions of neurons. These networks have varying levels of stability and flexibility depending on the type of encoding and the person's life exposure.

How does the brain create these firing patterns? Researchers are still not 100 percent sure; deciphering the complete code to all of the various separate (yet related) memory processes is a challenge. The current understanding includes the following steps:

1. An electrical impulse travels down the axon of a neuron and triggers the release of chemicals known as neurotransmitters. Included with these chemicals are messenger ribonucleic acids (mRNAs). These are the molecules that carry information. Simultaneously, a process known as synaptic adhesion takes place that uses protein "strings" to help bind the two neurons at the synapse.

2. The mRNAs and the other neurotransmitters dock into receptor sites on the surface of the receiving dendrite.

3. When the electrochemical threshold is reached, an event known as long-term potentiation (LTP) is created. That's simply a use-dependent alteration in the strength of the synaptic connections.

4. The LTP reaction stimulates new electrical activity in the dendrite, sending it toward the cell body of the receiving neuron. Many factors influence the efficacy of this connection, including chemicals known as neuromodulators (i.e., stress hormones). Learning is the result of the strengthening of the connection between two neurons. Typically, a single memory will involve thousands of neurons.

Figure 10.3 is a highly simplified illustration of the process of creating memory.

The details of the process have been a baffling intellectual labyrinth, and researchers have had to deal with exceptions to the rules, myths exposed, and continual discovery. Nevertheless, the research has uncovered some critical principles about encoding, maintenance, and retrieval of memories.

Encoding. Memory-making is well distributed in multiple pathways. Different types of memories form at different speeds. Multiple factors can enhance encoding.

Figure 10.2

THE NEURAL NETWORK OF MEMORY

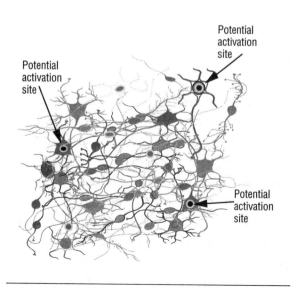

Figure 10.3

THE CREATION OF MEMORY

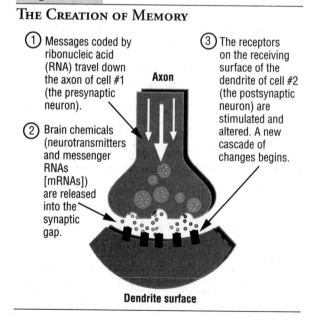

Maintenance. Memories are malleable. Activating memories helps maintain them. Implicit memories are more fixed; explicit memories are less fixed.

Retrieval. Not all memories can be retrieved. Multiple factors enhance retrieval. We are good at retrieving survival-based memories.

The Distribution of Memory

There is no single, all-purpose "resting" location for all our memories. Our best learning and recall involves multiple memory locations and systems (Schacter, 1992) (see Figure 10.4). However, most encoding, regardless of its location in the brain, is

Figure 10.4

LOCATIONS OF MEMORY ACTIVATIONS

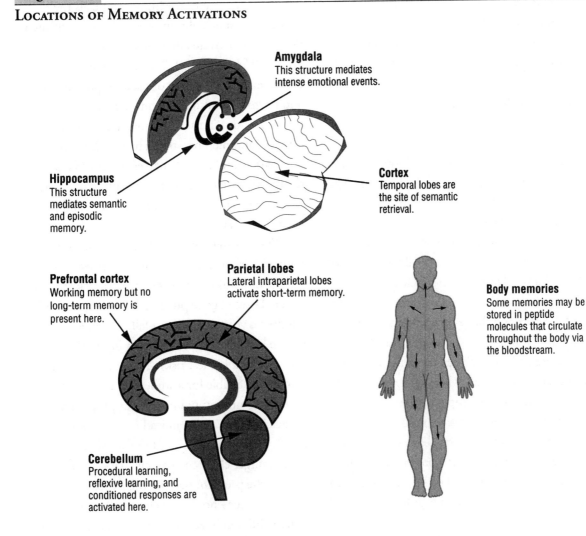

Amygdala
This structure mediates intense emotional events.

Hippocampus
This structure mediates semantic and episodic memory.

Cortex
Temporal lobes are the site of semantic retrieval.

Prefrontal cortex
Working memory but no long-term memory is present here.

Parietal lobes
Lateral intraparietal lobes activate short-term memory.

Body memories
Some memories may be stored in peptide molecules that circulate throughout the body via the bloodstream.

Cerebellum
Procedural learning, reflexive learning, and conditioned responses are activated here.

enhanced by a good night's sleep. And the more complex the learning, the more helpful sleep is (Piegneux et al., 2001).

In general, memories seem to be encoded in the areas of the brain that originally processed them (Moscovitch, 1995). Hence, visual memories are stored in the occipital lobe, language memories in the temporal lobe, and spatial memories in the parietal lobe. Learned skills involve both the cerebellum and the striatum (Doyon, Owen, Petrides, Szliklas, & Evans, 1996). Think of the striatum, a small structure located in the top of the mid-brain area, as an automated habit-preserver; it's the part of your brain that, for example, allows you to walk across a room with a full cup of coffee—and not spill it—without looking constantly at the cup. The basal ganglia (mid-brain) structures may also be linked to intention, nonverbal information, and social references (Lieberman, 2000). The more spatial, episodic memories are stored in the right medial temporal lobe (Shimamura, 2002). The parietal and frontal areas of the brain help us determine whether a memory is new or old (Wheeler & Buckner, 2003). Many "classroom facts" (vocabulary, terms, textbook data) are stored in parts of the prefrontal cortex and the temporal lobes (Wagner, 2003). Some "number sense" is activated in an area of the left parietal lobe (Cohen & Dehaene, 1996), whereas higher math skills will likely create activity in both the parietal and temporal lobes.

The fact that memory resides in so many different locations in the brain means that a single event, such as teaching a class, will activate multiple pathways: What someone saw will be stored in one area of the brain, what was said and heard will be stored in a different area of the brain, and so on. When we recall memories, our brain has to reconstruct the fragmented "Humpty-Dumpty" memory pieces (Shimamura, 2002) and make sense of them. An area of the inner brain, the hippocampus, is quite active in forming and eliciting spatial and other explicit memories, such as memory for speaking, reading, and even recalling an emotional event. As we learned earlier, the hippocampus is a small, C-shaped structure located in the medial temporal lobe (there's one in each side of the brain). At the end of the hippocampus is the amygdala—small, almond-shaped, and exquisitely designed to activate and remember emotional events (Whalen, 2003). These include experiences characterized by feelings of fear, disappointment, and horror, but also of joy and celebration. The more locations in the brain that are engaged in learning and memory, the better the learning and the sharper the recall (Schacter, 1992). Having different memory systems may explain why a student can have great recall for sports statistics and poor recall for other things.

The fact that our memories are distributed is both a blessing and a curse. It means that narrow subsets of memories may be easily impaired while larger classes may be preserved. Over one million children a year experience a fall, a kick, or a thump on the head that leads to a brain injury (boys ages 3 to 17 are at highest risk). The brain injury means it may be possible for a student to retrieve, for example, common nouns but not proper nouns. Understandably, this can lead to very uneven academic performance . . . and to frustrated teachers. And younger children generally have no way to express the problem because their vocabulary or life history may not be developed enough to do so. When children have unusual or specific memory patterns, it's wise to refer them to a specialist.

Memories' Multiple Pathways

Because different kinds of life experiences encode differently (Fuster, 1995), each has a different likelihood of being recalled. It's important to have realistic expectations about what can and what should be recalled and to appreciate the differences among learners and their preferred style of learning. Here's another important thing to keep in mind: Encoding and strengthening multiple pathways gives your students a far better chance of retrieving a classroom memory. Researchers have described various memory processes, each with particular encoding and retrieval characteristics, strengths and weaknesses, and locations in the brain.

Generally, the two broadest categories for memories are "explicit" and "implicit," also known as "declarative" and "nondeclarative." Explicit learning may be either semantic (words and pictures) or more episodic (autobiographical, or a personal rendition of the memory versus learning about it second or third hand). Implicit memories include so-called reflexive memories and procedural, or motor, memories (see Figure 10.5).

Figure 10.5

MEMORY PATHWAYS

All of our learning and life experiences are stored in multiple pathways (for example, music could be in semantic, episodic, and reflexive pathways).

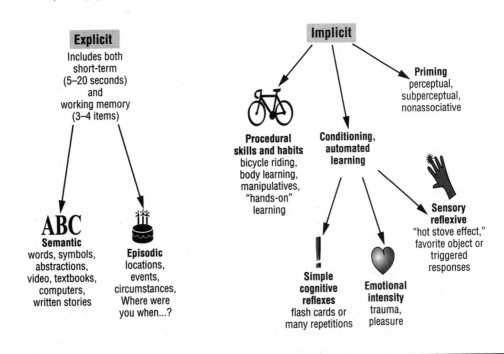

Semantic Memories

Semantic memory, one of the kinds of explicit memory, is also known as declarative, factual, taxon, or linguistic memory. It includes the names, facts, figures, and textbook information that seem to frustrate us the most. It may develop when we are taught, spoken to, or observe something (such as pictures or movies). Semantic memories commonly consist of the kinds of information we pick up from conversations, lectures, DVDs, reading, and visual aids. Teachers who use most of their class time lecturing are hoping this style of learning sticks—but it rarely does. Students retain little of what is said. In one study, college students who listened to lectures knew only 8 percent more than those who skipped class (Rickard, Rogers, Ellis, & Beidleman, 1988). This is, as you might guess, the weakest of our retrieval systems.

Semantic memory has limitations in both time and capacity. These limitations are expressed in descriptions of our short-term or "working" memory, a time-sensitive process referring to the online maintenance and manipulation of information. Working memory is a critical contributor to cognition and intelligence (Jonides, 1995). An item in working memory usually lasts for 5 to 30 seconds before either disappearing or being reactivated (see Figure 10.6). For example, we meet someone at a social gathering and forget the person's name mere seconds after an introduction. Or the mind goes blank after reading a single page of a book, and we recall nothing.

The capacity limitations of semantic memory are influenced by both the strength of associations and the sheer quantity of items. We remember information better in chunks than in the form of random, single thoughts, words, ideas, or groups of unrelated ideas. George Miller's often-cited study (1956) suggests that working memory can hold seven items, plus or minus two. This outdated notion has persisted despite contrary everyday experiences in which we are lucky to recall more than one or two ideas at a time. The reality is that for most items, students under age 12 can handle one item at a time. On a good day, those older than 12 can hold two or three things at a time.

Practical suggestions. The time limitations of semantic memory suggest that students will remember very little past a few seconds of input. When you ask students to read a chapter, insist that they stop after each page and take some notes. Use a variety of activities that engage partners, such as having one student read while the other maps out the content. If you are lecturing, after just a few minutes let students pair up and reteach. If they struggle, add a larger-group activity that lets students correct errors and consolidate information; a group discussion with a prompting handout is one possibility.

Figure 10.6

THE LIMITS OF SEMANTIC MEMORY

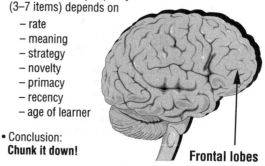

- Explicit learning is held in the frontal lobes for 5–30 seconds unless processed for meaning

- Working memory capacity (3–7 items) depends on
    - rate
    - meaning
    - strategy
    - novelty
    - primacy
    - recency
    - age of learner

- Conclusion:
  Chunk it down!

Frontal lobes

Capacity limitations should also be an important consideration. For a 2- or 3-year-old with a healthy brain, the normal limitation is about one chunk of information ("Put your shoes away, please."). For a 5- to 12-year-old, the limit is usually one or two bits of data. But as a practical matter, many students have poor short-term memory because of conditions such as attention deficit disorder, learning delays, and auditory-processing deficits, and it's better to stick with one piece of information for all students. In a classroom, give directions just one at a time:

1. "Boys and girls, please stand up." (pause)

2. "Now, slide your chairs in gently." (pause)

3. "In 10 seconds, when I say 'go,' please line up at the door."

4. "Is everyone prepared?" (pause, check for understanding)

5. "Ready, get set, go!"

Teachers who require moderate to large amounts of recall from texts are, at best, developing self-discipline in the learners. At worst, they are creating discouraged learners who feel unnecessarily incompetent. Should we throw out traditional "book learning"? No. Students still need facts, directions, references, and safety information. They still need to read poetry, novels, letters, and textbooks. However, if you ask students what they have learned that was interesting in the past year, little of it will be semantic. This type of memory requires strong intrinsic motivation—something that's usually missing from learning that's based on textbooks and handouts. Ways to help students better encode their word-based semantic system include asking them to

• Compare and contrast the material.

• Summarize what was learned.

• Make a rhyme out of key ideas and teach it to a classmate.

• Turn the learning into a nonlinguistic representation—a drawing, a comic strip, and so on.

• Analyze and critique the material.

• Consider the material from different points of view.

• Group and regroup the material into different categories.

Episodic Memory

Episodic memory is another kind of explicit memory. The system of episodic memory pathways is also known as the autobiographical, loci, spatial, event-related, or contextual recall process. It's a thematic map of (or "a place in space" for) your daily experiences. In this case, learning and memory are prompted by the particular location or circumstance—with one caveat: *You must have been there personally.* Consider this example. Reading about a safari in Africa is far different from actually experiencing one. I personally knew plenty about elephants before I went on an African safari. But, trust me, until you stand just 25 feet from an agitated African bull elephant with no fence, no protection, or defense, you have no idea what wild elephants are really like (or how much adrenaline you have!). Now, that's a very different memory (it's episodic) than the memory created as a result of reading about elephants. Episodic memory formation involves the hippocampus and the medial temporal lobe. Curiosity, novelty, and expectations motivate it, and it's enhanced by intensified sensory input, such as sights, sounds, smells, taste, and touch.

The episodic memory process has unlimited capacity, is effortless, and is used naturally by everyone. Ask a content question like "What did you have for dinner last night?" and most people first ask themselves, "Where was I?" The *location and the fact of being there* trigger the content recall. A common example of this focus on location is the question "Where were you when 9/11 happened?"

How does the episodic memory process work? Surprisingly, our visual system has both "what" (content) and "where" (location) pathways (Kosslyn, 1992). Many researchers believe this information is processed by the hippocampus in a visual fabric, or "weave of mental space." We possess a backup memory system based on locational cues because every life experience has to be, in some way, contextually embedded. All learning provides contextual cues as long as "you were there."

Episodic processing does have a major drawback: contamination, which can take place when you have too many event memories embedded in the same location memories (say, months of reading a textbook in the same seat in the same classroom in the same school). Contamination is like when a virus renames all the files in your computer with the same file name—the information is there, but because you can't distinguish it, it's nearly useless. This often happens to students who really do know their material but lack the specific "hooks" or mental "file names" to retrieve all their learning.

Practical suggestions. Use teaching strategies that incorporate mobility to remove the staleness

that comes with the same learning location: same desk, same seating arrangement, same classroom. Some options include using stand-up reviews, learning stations, labs, or regrouping; going outside; trading rooms with another teacher; and allowing students to stand or lean against a far wall or desk.

Reflexive Memory

Reflexive memory is one kind of implicit memory. Some of our responses in life are reflexive (see Figure 10.7). You jerk your leg when a doctor taps your knee, you cover your ears at the sound of a blaring siren, and you blink to protect your eyes from a thrown object. (Those actions are instinctive as well as reflexive.) What we learn can become reflexive, too.

Figure 10.7

REFLEXIVE MEMORY

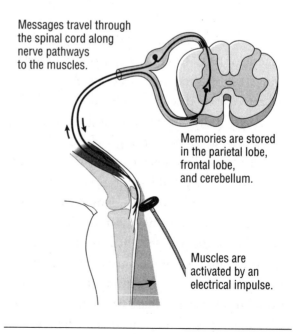

Messages travel through the spinal cord along nerve pathways to the muscles.

Memories are stored in the parietal lobe, frontal lobe, and cerebellum.

Muscles are activated by an electrical impulse.

The pathway for reflexive memory can be sub-divided into emotional memories (such as a favorite song from high school, a first kiss, a car accident) and nonemotional associative memories. There are only two ways that new learning can become reflexive: either through intense sensory input (the kind experienced through trauma, celebrations, and other emotion-laden events) or through repetition.

Practical suggestions. In the classroom, reflexive retrieval can happen with flashcard repetition or other forms of "over learning," which may explain why a student who struggles to retain information read in a textbook can often excel with content-laden raps. The raps trigger the implicit reflexive memories of stored material and engage a different part of the brain than reading, note taking, or essay writing would. The automatic nature of a rap means that it can also trigger implicit memories through both the physical motions and the auditory cues. The blank on a fill-in-the-blank test can be the prompt for semantic or reflexive retrieval, depending on how the student learned the material and how much review was done. The more practice and the more "automated" the learning, the more likely it will become reflexive. Celebrations and other events with an emotional component are another way to encourage reflexive memory.

Emotions and Memory

We've discussed the importance of emotions in several other chapters, so it should come as no surprise that emotions get privileged treatment in the brain's memory system. The correlation between the strength of the original emotional event and the likelihood of retrieval of that event is astonishingly high,

around 90 percent (Christianson & Loftus, 1990). Several scientists at the Center for the Neurobiology of Learning and Memory at the University of California–Irvine have tested the effects of emotions on memory. Norepinephrine (also known as noradrenaline) is a hormone released from the peripheral nerve endings of the sympathetic nerves. Typically it's released in an emergency, but on a broader level, increased risk, excitement, and urgency will prompt its release. Amazingly, it acts as a memory fixative, locking up memories of exciting or traumatic events (Cahill et al., 1994). Students who get a standing ovation or a harsh rebuke from a teacher—or who enjoy and celebrate the completion of a project—are likely to recall that moment for years.

Practical suggestions. Teachers can and should orchestrate emotions in the classroom. Ways to do this may include introducing unusual aromas (from freshly baked cookies or bread, for example); emphasizing happy occasions, such as celebrations, positive rituals, and acknowledgments; incorporating "gross" things, such as wet, bubbly, slippery, gooey science displays; and mixing in storytelling and other experiences where suspense or surprise may be a feature. Emotional responses triggered during or immediately after the learning will help embed the memories.

Procedural Memory

Procedural memory is another kind of implicit memory. It is often known as motor memory, body learning, or habit memory. (Riding a bike is one example. Even if you haven't ridden for years, you can usually do it again without practice.) Procedural memory is expressed by student responses, actions, or behaviors. It's activated by physical movements, sports, dance, games, theater, and role-play. Procedural memory appears to have unlimited storage, requires minimal review, and needs little intrinsic motivation.

Memories of learned skills involve the striatum, the pons, the globus pallidus (located near the lower middle area of the brain), and the cerebellum (Duyon & Ungerleider, 2002). To the brain, the body is not a separate, isolated entity. Body and brain are part of the same contiguous organism, and what happens to the body happens to the brain. This dual stimulus creates a more detailed "map" for the brain to use for storage and retrieval (Squire, 1992). Maybe that's why most students will tell you that their most memorable classroom experiences were based on hands-on learning.

Physical activities, like role-playing, doing a hands-on science experiment, or creating a project in an industrial arts class are highly likely to be recalled. These are, in fact, the most commonly used methods for early childhood learning. A child's life is full of actions that require standing, riding, sitting, trying out, eating, moving, playing, building, or running. These activities create a wider, more complex, and overall greater source of sensory input to the brain than mere cognitive activity. At school, this type of learning diminishes each year until it's virtually absent from all but a physical education, industrial arts, or drama curriculum. Yet a summary of the research tells us that this learning is robust. It is age and IQ independent and has less variance once learned (Reber, 1993).

Practical suggestions. A variety of approaches can engage procedural memory. The use of hands (with puppets, charades, or manipulatives) can do it. You can the use the whole body (dance, movement, theater, drama) to get a strong effect. Activities that promote procedural memory can occur outdoors (during recess, physical education, sports) or indoors (games, visual arts, music, puzzles, learning stations). Learning that involves any of these strategies is likely to be remembered for a long time, which suggests that you should allow students to have time for error correction and add a celebration at the end to enhance the "right" memory.

Here's just one example of using simple movement to reinforce learning. If you have three points to make, begin by asking students to rise. Then ask them to take three steps in any direction. Introduce the first of the three points briefly as a preview. Include an action that links with the topic. Ask students to walk three more steps. Introduce the second point, including an action. Repeat this step for the third point. After you've introduced all three points, ask the students to sit down.

Memory Maintenance

Why do we have to "work" to maintain memories? The answer is simple: Memories are malleable. As a general rule, most of what we are exposed to we don't remember. Of the things we do remember, it is highly unlikely that they will remain in our memories intact. Memory expert Daniel Schacter (2001) of Harvard University posits seven reasons for why memories fail us: transience (memory erosion over time), absent-mindedness (we weren't really paying attention), blocking (it's on the tip of our tongue), misattribution (we're confused by similar memories), suggestibility (alternative thoughts unintentionally contaminate memories), bias (existing prejudices influence our memory), and persistence (a negative memory becomes pervasive). Each of these reasons alone is enough to create problems, but all seven make consistent, accurate retrieval a very unlikely prospect (see Figure 10.8). You might think you have some memories that will *always* be with you, but research is showing why and how even traumatic memories can be altered.

As an example, let's use the events of 9/11 once again. Will you always remember where you were when you first became aware of the terrorist incidents of September 11, 2001? The research suggests that unless you lived near the sites of the attacks, you either won't recall exactly where you were, or what you *do* recall may be wrong. Before you cry foul and insist that you would *never* forget, consider the results of a couple of studies. The memories of graduate students who kept a diary after the 1986 *Challenger* space shuttle disaster were riddled with major errors just 12 months later (Neisser & Harsch, 1992). Three years after the O. J. Simpson trial verdict, less than 30 of a large group of California undergraduates had accurate recall of where they were when the verdict was announced and what happened (Schmolk,

Figure 10.8

SEVEN PRIMARY SOURCES OF MEMORY MALLEABILITY

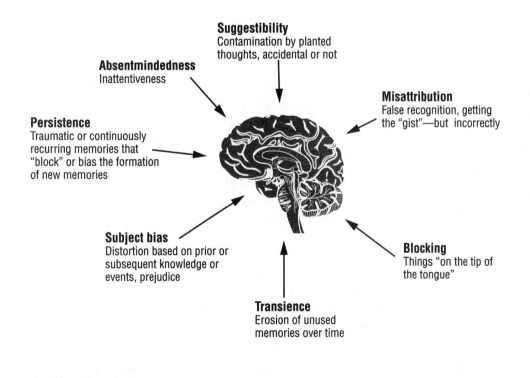

Suggestibility
Contamination by planted thoughts, accidental or not

Absentmindedness
Inattentiveness

Misattribution
False recognition, getting the "gist"—but incorrectly

Persistence
Traumatic or continuously recurring memories that "block" or bias the formation of new memories

Subject bias
Distortion based on prior or subsequent knowledge or events, prejudice

Blocking
Things "on the tip of the tongue"

Transience
Erosion of unused memories over time

Source: Adapted from Schacter (2001).

Buffalo, & Squire, 2000). In short, time is a serious challenge, even with so-called "unforgettable" memories.

Consider the experiments of New York University neuroscientist Joseph LeDoux and colleagues (2003), who found that when subjects "relived" fearful memories, the memories reverted to a volatile, unconsolidated state, as if the fear-inducing events has just occurred. In other words, reactivating a memory means it has to be reprocessed for storage all over again. LeDoux used a protein blocker to prevent the reconsolidation process and found that long-time, fear-invoking memories became tame and unemotional. This finding suggests that *all* memories, even traumatic ones, are subject to alteration and may even be erasable

That said, some memories are not as malleable as others. After Tiger Woods burst onto the golf scene with major victories early in his career, he hit a well-publicized slump. To recapture his game, he undertook a retooling of his golf swing—the same swing that had served him since he began golfing as a tot. The memories were procedural and, originally, highly implicit. To change them, he had to make the alterations explicitly, and the procedure took almost a year to implement. This suggests to us just how robust this memory system is. It can be changed, but even with practice, the change takes time.

The Impact of Activation

Memories are not stored intact, and that creates a problem. Because some attributes of memory may experience different fates over time, memories are very likely to be incomplete or erroneous (Land & Riccio, 1998). This suggests that more consolidation makes sense: "Reconsolidation, as a function of

reminding and reactivation, can then be viewed as a means by which specific attributes are selectively strengthened, and memory as a whole made more retrievable" (p. 280). Naturally, if the activation is accurate (the correct information is retrieved or it is corrected after inaccurate retrieval), it will strengthen the memory. Anderson (1995) found that reviewing material is most beneficial when done immediately or soon after the initial learning. Because various attributes of memories become strengthened by use, greater frequency of activation will influence them. If the information retrieved is faulty and left uncorrected, the resulting "false" memory will be strengthened. In other words, we may need to make even greater efforts to ensure that students retrieve and maintain accurate memories.

Practical Suggestions

From a practical standpoint, it's important to realize that even with supposedly unforgettable classroom learning experiences, students' memories will unravel or change. Plan on students remembering the wrong things or completely forgetting some things. Why? You'll be right more often than you'll be wrong, and you'll be inspired to invest a few minutes in daily and weekly reviews. You can review via mind maps, paired sharing, group discussions, and countless other tools.

Memory Retrieval

Memories that are more active (that were either formed or accessed recently) are considered less consolidated than inactive ones: more fragile and subject to change and harder to retrieve (Nader, Schafe, & LeDoux, 2000). Interestingly, one set of variables is involved in making memories and another set is involved in retrieving them. The synaptic consolidation happens within minutes to hours after initial learning occurs. This two-part process of making and retreiving memories is *activity dependent* for short-term memory, meaning that it requires repetition. The long-term memory mechanisms that lead to encoding, transcription, and synaptic growth are *modulatory dependent*, meaning that they need the presence of emotions.

A host of factors influence whether and how well we recall something. One is chemical arousal within the brain. Hormones, certain kinds of food, and neurotransmitters can all enhance or inhibit recall if they are present at the time of learning. For example, the brain uses the neurotransmitter acetylcholine in long-term memory formation (Kilgard & Merzenich, 1998; McGaugh, 1992). Levels of this neurotransmitter are greater at night, during memory consolidation, and agents that reduce the deterioration of acetylcholine—known as acetylcholinesterase inhibitors—are linked to improved recall (Woodruff-Pak, Vogel, & Wenk, 2001).

Ideally, learning brains have high levels of the chemical choline, a key ingredient in the production of acetylcholine. Lecithin, found in eggs, salmon, and lean beef, raises choline levels; many studies have shown that lecithin intake boosts recall. Other nutrients found to support memory function include folic acid, lipoic acid, and vitamins B, C, and E (Carper, 2000), which are found in spinach, lean proteins, most vegetables, and salmon. Studies show that even the presence of just 100 mg/kg of household sugar in the bloodstream can enhance memory if given after a nonemotional learning event (Mohanty & Flint, 2001). Sugar has no effect on memories of emotional events, because it

works on a very different mechanism in the brain, the stress response system (Thompson, 1993).

Admittedly, educators have limited influence over students' diets or their brain chemistry in general. The good news is that we have potentially much more influence over many of the other factors that affect memory retrieval. Here are just a few of the strategies for doing so.

Matching the Original Memory State or Context

Recall is stronger when we are in the same emotional state we were in when the memory was formed. What's more, learning acquired under a particular state (happy, sad, stressed, or relaxed) is most easily recalled when the person is in that same state (Eich, 1995). The strategy for teachers, then, is to try to engineer matching states when it's necessary for students to recall something that they've learned.

Practical suggestions. The discrepancy between learning states and testing states is widely known among researchers as a source of performance loss (Bower, 1981; Overton, 1984). There are two ways to affect this phenomenon. First, we can teach students how to better manage their own emotional states at test time (for example, through relaxation methods or positive self-talk). Second, we can rehearse the learning in a variety of states to promote "recall resiliency"—acclimation to the range of emotions students might feel at test time. Savvy teachers use timed quizzes, public quizzes, or small-group presentations, and they provide structured practice taking timed mock tests. This approach lets students practice in many states, one of which may match the testing one.

A third powerful strategy is matching locations or learning contexts. Within the brain, the hippocampus makes a spatial map of where we are and embeds the learning within that location (Rosenzweig, Redish, McNaughton, & Barnes, 2003). The use of retrieval clues—spatial or sensory—can produce astonishing results. Subjects in studies by Bahrick (1975, 1983, 1984) and Bahrick and Hall (1991) demonstrated remarkable recall for diverse content (from Spanish to mathematics to locations, name, and faces) when careful attention was paid to replicating learning contexts. For example, given context stimuli, even elderly subjects scored 80 to 90 percent correct on tests that measured the ability to recognize former classmates that they had not seen for years. And Schab (1990) found that if students eat chocolate (or another aromatic, sensory-stimulating food, like peppermint) while they are learning, they'll recall more of that learning if they are again given chocolate (or the same matched food) during the test.

Research clearly demonstrate that matching the original learning location and circumstances can improve the chances for recall. Many schools have paid particular attention to this principle when administering state tests, ensuring that students take these tests in the same classroom where they reviewed for it. The theory is that the room is full of invisible retrieval "cues" and is also emotionally more comfortable than an unfamiliar room, which may arouse stress.

Priming

Memories often form while we are not paying attention (Schacter & Tulving, 1994). As an example, we drive home from work, thinking about our day. Later on, we decide we want to go to our favorite Italian restaurant. It just so happened that we saw

an Italian resturant on the way home; it wasn't something that registered consciously, but the visual nevertheless triggered a memory of how much we enjoy the spaghetti alle vongole at Nunzio's.

This memory process is known as priming—in this example, *incidental* priming. The other kind of priming is *intentional* priming, which, from an educational standpoint, is even more effective at supporting memory than incidental priming. Intentional priming simply means you provide cues in advance of the actual learning. Even patients with amnesia can usually recall something with a bit of priming (Martin & Van Turenout, 2002). What's at work here is the implicit memory system: We know it, but we don't *know* we know it.

Priming is a good strategy for another reason. Memories are frozen patterns waiting for a resonating signal to awaken them. They're like ripples on a bumpy road that make no sound until a car drives over them. Neurobiologist William Calvin (1996) says the content may be embedded in "spatiotemporal themes" that will resonate and create a critical mass needed for retrieval. This theory explains why a student trying to remember information for a test comes up with the answer a half hour too late. It may take that long for the "intention to recall" to create enough "activated thought patterns" to hit critical mass. Earlier, the brain may not have been able to retrieve the information because too much other competing information processing was going on. Support for this theory comes from a recent study showing that different types of glial cells (interneurons) display memory-specific firing patterns that contribute to activating neural networks (Klausberger et al., 2003).

Practical suggestions. The phenomena described by Calvin and other researchers suggests the value of priming and a related strategy—"wait time." First, with regard to priming, it's important to realize that giving students hints about upcoming things is not cheating. I'll often give simple "letter primes" such as "Earlier we talked about memories being located in different areas of our _____ (*fill-in*). The word starts with the letters BR." The cues don't even need to be exact, just related (Schacter, 1996). Awareness of the value of priming helps us understand why students like multiple-choice tests; the format provides the prompts that the brain needs. Forgetting occurs because such cues are rarely present when the recall is needed. With regard to "wait time," remember that students' brains are busy with many things and need time for activation. If you're not going to "prime" students, at least give them time to think over ideas or retrieve memories.

Other Suggestions for Improving Memory

Intentional wordplay. Rhymes, visualization, mnemonics, peg words, music, and discussion help us recall semantic information. Without such strategies, reading a chapter can become an all-too-forgettable event. Remind students to stop after every quarter or half page to take notes, discuss what they've read, or reflect. Conduct oral or written review, both daily and weekly. Students can pair up or rotate in teams to present daily reviews. Consider repeating key ideas within 10 minutes of the original learning, again 48 hours later, and then tie it all together 7 days later. Remember, spaced learning—with pauses and intervals for reflection—is valuable. Without the quiet processing time, much learning is never transferred to long-term memory.

Teach students how to use acrostics—phrases or sentences in which the first letter of each key

word forms a new word. For example, we remember the names of the planets (Mercury, Venus, Earth, Mars . . .) by reciting, "My very energetic mother just served us nine pizzas." For years, we've learned the musical notes on the lines of the G-clef by memorizing "every good boy does fine." We learn the names of the Great Lakes by making one word of their first letters: HOMES (Huron, Ontario, Michigan, Erie, and Superior).

To help students learn definitions, ask them to create action pictures that tie the two words together. To remember the word *semantic,* we could picture a "sea man, with ticks on his face" (se-man-tic) holding up a long list of words to memorize. That effectively unifies the two concepts in memory.

Analysis. Studies (Matthews, 1977) show that it is the analysis of the material that aids in the recall of it. Many successful teachers find that mind maps or other graphic organizers not only improve students' understanding of material, but also keep learning fresh. The mind map has a central organizing theme (such as an author, a science topic, or a math concept). Studies show that when students organize the material (instead of the teacher doing it for them), they recall it better (McDaniel, Waddell, & Einstein, 1988). Students benefit from analyzing a topic from varying perspectives; for example, they might learn about weather by considering it in terms of the benefits of varying types of weather and from the perspective of the kinds of damage it can do. They might explore the typical weather patterns of various geographic locations, the mythology related to weather, and the effect that technology has had on our ability to predict weather and manage its consequences.

A great, analysis-focused recall strategy is to allow students to create their own visual images

(Weinstein & Mayer, 1986). Use poster-type displays to create more visually effective overviews of a topic. Have students draw out, organize, or symbolize key points on poster paper. Make sure the posters are easy to read, use illustrations, and feature strong colors. Put them on the wall, and leave them up weeks after the learning. Make and use storyboards—oversized comic strip panels of your key ideas. Better yet, ask students to make them.

Lesson presentation. Presenting the most important material in a lesson first thing and last thing can improve recall. Open and close the class with the three most important words or concepts for the day. Use music, props, or costumes to introduce the words or concepts. Or use openings for personal or controversial discussions that engage students emotionally. At the close, ask students to share what they have learned with their classmates.

In addition, wholes taught before parts are recalled better. Whether the subject is a Shakespearean play or an assignment in anatomy, our mind recalls best with context, a global understanding, and complete pictures to remember. You might introduce Shakespeare by showing a modern video first or by making a pictorial overview map. Once students understand the relevance and overall themes, the details and deeper studying make more sense. In anatomy, studying the whole body first will yield a better grasp of the parts.

We also remember almost any learning that was temporarily interrupted. In other words, cliffhangers do work! Introduce a pressing, relevant problem to solve and leave brainstorming for solutions until the next day.

Use of peer teaching. Ask students to teach others what they've learned. They can pair up with others in different grade levels or with an adult.

Create opportunities for students to discuss their learning, to debrief it, and to teach small chunks of it. Students can summarize in their own words what they have just learned. This approach is most effective when they analyze or break down their learning into smaller parts.

Figure 10.9 consolidates much of what we know about ways to strengthen memory. Use it as a guide for organizing your teaching.

Figure 10.9

RULES FOR STRENGTHENING LEARNER MEMORY

More attentional resources = Greater content accuracy
- Foster attention
- Ask questions
- Use novelty
- Personalize the learning
- Introduce some stress
- Focus on details

More neurons = More stable memory
- Use movement
- Group and regroup

Greater number of networks = Greater accessibility
- Use rhyme and songs
- Use repetition
- Create associations
- Introduce other perspectives

More stable synapses = Robust recall
- Allow settling time
- Engage emotions
- Rehearse, review
- Use error correction with feedback
- Match earlier states and context

Summary

If attitude isn't everything in learning, it certainly still counts for a lot. Tell students, "Yes, you can." Start by modeling a new attitude about memory and recall. Instead of saying, "Oops, I have to go back. I forgot something," make this, more accurate statement: "Hey, I just *remembered* something; I've got to go back." In other words, make it a point to celebrate the act of remembering, even if you remember that you left something behind!

Certainly, a better education involves more than memory. Larger issues include questions such as how much memorization should schooling require? Or, is the teacher's role essentially content-driven (leaving it up to the students to figure out *how* to improve their recall) or catalytic (empowering students with knowledge of *how* to learn by teaching them these strategies)? Although there's certainly less emphasis on the necessity to memorize volumes of material—except at the university levels in science, medicine, and law—it's still a critical skill. And as long as it remains critical, educators have an obligation to share research-based strategies with students.

Brain-Based Teaching

How do we put together everything we know about the brain and learning? What does a "brain-based" classroom look like, sound like, and feel like? The truth—and the first and shortest answer—is that there is no "perfect" or "best" way to teach. Millions of children have already been educated over the centuries, some of them very well, by teachers whose careers preceded this revolution in teaching and learning. But given what we know about the realities of teaching *today*, what can and should you do that is aligned with the latest research? What is the reality of "teaching with the brain in mind"?

To answer that question, I've sequenced the book's information into a model (see Figure 11.1). As we learned in Chapter 3, models are a useful way to begin to understand and think about things, but they are not the end of thinking about them. Take the model presented here and think about how it might work for you. Instead of either embracing or rejecting it, make it part of your exploration of this question: What do we mean by brain-based learning?

One more thing: We all tend to look at something and relate it to something else we

Figure 11.1

THE TEACHING MODEL

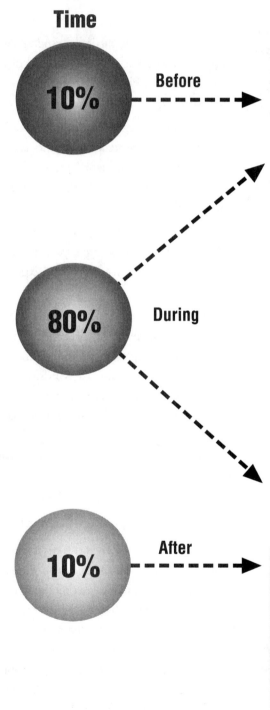

Time

10% — Before

80% — During

10% — After

Process

PREPARE
your learners.

CREATE
an optimal environment.

ENGAGE
learners by getting them vested
emotionally with an attentional
bias.

FRAME
learning to make it relevant,
important, and compelling.

ACQUIRE
knowledge, skills, values, and
experiences.

ELABORATE
and deepen the learning through
trial-and-error time, with feedback and active processing.

CONNECT
learning to other content,
processes, and self.

SETTLE
the learning with time for
passive processing.

**REHEARSE AND
INCORPORATE**
by revising learning and
using it.

know. For example, some see this teaching model and immediately see theories from their favorite icon—perhaps John Dewey, David Kolb, Madeline Hunter, or Bernice McCarthy and her 4-MAT system. I would discourage the natural tendency to overlay your past understandings onto this model. First, each model or theory from educational history can stand on its own. That doesn't mean all are perfect, but each was designed a specific way for certain reasons. Honor and respect those reasons, and don't try to make a model into something that it's not. Second, most theorists or practitioners have based their work on philosophy or pedagogical research. This book is based on research on the brain and the mind. That gives the model a unique perspective that I hope you'll appreciate and accept as is.

The model is sequential, with three distinct stages. The first stage concerns what to do before any class begins and focuses on the prep time that increases your odds of instructional success. The middle stage is focused on the bulk of the learning process. Finally, the last stages help ensure the learning is the best it can be and stays intact as long as possible.

Before Class

There are two steps in this stage: *pre-exposure* and *the physical learning environment.*

Pre-exposure

Some of these suggestions are intended to help you, and others are intended to help both you and your students. Begin by preparing for each class long in advance. Prepare yourself mentally,

academically, and emotionally. Here are some guidelines:

• Think about particular students who need extra help, whether they are ahead of or behind the rest of the class. Plan well ahead of time to ensure their success.

• Walk through your lessons in advance. Review each of the steps below and ask yourself: How will I engage students? How will I make the content come alive? How will I ensure it is memorable?

• Get yourself in a good emotional state. When you're in a good state, your students notice the positive energy. It makes their experience better.

• For the benefit of your students, use the days and weeks ahead for priming their brains with content. This step asks you to influence content areas (using new vocabulary words, working models, and key ideas) as well as processes (doing activities that allow for scaffolding and for teaching social or emotional skills). Post key ideas with pictures or words on the walls so students can become familiar with them.

The Physical Learning Environment

Your ability to change the environment you work in has some limits. Focus on the greatest contributors to student success that are within your power to change. What you cannot influence, let go. In some countries, students in secondary schools stay put and the teachers move from class to class. If you and your colleagues adopt this approach, you can personalize the learning environment by bringing music (via a portable CD player) and posters or placards, and moving or rearraging seating to make the room better for learning. Here are other suggestions for making the most of your physical environment:

- *Promote feelings of safety.* Ensure that students feel physically and emotionally secure.
- *Incorporate kinesthetics.* Allow flexible steating arrangements and movement.
- *Monitor room temperature.* Keep it in the range of 68 to 72 degrees Fahrenheit.
- *Monitor visual environment and lighting.* Brighter is better for most students.
- *Monitor acoustics.* If you don't have a sound system, move around the room as you speak, use your voice theatrically, and prime students for key directions.

Once you've done what you can to positively influence pre-exposure and the environment, you're ready for the next steps.

During Class

This is the most complex stage, consisting of five steps: *engagement, framing, acquisition, elaboration,* and *memory strengthening.*

Engagement

This step is about engaging the mind and body. We all know physical or emotional activation readies the student for learning. It increases the heart rate and it raises levels of cortisol and, depending on the event, dopamine or epinephrine. Assume that you've built the best physical and emotional environment you can. Some students now entering your positive environment will improve their own emotional state for learning. But other students will need something much stronger. The bottom line is that unless students are in a good emotional state for learning, you have no other more important job. All learning is state dependent. Unless you manage students' states, you'll always be dealing with the effect of what happens, not influencing the cause of it. Use the first few minutes of class to positively influence your students' states. This step could be the primary learning experience of the day, but more often it is the setup. Create a positive social climate, keeping in mind that your students are highly influenced by their peers. You might use journaling, humor, affirmations, art, group rituals, activities, or stretching.

Framing

Once students are awake, alert, and aroused, you're ready to address the tricky part. Framing activates neuronal assemblies, or networks, in particular ways that influence states. It is a powerful tool that creates an intentional bias toward what follows. Framing is the "spin" that you put on something—a word, an activity, an assignment, even a disaster. Framing creates the emotional invitation to learn. This step is "the frame" around the picture, the setup for a story, the background for an activity, or anything that "hooks" the learner mentally. You've already hooked them physically; now get their curiosity and wonder engaged. Any time your students show resistance, demotivation, or boredom, framing is one of your top options.

Acquisition

In a way, acquisition is something that's going on all the time. Implicitly, the world is a teacher and so is the classroom—with or without the teacher. The words you choose, the environment you build, and the social influences that students are exposed to are all "teachers." But, in a more explicit way, this step is the part of your instructional day that focuses on input. It's when you orchestrate an activity, an experience, a field trip, a guest speaker, or a simulation. Ideally, learning should have active components to it, and this is the time for them. Could it be research, a lecture, or just reading? Yes, but not ideally. You'll have to decide whether or not the learning is better done socially or individually. The real world typically offers opportunities for both. This suggests cooperative or collaborative learning may be appropriate close to half of the time.

Elaboration

Elaboration is about deepening learning through integration and error correction. It's about students developing more comfort within and confidence in their learning. With this step, the first thing you want to do is ensure that students really have developed a deep understanding of the material and that their understanding is accurate. Students often don't know when they have learned something correctly or not. Connections made at the synapse from the previous step (acquisition) will be solidifying in the first hour after learning. The sooner you allow for error correction, the less "fixed" the synapse is. In other words, mistakes are easier to correct earlier in the process than later. Second, it's important to remember that there are serious limitations to how much students can hold in their short-term, or working, memory. They often turn facts into the "gist" of things—sometimes

accurately, other times not. Mental or physical models that students develop about their learning can reveal inaccuracies. Helpful error-correction strategies include partner quizzes, checklists, peer editing, presentations with feedback, and competitions.

Memory Strengthening

At this point, students' knowledge should be accurate. Now is the time to take a few moments to ensure that the right content will be recalled. Traditionally, teachers have left this memory work up to the students. But the teachers who develop high-performing students, students who are confident and love to excel, also help them recall their material. Learners will develop their recall of the learned material more in the first hour after learning than in the next few days. Use this time wisely. In this segment, using drama, sharing with a partner, or testing mental models can be powerful ways to encapsulate the learning in an easy-to-recall format. Other devices include the use of acronyms, student-developed visual representations, partner reviews, quizzes, or rhymes. Take the time to do this step right. You'll never regret it.

After Class

This final stage has two steps: *settling time and rest* and *review and revision.*

Settling Time and Rest

The evidence is strong that interval learning is superior to "massed" learning. After a learning session, do what you can to give students a way to let the content settle. Ideas include taking time for breaks, walks, or lunch, or orchestrating the learning so that students complete an important learning task just before the end of class or the end of the day. For younger students, short naps also prevent a decline in task performance after new learning. You have some limitations to what you can do, but remember the aphorism from Chapter 3: *Too much, too fast, it won't last.*

Review and Revision

Connections have been made at the synapse by now, but those connections are constantly being modified. Some of the changes happen as a result of the introduction of new, dissonant content, and other changes happen by erosion. Assume that your students won't get things right the first time, that they won't recall what they learned and what they got right, and that memories will deteriorate or get warped. You'll be right more often than you'll be wrong. Incorporate some revision time into every day. Remember, synapses are not static; they constantly adapt in response to activity.

Summary

This short chapter has been an attempt to answer the question "Where?" Where would you put the suggested ideas, concepts, and challenges of brain-based teaching and learning? The answer: "In every part of the curriculum." As our understanding of how the brain works deepens and becomes more attuned to the needs of the educational community, future revisions may be necessary. But for now, you can begin with some confidence in the knowledge that you are supporting optimal student learning.

Schools with the Brain in Mind

This chapter is about strengthening connections.

Attending school from kindergarten through grade 12 takes up more than 13,000 hours of the developing brain's time. During that time, the brains of our students will be altered by the entire school experience. It's not a "maybe," it's a fact: Schools change brains. Brains are being changed by the decisions educators make and by the policies we carry out. Ethically, morally, and opportunistically, we have to pay attention to how we ask students to spend time with us. Yes, this paradigm shift brings with it a whole new understanding of the elevated role of education and educators. I hope you've been "connecting the dots" throughout this book. In fact, you may have already thought of many new tie-ins that your colleagues have yet to make.

There is a caveat, however. I have never advocated running a school based solely on brain research, and I never will. Taking the brain into consideration for almost all of our decision making is a very good idea, but other factors deserve consideration, too. We must consider the interests of parents, districts, school boards, and staff. We must consider state standards. We must consider the safety, weather, and local culture. In short, I advocate schools with the brain in mind, not schools with nothing but the brain in mind. The latter just doesn't make sense.

"Outside the Box" Thinking

Once you start thinking of schools with the brain in mind, a whole realm of possibility comes into view. Suddenly, you become more interested in making mind/brain connections with nutrition, violence prevention, curriculum development, stress management, technology infusion, special education programs, school design, parenting, school sports, assessment, field trips, standardized testing, arts programs, child abuse prevention and intercession, and even the effect of environmental toxins on student achievement. The fact is every one of these topics has some clear connections with brain function and performance. Earlier in this book you read about nutrition, stress, and parenting connections. There are several more connections that merit discussion, and instead of devoting an entire chapter to each new topic, I want to talk about three of the most significant here. They are curriculum connections, assessment connections, and staff development connections. My goal for this chapter is to provide an overview of the connection-making process and to ask some questions that may help you leverage these connections within your own school.

Curriculum Connections

Questions about how to explicitly connect brain research to school curriculum are more likely to lead to further questions than to definitive answers. For example, it's a very relevant question to ask, "At what age is the brain mature enough for abstract reasoning?" But the answer is that there's a wide range in human development; some children are capable of abstract reasoning at age 10, while others don't develop the capacity until they are closer to 15. The wide range of developmental maturity makes it tough to develop a specific schedule for curricular mastery. Unfortunately, we see many schools enacting policies that try to do exactly that. We know too that the brain development necessary for reading also takes place along a multiyear continuum. Some children are reading by age 3 or 4, and others are not ready until they are 7 or 8. Likewise, geometry: Some are ready to grasp the abstract spatial relations of it at age 12, and others need until 14 or 15. Have you also seen these ranges in student performance? Are you subject to policies that are at odds with these realities ("We want every student to have mastered the material on page 50 by Wednesday.")?

Research on brain maturation clearly indicates that the commonly mandated policy of "everybody on the same page on the same day" makes little sense. Until we have a better fix on the factors that contribute to certain kinds of development, we should continue to focus on accommodating all our learners. How does your school successfully accommodate your students' variability in learning differences? How well do you support "learning at one's own pace"? Do you support mastery learning? Can a student who has mastered a topic move ahead to new content? If not, you're going to have frustrated students who will either lose interest or act out.

In light of what we now know about the brain, we also need to ask questions about curriculum content. The human brain is always concerned with survival. Why, then, have so many schools removed the parts of the curriculum that offer the greatest real-world survival value: creativity (the arts), health intelligence (physical education), and financial intelligence? It's a mistake to remove what students care about the most, then grumble that they're not motivated and they often drop out. What about how to develop and strengthen personal and parental relationships? Remember, there is a strong research base for the value of emotional intelligence and its impact on cognition (Maree & Ebersohn, 2002; Petrides, Frederickson, & Furnham, 2004). But this topic—although critical to our students' survival—is usually absent from the curriculum; if it's addressed at all in school, it's usually due to the efforts of a caring teacher or school counselor.

Finally, the world has changed dramatically. With overworked parents having less time to invest in child rearing, today's students have weaker social and emotional skills. Disruptive behaviors are on the rise. Schools ought to respond by offering more social and emotional skill-building, not less. These life skills are easier to teach earlier—in grades K through 5—than in later years. But the substantial pressure to have students succeed on high-stakes tests means that even elementary school teachers are dropping these skills in favor of test-prep skills.

We can all agree that students ought to be able to read and count by the time they take the national standard tests in 4th grade. But can we also agree that we'd like them to show empathy, fairness, and honesty as well? Many studies support the conclusion of Goleman (1995): that emotional IQ matters more than intellectual IQ. Have you come to this conclusion, too?

Assessment Connections

The problem of creating fair assessment is still challenging for even the best of minds. After all, assessment is essentially trying to "read" what's in a student's brain—quite a feat! Assessment has come a long way from the apple-sorting, paper testing of 50 years ago. But considering what we now know about the brain, it's clear that we still have a long way to go. Here are some of the challenges we still have to solve:

1. Memories are highly malleable and need constant revising, meaning that students can learn something and then not remember it. Memory is also highly variable, affected by a range of factors including attention deficit disorders, brain injuries, learning delays, and poor nutrition. At the very least, this suggests that if a testing model is based on recall—as so many are—students must have more practice time.

2. Learning-to-learn strategies are far more essential to real-world success than are amassed facts. So where are the tests that give students opportunities to show these skills?

3. Much of what we ask students to learn is not behaviorally relevant, so how realistic is it to ask them to be vested in the test taking? As it turns out, "Will this be on the test?" is a very smart question to ask!

4. There is little evidence that better test takers do better in life or that the testing skills are transferable (Koretz, Linn, Dunbar, & Shepard,

1991), so what is the incentive for students to get highly motivated about achieving high test scores?

    5. Mental models are highly critical in thinking, yet schools never test for them. Why not? And why is it that that over 99 percent of schools never try to measure students' love of learning, perhaps the most valuable thing they could gain from schooling? It would be easy to develop instruments to measure these factors, and the feedback from them would definitely be useful.

    If *learning* is what we value, then we ought to value the process of learning as much as we value the result of it. A typical classroom narrows both thinking strategies and answer options. Educators who insist on singular approaches and the "right answer" are ignoring the history of our species: Human beings have thrived because we continually seek viable alternative solutions instead of being bound to a single path. The human brain survives on effectiveness, not efficiency. Limiting education to the search for the right answer—as we do when we focus on standardized testing—violates the law of the adaptability of the developing brain. Quality education encourages a wide-open, creative problem-solving approach, thereby exploring alternative thinking options, multiple right answers, and creative insights. These are *not* valued on standardized tests.

    Having said all this, I believe things are getting better in some areas of assessment. For example, today, special education students are usually provided with special testing setups that give them more time, a quiet location, alternative test formats, and so on. (Of course, the huge population of students who don't qualify for special education testing accommodations would also benefit from

these things!) Another positive change is the increasing use of portfolio assessment—a much better way to measure student progress, because it measures a variety of skills over time. We have also come to understand the benefit of providing more choice in the assessment process, and we recognize the legitimacy of allowing students to show what they know in a variety of ways.

    In the near future, I look forward to even better assessments that take on some of the challenges listed above. But until we start measuring what's important to both teachers and students, we'll continue to lose good teachers and to disenfranchise many students. My question to you is, "Can you address some of the assessment issues I've raised in your own work?"

Staff Development

The simplest, most effective way to improve student achievement is to improve teacher effectiveness (Wright, Horn, & Sanders, 1997). The strategies discussed in each of the preceding chapters are things that most teachers can use. Instead of my repeating them here, it's more productive to step back and think in terms of the general principles that underlie them. The following are the most critical brain-based instructional principles. All are great reminders for experienced teachers. My hope is that they'll affirm what you may already know and help you update your teaching knowledge. Can you find additional ways to connect and integrate these principles into your instructional practices?

    1. *Memory malleability.* Memories may be encoded poorly or not at all, changed, confused, or

not retrieved. Your instructional strategies should include ways to strengthen memories.

2. *Nonconscious experience's effect on automatic behaviors.* Most of our behaviors are things we've done so long that we don't even think about doing them. They often are a manifestation of "undisputed downloads," which is learning acquired from role models whom we did not question, internalized when we weren't paying critical attention, or internalized when we were young and our frontal lobes were too immature for critical analysis. As an example, a 3-year-old might experience being ignored in a supermarket for a minute too long and get scared. Soon there are tears, then the fear that she's being "abandoned." Traumas resulting from simple mistakes or minor life incidents are huge to a child who cannot cognitively debrief the situation. Automatic behaviors, which often seem rude or antisocial, manifest when students are not paying full attention to what they do. As teachers, we have to know our students well enough to not take those comments or actions personally. Yet, at the same time, we should work to continually infuse better social skills into the classroom.

3. *Reward dependency.* Human beings naturally crave positives, including novelty and excitement, and they always try to limit pain. Teach your students the skills of deferred gratification (patience, withholding judgment, the ability to go without a reward), and you will give them an advantage in the world.

4. *Attentional limitations.* We rarely maintain a focus on any one thing for very long, except when we are in "flow" states. We cannot hold much in our short-term memory, and mentally, we fatigue very easily. Teach in shorter bursts and do what you can to stress the relevance of the content to your students' lives.

5. *Emotional state dependency.* Emotional states influence attention, memory, learning, meaning-making, and behavior. Manage your learners' states and you'll get better buy-in, with more students caring about the learning goals, the learning process, and the learning outcomes.

6. *Rough drafts.* Our brains rarely get it right the first time. We make "rough" templates and hold them until we either abandon or improve them. Improve your students' depth of understanding by allowing them time to organize and map their learning, dig for details, and make models. They will learn faster and better with opportunities for trial and error and elaboration, and with informal testing to ensure quality and accuracy.

7. *Input limitations.* Complex encoding takes time. Breaks, sleep, and orchestrated pauses all help solidify learning. Design your lesson plans accordingly. Remember, you can teach faster, but your students will just forget it faster.

8. *The influence of perception on experience.* Prior knowledge changes how our brains organize information, either for better or worse. Understand the huge effect of prior knowledge, and deal with it up front. To change the way your students perceive the world is to change their experience of it.

9. *Neural plasticity.* Brains are constantly changing. Be aware of the factors that drive change. Keep in mind the old concept of fixed systems (like homeostasis) or structures (our brains make new connections, form new synapses, and grow new neurons). Every one of your students can change and grow.

10. *Uniqueness.* Brains vary from individual to individual, as a result of both genetic makeup and the influence of environment and life experience. Expect that what works for one student may not work for

another. Make differentiation and customization the norm in your classroom, not the exception.

These principles are probably familiar to you, and I offer this list not as a new way to boggle your mind or revolutionize your teaching practices, but as a support to help you maintain your focus on these key ideas. Try taking just one of the principles in the list and investigating the various instructional strategies related to it. Make it a discipline to integrate those changes into your work over a few weeks' time. Do this, and over a school year, your persistence will work miracles. You can move your teaching to a stronger biological foundation. What you're doing will make sense, and it will be practical too.

Teacher Support and Retention

To get the best from teachers, administrators need to remind themselves that the work teachers do is demanding and can be crazy-making, draining, and stressful. Although teacher salaries are often not what they should be, a bigger problem is working conditions. (After all, most educators choose the profession to make a difference, not to get rich.) Administrators, to keep your staff healthy and keep job performance high, provide the following:

• *Quality professional development.* It improves competency and satisfaction.

• *Better career ladders.* They enhance motivation.

• *Time and structure for both collegial sharing and support.* This keeps morale high and proficiency strong.

More support for teachers might include *stress reduction tools,* which contribute to better health

and less absenteeism. Examples include quiet areas where teachers can de-stress while still at work; loungelike areas separate from a lunchroom where teachers can share helpful professional practices; and even a space with a treadmill so that teachers can run off some of the daily stress. Most important, teachers need the time to use these facilities. For this reason, I'm a strong advocate for a restructured work week that gives teachers more time to think and plan. It makes sense for K–12 teachers to teach no more than four to four and a half days per week. Do you think that's crazy? No one thinks it's crazy for college professors, many of whom balance teaching time with office hours, department meetings, and writing and research. Imagine the rebellion if universities asked professors to teach five hours a day, five days a week.

Teachers need time for renewal and for restoring the physical and emotional soul that they are asked to give their students. Schools districts that say that they can't afford to give staff one half or one full nonteaching day a week would do well to consider the math. It's always cheaper to take care of the good people you have than to recruit (in some cases, internationally or with bonuses) to replace those that you chased away. In a nutshell, administrators need to take care of teachers so that the teachers will take care of the students.

It's necessary to add a quick word about support for new teachers. Our brains are designed to respond to threat, and new teachers can perceive a great deal of threat in their environment. There is the pressure from students, pressure from other staff members, economic pressures associated with choosing teaching as a profession, and the realization that they are accountable for students' performance on high-stakes tests even though they may have limited influence over the many factors that determine how students will score. New teachers are often given the worst classrooms with the least lighting, most noise, and least access to resources (Heschong Mahone Group, 2003). They are frequently assigned the toughest multilevel classes with the least experienced help. The number-one reason teachers leave a school is for a better teaching assignment (Chandler, 2004). Why would any principal do this to a new teacher, knowing that too many new ones are more likely to quit within the first three years of teaching—simply out of frustration? New teachers need less of the "hazing" that goes on and the best conditions possible, not the worst.

To reduce threat to new teachers (and to increase the odds of retaining them past the critical three-year mark), many schools do provide additional support (Renard, 2003). New teachers need accountability (best provided through mentor supervision) and require continuous coaching and feedback. The best way to keep good teachers is to remember that the climate they need is (1) full of hope and opportunity, (2) empowering, (3) challenging, and (4) supportive (Nieto, 2003). The research is very clear: When we don't support teachers, everybody loses.

Changing with the Brain in Mind

A while back, I visited a school district that was very proud about being "brain-based." Do you know what this district had done? Staff members had put a bottle of water on every kid's desk! It was hard for me to keep from laughing. Water will *not* turn anyone's students into an Einstein, and no responsible person would ever claim that it could. Another time, I ran into a teacher who asked me

what I did for a living. When I replied that I did staff development on the applications of brain research, she smiled and said, "Oh, that brain stuff? Yeah, we did that last year." She seemed so pleased that her school had already checked that task off their pedagogical list, as if it were an errand to the post office.

My message for that teacher is that you *haven't done it,* no more than a teacher who has attended a six-hour workshop on cooperative learning or differentiated instruction can be said to have "done" cooperative learning or differentiated instruction. Learning anything well enough to be able to implement it and show reliable results is an extended process of trial and error plus reflection. The level of competence that most of us really need comes after hundreds and often thousands of hours of practice.

Let's all be in the process of improvement. Schools do many things right, but all educators know that there are many things that can be done better. We know it's possible to do some things imperfectly and *still* have a great school. The hungry attitude of continuous improvement is what's most important. The Japanese word for it is "kaizen," meaning "continuously improving." It's a good motto to have.

Summary

The brain-based education movement is now more than 20 years old. It's no longer a flash in the pan, no longer a topic to ignore; it's definitely here to stay. In recent decades, nearly every responsible academic discipline has turned to the brain to learn something new, and those that have not explored this option run the risk of falling behind. A recent international conference in

Granada, Spain, asked neuroscientists to link their work to the work of educators. After listening to three days of scientists sharing their research, the host of the conference said this:

> We need a science of pedagogy. . . . If I can learn in a way that satisfies me, I will learn anything you want me to. But if I cannot learn in a way that is comfortable for me, then I will not learn anything, even if I want to learn it, let alone if you want me to learn it. The "how" of my learning governs the "what." The pedagogy is more important than the curriculum. . . . Knowing what we now think we know as a result of this forum, schooling as we know it may be unsustainable as a strategy for raising and developing our young people . . . because the model we have inherited from the past is not working satisfactorily. (Ball, 2001, p. 19)

The new research into the brain is helping us better understand curriculum, discipline policies, assessment challenges, special education students, cafeteria food, the role of arts, retention policies, and countless other aspects of the teaching profession. In light of brain research, school districts have changed their start times (earlier for younger students, later for high school students), reexamined vending machine and cafeteria food, and altered reading programs (Berninger & Richards, 2002). This is an exciting time! There is a parade of even more new discoveries coming our way. The best way to avoid being run over by the parade is to join in and bring your friends.

Glossary of Brain Terms

Acetylcholine. (uh-see-til-KO-lene) A common memory *neurotransmitter,* particularly involved in long-term memory formation. Specifically released at key junction points, it's present at higher levels during sleep.

ACTH. Also called adrenal-corticotrophin release hormone, this stress-related hormone is produced by the pituitary gland. It's released into the bloodstream when a person experiences injury, emotion, pain, infection, or other trauma.

Adrenaline. The hormone of risk and urgency. Under conditions of stress, fear, or excitement, this hormone is released from the adrenal gland into the bloodstream. When it reaches the liver, it stimulates the release of glucose for rapid energy. Abrupt increases caused by anger can constrict heart vessels, requiring the heart to pump with higher pressure. Also known as *epinephrine.*

Amygdala. (uh-MIG-da-la) Located in the middle of the brain area (there are two of them—one in each anterior temporal lobe), this almond-shaped complex of related nuclei may be the critical processing area for the senses. It's connected to many areas of the brain and plays a critical role in learning, cognition, and the processing of emotional memories.

Axons. These long fibers extending from the brain cells (*neurons*) carry the output (an electrical nerve impulse) to other neurons. They can be up to a meter long. When used often enough, axons build up a fatty white insulation called *myelin.*

Brain stem. Located at the top of the spinal cord, it links the lower brain with the middle of the brain and the cerebral hemispheres. Often referred to as the lower brain, or reptilian brain, in MacLean's older (now out-of-date) "triune" model.

Broca's area. Part of the frontal lobe in the *cerebrum*, it converts thoughts into sounds (or written words) and sends the message to the motor area. Impulses go first to *Wernicke's area*, then to Broca's area.

Cerebellum. A cauliflower-shaped structure located below the *occipital lobe* and next to the *brain stem*. The word is Latin for "little brain." Traditionally, research linked it to balance, posture, coordination, and muscle movements. More recent research has linked it to cognition, novelty, and emotions.

Cerebral cortex. This is the newspaper-sized, 1/4-inch thick, outermost layer of the *cerebrum*. It's wrinkled, six layers deep, and packed with brain cells (*neurons*). *Cortex* is the Latin word for "bark" or "rind."

Cerebrum. This is the largest part of the brain, composed of the left and right hemispheres. It has *frontal, parietal, temporal,* and *occipital lobes.*

Cingulate gyrus. (SIN-gue-lit gye-rus) This structure lies directly above the *corpus callosum.* It mediates communication between the cortex and midbrain structures. It is involved with right–wrong, decision making, and emotions. It helps us shift from one mind–body state to another.

Corpus callosum. A white-matter bundle of millions of nerve fibers that connect the left and right hemispheres. Located in the middle of the brain area.

Dendrites. These are the strandlike fibers emanating from the cell body of *neurons.* Similar to spider webs or cracks in a wall, they are the receptor sites for *axons,* creating a junction at the *synapse.* Each neuron usually has many, many dendrites.

Dopamine. A powerful and common *neurotransmitter* primarily involved in producing a positive mood or feelings. Secreted by *neurons* in the substantia nigra, midbrain, and *hypothalamus,* it also plays a role in movement. It's commonly deficient in patients with Parkinson's disease.

Endorphin. A natural opiate, this *neurotransmitter* is similar to morphine. It is produced in the pituitary gland. It protects against excessive pain and is released with *ACTH* and enkephalins into the brain. It is released to create the "runner's high," which dulls the pain of running.

Epinephrine. (eh-puh-NEFF-rin) Also known as adrenaline, it's a common *neurotransmitter,* hormone, and *neuromodulator.* It is primarily involved in arousal states such as "fight or flight," thus affecting metabolic rate, blood pressure, emotions, and mood.

Frontal lobes. One of four main areas of the *cerebrum,* the upper brain area (the others are the *occipital, parietal,* and *temporal lobes*). Controls voluntary movement, verbal expression, problem solving, willpower, and planning.

GABA. Gamma-aminobutyric acid. This *neurotransmitter* acts as an inhibitory agent, an "off" switch.

Glia. (GLEE-uh) These are one of two critically important types of brain cells (the others are *neurons*). Glia, also known as interneurons, outnumber neurons five to one. They carry nutrients, speed repair, help myelinate *axons,* and may form their own communication network. They are also involved in *neurogenesis.* "Glia" is a shortened form of "neuroglia."

Hippocampus. (hip-uh-CAM-pus) A crescent-shaped structure deep in the *temporal lobe,* in the central brain area. It is strongly involved in learning and memory formation.

Hypothalamus. Located in the bottom center of the midbrain area, this is a complex, thermostat-like structure that influences and regulates appetite, hormone secretion, digestion, sexuality, circulation, emotions, and sleep.

Lateralization. Refers to the activity of using one hemisphere more than another. The term "relative lateralization" is more accurate because we are usually using at least some of the left and right hemispheres of the brain at the same time.

Limbic system. An older term coined by Dr. Paul MacLean in the 1950s to refer to a group of connected structures in the midbrain area, including the *hypothalamus, amygdala, thalamus,* fornix, *hippocampus,* and *cingulate gyrus.* The term is no longer commonly used.

Lower brain. This is the lower portion of the brain, which is composed of the upper spinal cord, *medulla, pons,* and, some say, the *reticular formation.* It sorts sensory information and regulates such survival functions as breathing and heart rate.

Medulla. Located in the *brain stem,* it channels information between the cerebral hemispheres and the spinal cord. It controls respiration, circulation, wakefulness, breathing, and heart rate.

Myelin. A fatty white shield that coats and insulates *axons.* It can help make *neurons* more efficient, allowing electrical impulses to travel up to 12 times faster. Habits may be a result of myelinated axons.

Neurogenesis. The process of growing new brain cells. It is known to occur in birds, rats, monkeys, and humans. Typically, the growth involves hundreds to thousands of new cells per day.

Neuromodulators. Chemicals that influence the quality of transmission at the *synapse.* Examples are cortisol and *adrenaline.*

Neurons. One of two types of brain cells (the others are *glia*). We have about 30 to 50 billion of these. Neurons receive stimulation from their branches, known as *dendrites.* They communicate with other neurons by firing a nerve impulse along an *axon.*

Neurotransmitters. These are the brain's biochemical messengers. There are more than 50 types of neurotransmitters. They usually act as the stimulus that excites a neighboring *neuron* or as an inhibitor to suppress activation.

Norepinephrine. (nor-EH-pi-neff-rin) A common *neurotransmitter,* hormone, and *neuromodulator* that is primarily involved in arousal states such as "fight or flight," affecting the regulation of metabolic rate, blood pressure, emotions, and mood. (This is *epinephrine* that has reached the brain.) Also called *noradrenaline.*

Nucleus basalis. (NEW-clee-us bah-SAL-us) Located in the lower midbrain area, this structure is highly implicated in learning and memory. If activated, it seems to tell the rest of the brain that what is being learned is important and to save it. It projects to the *amygdala* and the *cerebral cortex.* It triggers the release of *acetylcholine* to strengthen memories.

Occipital lobe. Located in the rear of the *cerebrum,* this is one of the four major areas of the upper brain (the others are the *parietal, frontal,* and *temporal lobes*). The occipital lobe processes vision.

Oligodendrocyte. (Oh-lig-oh-DEN-dro-cyte) An especially important type of *glial* cell involved in the support of cells following *neurogenesis.*

Oxytocin. (OX-ee-toe-sin) A peptide also known as the "commitment molecule." It's released during sex and pregnancy and influences pair bonding. Females have more than males.

Parietal lobe. (puh-RYE-uh-tal) The top of the upper brain, it's one of four major areas of the cerebrum (the others are the *occipital, temporal,* and *frontal lobes*). This area deals with reception of sensory information from the contralateral (opposite) side of the body. It also plays a part in reading, writing, language, and calculation.

Pons. A structure located near the top of the *brain stem,* above the *medulla.* It's a critical relay station for sensory information.

Reticular formation. A small structure, located at the top of the *brain stem* and near the bottom of the middle of the brain. It's the regulator responsible for attention, arousal, sleep–wakefulness, and consciousness.

Serotonin. A common *neurotransmitter,* most responsible for inducing relaxation, regulating appetite, mood, learning, consciousness, and

sleep. Antidepressants (such as Prozac) usually suppress the absorption of serotonin, making it more active.

Synapse. The junction area between *neurons.* When an *axon* of one neuron releases *neurotransmitters* to stimulate the *dendrites* of another neuron, the resulting junction area of reaction is a synapse. The adult human has trillions of synapses. Some say a synapse is an actual "unit," not just space.

Temporal lobes. One of the four major areas of the *cerebrum* (the others are the *frontal, occipital,* and *parietal lobes*). Located on the left and right sides of the *cerebrum* (in the middle of the upper brain, near the ears), this area is believed to be responsible for hearing, senses, language, learning, and memory storage.

Thalamus. Located deep within the middle of the brain, it is a key sensory relay station for all senses except smell. It is critical to daily consciousness.

Vasopressin. A stress-related hormone that is synthesized in the *hypothalamus.* It is correlated with vasoconstriction, blood pressure regulation, conservation of water in the body, memory, and distress.

Wernicke's area. (WERE-nick-eeze) The upper back edge of the *parietal lobe* and the left *temporal lobe.* Here the brain converts thoughts into language.

REFERENCES

Abercrombie, H. C., Kalin, N. H., Thurow, M. E., Rosenkranz, M. A., & Davidson, R. J. (2003). Cortisol variation in humans affects memory for emotionally laden and neutral information. *Behavioral Neuroscience, 117*(3), 505–516.

Ackney, C. (1992). Sex differences in relative brain size: The mismeasure of women, too? *Intelligence, 16,* 329–336.

Adlard, P. A., Perreau, V., Engesser-Cesar, C., & Cotman, C. (2003). *Voluntary exercise differentially induces brain-derived neurotrophic factor across lifespan and protects against behavioral depression.* Poster, Program #633.1, Society for Neuroscience, New Orleans, LA.

Adolphs, R. (1998). The human amygdala in social judgment. *Nature, 393,* 470–474.

Ahissar, E., Vaadia, E., Ahissar, M., Bergman, H., Arieli, A., & Abeles, M. (1992). Dependence of cortical plasticity on correlated activity of single neurons and on behavioral context. *Science, 257*(5075*)*, 1412–1415.

Allen, L., & Gorski, R. (1991). Sexual dimorphism of the anterior commissure and massa intermedia of the human brain. *Journal of Comparative Neurology, 312,* 97–104.

Altmann, G. T. (2002). Learning and development in neural networks—the importance of prior experience. *Cognition, 85*(2), B43–50.

Anderson, B. J., Eckburg, P. B., & Relucio, K. I. (2002). Alterations in the thickness of motor cortical subregions after motor-skill learning and exercise. *Learning and Memory, 9,* 1–9.

Anderson, C. A., & Bushman, B. J. (2001). Effects of violent video games on aggressive behavior, aggressive cognition, aggressive affect, physiological arousal, and prosocial behavior: A meta-analytic review of the scientific literature. *Psychological Science, 12*(5), 353–359.

Anderson, J. (1995). *Learning and memory: An integrated approach.* New York: Wiley & Sons.

Antoniadis, E. A., Ko, C. H., Ralph, M. R., & McDonald, R. J. (2000). Circadian rhythms, aging, and memory. *Behavioral Brain Research, 111*(1–2), 25–37.

Aoki, H., Yamada, N., Ozeki, Y., Yamane, H., & Kato, N. (1998, August 14). Minimum light intensity required to suppress nocturnal melatonin concentration in human saliva. *Neuroscience Letters, 252*(2), 91–94.

Armony, J., & LeDoux, J. (2000). How danger is encoded: Toward a systems, cellular and computational understanding of cognitive–emotional interactions in gear. In M. Gazzaniga (Ed.), *The new cognitive neuroscience* (pp. 1067–1080). Cambridge, MA: MIT Press.

Ashby, F. G., Isen, A. M., & Turken, A. U. (1999, July). A neuropsychological theory of positive affect and its influence on cognition. *Psychological Review, 106,* 529–550.

Aslin, R., & Hunt, R. (2001). Development, plasticity and learning in the auditory system. In C. Nelson & M. Luciana (Eds.), *Handbook of developmental cognitive neuroscience* (pp. 205–220). Cambridge, MA: MIT Press.

Aspinwall, L. G., & Richter, L. (1999). Optimism and self-mastery predict more rapid disengagement from unsolvable tasks in the presence of alternatives. *Motivation and Emotion, 23,* 221–245.

Atwood, H., & Karunannithi, S. (2002). Diversification of synaptic strength: Presynaptic elements. *Nature Reviews Neuroscience, 3*(7), 497–515.

Ayers, P. D. (1999, December). *Exploring the relationship between high school facilities and achievement of high school students in Georgia.* Unpublished doctoral dissertation, University of Georgia, Athens.

Bacanu, S. A., Devlin, B., & Roeder, K. (2000, June). The power of genomic control. *American Journal Human Genetics, 66*(6), 1933–1944.

Bahrick, H. P. (1975). Fifty years of memories for names and faces. *Journal of Experimental Psychology, 104,* 54–75.

Bahrick, H. P. (1983). The cognitive map of a city—Fifty years of learning and memory. In G. H. Bower (Ed.), *The psychology of learning and motivation, 17* (pp. 125–163). New York: Academic Press.

Bahrick, H. P. (1984). Semantic memory content in permastore: Fifty years of memory for Spanish learned in school. *Journal of Experimental Psychology, 113,* 1–29.

Bahrick, H. P., & Hall, L. K. (1991). Lifetime maintenance of high school mathematics content. *Journal of Experimental Psychology, 120,* 20–33.

Bailey, D., Bruer, J., Symons, F., & Lichtman, J. (2001). *Critical thinking about critical periods.* Baltimore: Paul Brooks Publishing.

Ball, C. (2001, February 1–3). *Closing remarks.* Paper presented at a conference on Learning Sciences and Brain Research: Potential Implications for Education Policies and Practices, Granada, Spain. Available: www1.oecd.org/els/pdfs/EDSCERIDOCA110.pdf.

Bangert-Downs, R., Kulick, C., Kulick, J., & Morgan, M. (1991). The instructional effects of feedback in test-like events. *Review of Educational Research, 61*(2), 213–238.

Barber, B. L., Jacobson, K. C., Miller, K. E., & Petersen, A. C. (1998). Ups and downs: Daily cycles of adolescent moods. *New Directions for Child Development, 82,* 23–36.

Baumeister, R., & Sommer, K. (1997). What do men want? Gender differences and two spheres of belongingness: Comment on Cross and Madson. *Psychological Bulletin, 12,* 38–44.

Bechara, A., Damasio, H., & Damasio, A. R. (2003, April). Role of the amygdala in decision-making. *Annals of the New York Academy of Sciences, 985,* 356–369.

Benn, W. (2003, July). *New evaluation study of quantum learning's impact on achievement in multiple settings.* Independent assessment by William Benn and Associates, Laguna Hills, CA.

Bennett, S. N., & Blundell, D. (1983). Quantity and quality of work in rows and classroom groups. *Educational Psychology, 32*(2), 93–105.

Benton, D., Fordy, J., & Haller, J. (1995). The impact of long-term vitamin supplementation on cognitive functioning. *Psychopharmacology, 117,* 298–305.

Benton, D., & Roberts, G. (1988, January 23). Effect of vitamin and mineral supplementation on intelligence in a sample of school children. *Lancet, 1*(8578), 140–143.

Berg, F., Blair, J., & Benson, P. (1996, December). Classroom acoustics: The problem, impact, and solution. *Praxis der Kinderpsychologie und Kinderpsychiatrie, 45*(10), 16–20.

Berglund, B., Hassmen, P., & Job, R. F. (1996, May). Sources and effects of low-frequency noise. *Journal of the Acoustic Society of America, 99*(5), 2985–3002.

Berninger, V., & Richards, T. (2002). *Brain literacy for educators and psychologists.* San Diego: Academic Press.

Berridge, K., & Robinson, T. (2002). The mind of an addicted brain: Neural sensitization of wanting versus liking. In J. Cacioppo et al. (Eds.), *Foundations in social neuroscience* (pp. 565–572). Cambridge, MA: MIT Press.

Billings, A. G., Cronkite, R. C., & Moos, R. H. (1983, May). Social–environmental factors in unipolar depression: Comparisons of depressed patients and nondepressed controls. *Journal of Abnormal Psychology, 92*(2), 119–133.

Black, J. E., Isaacs, K. R., Anderson, B. J., Alcantara, A. A., & Greenough, W. T. (1990). Learning causes synaptogenesis, while motor activity causes angiogenesis, in cerebellar cortex of adult rats. *Proceedings of the National Academy of Sciences, 87,* 5568–5572.

Bliss, T. V. P., & Lomo, T. (1973). Long lasting potentiation of synaptic transmission. *Journal of Physiology, 232,* 331–356.

Bodizs, R., Bekesy, M., Szucs, A., Barsi, P., & Halasz, P. (2002, September). Sleep-dependent hippocampal slow activity correlates with waking memory performance in humans. *Neurobiology of Learning and Memory, 78*(2), 441–457.

Bouchard, T. (1988, June). Personality similarity in twins reared apart and together. *Journal of Personality and Social Psychology, 54*(6), 1031–1039.

Bower, G. H. (1981, February). Mood and memory. *American Psychologist, 36*(2), 129–148.

Bourgeois, J. P. (2001). Synaptogenesis in the neocortex of the newborn: The ultimate frontier for individuation. In C. Nelson & M. Luciana (Eds.), *Handbook of developmental cognitive neuroscience* (pp. 23–24). Cambridge, MA: MIT Press.

Bradley, M., & Lang, P. (2000). Measuring emotion: Behavior, feeling and physiology. In R. Lane & L. Nadel (Eds.), *The cognitive neuroscience of emotion* (pp. 242–276). New York: Oxford University Press.

Brennen, T., Martinussen, M., Hansen, B. O., & Hjemdal, O. (1999, December). Arctic cognition: A study of cognitive performance in summer and winter at 69° N. *Applied Cognitive Psychology, 13*(6), 561–580.

Brothers, L. (2000). The social brain: A project for integrating primate behavior and neurophysiology in a new domain. In J. Cacioppo et al. (Eds.), *Foundations in social neuroscience* (pp. 367–385). Cambridge, MA: MIT Press.

Brown, E., Rush, A., & McEwen, B. (1999). Hippocampal remodeling and damage by corticosteroids: Implications for mood disorders. *Neuropsychopharmacology, 21,* 474–484.

Bruer, J. (1998, November). Brain science, brain fiction. *Educational Leadership, 56*(3), 14–18.

Bruer, J. (1999). *The myth of the first three years.* New York: Free Press.

Bruner, A., Joffe, A., Duggan, A., Casella, J., & Brandt, J. (1996). Randomized study of cognitive effects of iron supplementation in non-anemic iron-deficient adolescent girls. *Lancet, 3488,* 992–996.

Byrnes, J. (2001). *Minds, brains and learning.* New York: Guilford Books.

Cacace, A. T., & McFarland, D. J. (1998, April). Central auditory processing disorder in school-aged children: A critical review. *Journal of Speech, Language, and Hearing Research, 41*(2), 355–373.

Cacioppo, J., Berntson, G., Sheridan, J., & McClintock, M. (2001). Multilevel analyses of human behavior: Social neuroscience and the complementing nature of social and biological approaches. In J. Cacioppo (Ed.), *Foundations in social neuroscience* (pp. 21–46). Cambridge, MA: MIT Press.

Cahill, L., Gorski, L., & Le, K. (2003, July–August). Enhanced human memory consolidation with post-learning stress: Interaction with the degree of arousal at encoding. *Learning & Memory, 10*(4), 270–274.

Cahill, L., Prins, B., Weber, M., & McGaugh, J. (1994, October). Adrenergic activation and memory for emotional events. *Nature, 371*(6499), 702–704.

Calvin, W. (1996). *How brains think.* New York: Basic Books.

Campbell, S. S., & Dawson, D. (1990, August). Enhancement of nighttime alertness and performance with bright ambient light. *Physiology & Behavior, 48*(2), 317–320.

Carper, J. (2000). *Your miracle brain.* New York: Harper Collins.

Carraher, T., Carraher, D., & Schliemann, A. (1985). Mathematics in the streets and in the schools. *British Journal of Developmental Psychology, 3,* 21–29.

Carskadon, M. A., Wolfson, A. R., Acebo, C., Tzischinsky, O., & Seifer, R. (1998, December). Adolescent sleep patterns, circadian timing, and sleepiness at a transition to early school days. *Sleep, 21*(8), 871–881.

Cash, C., Earthman, G., & Hines, E. (1997, January). Building condition tied to successful learning. *School Planning and Management, 21*(1), 48–53.

Castellanos, F. X., & Tannock, R. (2002, August). Neuroscience of attention-deficit/hyperactivity disorder: The search for endophenotypes. *National Review Neuroscience, 3*(8), 617–628.

Cave, B. (1997). Very long-lasting priming in picture naming. *Psychological Science, 8,* 322–325.

Ceci, S. J., & Roazzi, A. (1994). The effects of context on cognition: Postcards from Brazil. In R. J. Sternberg & R. K. Wagner (Eds.), *Mind in context: Interactionist perspectives on human intelligence* (pp. 74–101). New York: Cambridge University Press.

Cenci, A., Whishaw, I., & Schallert, T. (2002). Animal models of neurological deficits: How relevant is the rat? *Nature Reviews Neuroscience, (3)*7, 574–579.

Chandler, K. (2004). *Teacher attrition and mobility: Results from the Teacher Follow-up Survey, 2000–01.* (NCES Report # 2004301). Washington, DC: U.S. Department of Education, National Center for Education Statistics.

Chaouloff, F. (1989). Physical exercise and brain monoamines: A review. *Acta Physiologica Scandinavica, 137,* 1–13.

Chen, Z., & Klahr, D. (1999, September). All other things being equal: Acquisition and transfer of the control of variables strategy. *Child Development, 70*(5), 1098–1120.

Christianson, S. (Ed.). (1992). *The handbook of emotion and memory: Research and theory.* Hillsdale, NJ: Lawrence Erlbaum.

Christianson, S., & Loftus, E. (1990). Remembering emotional events: The fate of detailed information. *Cognition and Emotion, 5,* 693–701.

Churchill, J. D., Galvez, R., Colcombe, S., Swain, R. A., Kramer, A. F., & Greenough, W. T. (2002). Exercise, experience and the aging brain. *Neurobiological Aging, 23*(5), 941–955.

Cicerone, K. D., & Tanenbaum, L. N. (1997). Disturbance of social cognition after traumatic orbitofrontal brain injury. *Archives of Clinical Neuropsychology, 12*(2), 173–188.

Cohen, L., & Dehaene, S. (1996). Cerebral networks for number processing: Evidence from a case of posterior callosal lesion. *Neurocase, 2,* 155–174.

Coley, J. D., Hayes, B., Lawson, C., & Moloney, M. (2004, January). Knowledge, expectations, and inductive reasoning within conceptual hierarchies. *Cognition, 90*(3), 217–253.

Collie, A., Maruff, P., Darby, D. G., & McStephen, M. (2003, March). The effects of practice on the cognitive test performance of neurologically normal individuals assessed at brief test–retest intervals. *Journal of International Neuropsychology Society, 9*(3), 419–428.

Compton, R. J. (2003, June). The interface between emotion and attention: A review of evidence from psychology and neuroscience. *Behavioral and Cognitive Neuroscience Review, 2*(2), 115–129.

Courchesne, E., & Allen, G. (1997). Prediction and preparation, fundamental functions of the cerebellum. *Learning and Memory, 4,* 1–35.

Cox, D. J., Gonder-Frederick, L. A., Schroeder, D. B., Cryer, P. E., & Clarke, W. L. (1993, October). Disruptive effects of acute hypoglycemia on speed of cognitive and motor performance. *Diabetes Care, 16*(10), 1391–1393.

Cranz, G. (1998). *The chair: Rethinking culture, body, and design.* New York: Norton.

Crick, F. (1994). *The astonishing hypothesis*. New York: Macmillan Publishing Company.

Csikszentmihalyi, M. (1991). *Finding flow*. New York: Perennial.

Czoty, P. W., Morgan, D., Shannon, E. E., Gage, H. D., & Nader, M. A. (2004, July). Characterization of dopamine D_1 and D_2 receptor function in socially housed cynomolgus monkeys self-administering cocaine. *Psychopharmacology, 174(3)*, 381–388.

Damasio, A. (1994). *Descartes' error*. New York: Grosset/Putnam.

Damasio, A. (1999). *The feeling of what happens*. New York: Harcourt Brace.

Davidson, R. (1992). Emotions and affective style. *Psychological Science, 3*, 39–43.

Davidson, R. J., & Sutton, S. K. (1995). Affective neuroscience: The emergence of a discipline. *Current Opinion in Neurobiology, 5(2)*, 217–224.

Dawes, R., McTavish, J., & Shaklee, H. (1977). Behavior, communication and assumptions about other people's behaviors in a common dilemma situation. *Journal of Personality and Social Psychology, 35*, 1–11.

Denenberg, V. H., Kim, D. S., & Palmiter, R. D. (2004, January). The role of dopamine in learning, memory, and performance of a water escape task. *Behavioral Brain Research, 148*(1–2), 73–78.

DePorter, B., & Hernacki, M. (1992). *Quantum learning*. New York: Dell Paperbacks.

Desmond, J., Gabrielli, J., Wagner, A., Ginier, B., & Glover, G. (1997). Lobular patterns of cerebellar activation in verbal working-memory and finger tapping tasks as revealed by functional MRI. *Journal of Neuroscience, 17*(24), 9675–9685.

Dexter, D., Bijwadia, J., Schilling, D., & Applebaugh, G. (2003). Sleep, sleepiness and school start times: A preliminary study. *Wisconsin Medical Journal, 102*(1), 44–46.

Diamond, D., Park, C., Hemen, K., & Rose, G. (1999). Exposing rats to a predator impairs spatial working memory in the radial arm water maze. *Hippocampus, 9*, 542–552.

Diamond, M., & Hopson, J. (1998). *Magic trees of the mind*. New York: Dutton Books, Penguin-Putnam Group.

Dolcourt, J. L. (2000, Summer). Commitment to change: A strategy for promoting educational effectiveness. *Journal of Continuing Education in the Health Profession, 20*(3), 156–163.

Donevan, R. H., & Andrew, G. M. (1986). Plasma B-endorphin immunoreactivity during graded cycle ergometry. *Medicine and Science in Sports and Exercise, 19*(3), 231.

Donovan, A. M., Halperin, J. M., Newcorn, J. H., & Sharma, V. (1999). Thermal response to serotonergic challenge and aggression in attention deficit hyperactivity disorder. *Journal of Child and Adolescent Psychopharmacology, 9*(2), 85–91.

Doyon, J., Owen, A., Petrides, M., Szliklas, Z. V., & Evans, A. (1996). Functional anatomy of visuomotor skill learning in human subjects examined with position emission tomography. *European Journal of Neuroscience, 8*(4), 637–648.

Driskell, J., Cooper, C., & Moran, A. (1994). Does mental practice enhance performance? *Journal of Applied Psychology, 79*, 481–492.

Dugatkin, L. (2002). Prancing primates, turtles with toys: It's more than just (animal) play. *Cerebrum, 4*(3), 41–52.

Durston, S., Hulshoff Pol, H. E., Casey, B. J., Giedd, J. N., Buitelaar, J. K., & van Engeland, H. (2001, September). Anatomical MRI of the developing human brain: What have we learned? *Journal of the American Academy of Child & Adolescent Psychiatry, 40*(9), 1012–1020.

Duyon, J., & Ungerleider, L. (2002). Functional anatomy of motor skill learning. In L. Squire & D. Schacter (Eds.), *Neuropsychology of memory* (pp. 225–238). New York: Guilford Press.

Dwyer, T., Blizzard, L., & Dean, K. (1996, April). Physical activity and performance in children. *Nutrition Review, 54*(4), S27–31.

Dwyer, T., Sallis, J., Blizzard, L., Lazarus, R., & Dean, K. (2001). Relation of academic performance to physical activity and fitness in children. *Pediatric Exercise Science, 13*, 225–237.

Eckardt, M., Rohrbaugh, J., Rio, D., Rawlings, R., & Capola, R. (1998). Brain imaging in alcoholic patients. *Advances in Alcohol and Substance Abuse, 7*, 59–71.

Eich, E. (1995). Searching for mood dependent memory. *Psychological Science, 6,* 67–75.

Elman, J., Bates, E., Johnson, M., Karmiloff-Smith, A., Parisi, D., & Plunkett, K. (1996). *Rethinking innateness.* Cambridge, MA: MIT Press.

Evans, G., & Maxwell, L. (1997). Chronic noise exposure and reading deficits: The mediating effects of language acquisition. *Environment & Behavior, 29*(5), 638–656.

Evans, G. W., Lercher, P., Meis, M., Ising, H., & Kofler, W. W. (2001). Community noise exposure and stress in children. *Journal of the Acoustical Society of America, 109*(3), 1023–1027.

Feth, L. (1999, December 21). Many classrooms have bad acoustics that inhibit learning. News release published by Ohio State University.

Feynman, R. (1999). *The pleasure of finding things out.* London: Penguin Books.

Fine, I., Wade, A. R., Brewer, A. A., May, M. G., Goodman, D. F., Boynton, G. M., Wandell, B. A., & MacLeod, D. I. (2003, September). Long-term deprivation affects visual perception and cortex. *Nature Neuroscience, 6*(9), 915–916.

Fiorillo, C. D., Tobler, P. N., & Schultz, W. (2003, March 21). Discrete coding of reward probability and uncertainty by dopamine neurons. *Science, 299*(5614), 1898–1902.

Fischer, H., Andersson, J. L., Furmark, T., & Fredrikson, M. (2000, August). Fear conditioning and brain activity: A positron emission tomography study in humans. *Behavioral Neuroscience, 114*(4), 671–680.

Fischer, K., & Bidwell, T. (1991). Constraining nativist inferences about cognitive capacities. In S. Carey & R. Gelman (Eds.), *The epigenesis of mind* (pp. 199–236). Hillsdale, NJ: Lawrence Erlbaum.

Fisher, R. (1990). Why the mind is not in the head but in society's connectionist network. *Diogenes, 151*(1), 1–28.

Flanagan, J. R., Vetter, P., Johansson, R. S., & Wolpert, D. M. (2003). Prediction preceded control in motor learning. *Current Biology, 13,* 146–150.

Fordyce, D. E., & Wehner, J. M. (1993, August 13). Physical activity enhances spatial learning performance with an associated alteration in hippocampal protein kinase C activity in C57BL/6 and DBA/2 mice. *Brain Research, 619*(1–2), 111–119.

Foster, P. L., & Cairns, J. (1994, November). The occurrence of heritable Mu excisions in starving cells of *Escherichia coli. The EMBO Journal, 13*(21), 5240–5244.

Fox, M., Pac, S., Devaney, B., & Jankowski, L. (2004). Feeding infants and toddlers study: What foods are infants and toddlers eating? *Journal of the American Dietetic Association, 104* (supplement 1), 22–30.

Frank, D. A., & Greenberg, M. E. (1994). CREB: A mediator of long-term memory from mollusks to mammals. *Cell, 79,* 5–8.

Friston, K., & Price, C. (2001). Dynamic representations and generative models of brain function. *Brain Research Bulletin, 54,* 275–285.

Frith, C., & Frith, U. (1999). Interacting minds—biological basis. *Science, 286,* 1692–1695.

Fuster, J. (1995). *Memory in the cerebral cortex.* Cambridge, MA: MIT Press.

Gabbard, C. P., & Shea, C. H. (1979, February). Influence of movement activities on shape recognition and retention. *Perceptual and Motor Skills, 48*(1), 116–118.

Galinsky, E., Howes, C., Kontos, S., & Shinn, M. (1994). *The study of children in family child care and relative care: Highlights of findings.* New York: Families and Work Institute.

Gardner, H. (1991). *The unschooled mind: How children think and how schools should teach.* New York: Basic Books.

Gardner, H. (1995). Reflections on multiple intelligences: Myths and messages. *Phi Delta Kappan, 77,* 200–209.

Gaser, C., & Schlaug, G. (2003, October 8). Brain structures differ between musicians and non-musicians. *Journal of Neuroscience, 23*(27), 9240–9245.

Gazzaniga, M. (1988). *Mind matters: How mind and brain interact to create our conscious lives.* Boston: Houghton-Mifflin/MIT Press.

Gazzaniga, M. (2001). Brain and conscious experience. In J. Cacioppo, et al. (Eds.), *Foundations in social neuroscience* (pp. 203–214). Cambridge, MA: MIT Press.

Georgieff, M., & Rao, R. (2001). The role of nutrition in cognitive development. In C. Nelson & M. Luciana (Eds.), *Handbook of developmental cognitive neuroscience* (pp. 491–504). Cambridge, MA: MIT Press.

Glascher, J., & Adolphs, R. (2003, November 12). Processing of the arousal of subliminal and supraliminal emotional stimuli by the human amygdala. *Journal of Neuroscience, 23*(32), 10274–10282.

Goda, Y., & Davis, G. W. (2003, October 9). Mechanisms of synapse assembly and disassembly. *Neuron, 40*(2), 243–264.

Gogtay, N., Giedd, J. N., Lusk, L., Hayashi, K. M., Greenstein, D., Vaituzis, A. C., Nugent, T. F., Herman, D. H., Clasen, L. S., Toga, A. W., Rapoport, J. L., & Thompson, P. M. (2004, May 25). Dynamic mapping of human cortical development during childhood through early adulthood. *Proceedings of the National Academy of Sciences, 101*(21), 8174–8179.

Goleman, D. (1995). *Emotional intelligence.* New York: Bantam Books.

Gomes, L., Martinho, P., Pimenta, A., & Castelo Branco, N. (1999). Effects of occupational exposure to low-frequency noise on cognition. *Aviation, Space & Environmental Medicine, 70*(3), A115–118.

Gordon, H. W., Stoffer, D. S., & Lee, P. A. (1995, December). Ultradian rhythms in performance on tests of specialized cognitive function. *International Journal of Neuroscience, 83*(3–4), 199–211.

Gouchie, C., & Kimura, D. (1991). The relationship between testosterone levels and cognitive ability patterns. *Psychoneuroendocrinology, 16*(4), 323–334.

Gould, E., McEwen, B., Tanapat, P., Galea, L., & Fuchs, E. (1997). Neurogenesis in the dentate gyrus of the adult tree shrew is regulated by psychosocial stress and NMDA receptor activation. *Journal of Neuroscience, 17,* 2492–2498.

Greenough, W. T., & Anderson, B. J. (1991). Cerebellar synaptic plasticity: Relation to learning versus neural activity. *Annals of the New York Academy of Sciences, 627,* 231–247.

Greenspan, S. (1997). *The endangered mind.* Reading, MA: Perseus Books.

Greenwald, A., & Banaji, M. (1995). Implicit social cognition: Attitudes, self-esteem, and stereotypes. *Psychological Review, 102*(1), 4–27.

Greenwood, C. E., & Winocur, G. (2001, March). Glucose treatment reduces memory deficits in young adult rats fed high-fat diets. *Neurobiology of Learning and Memory, 75*(2), 179–189.

Grigsby, J., & Stevens, D. (2000). *Neurodynamics of personality.* New York: Guilford Publications.

Grunbaum, J. A., Kann, L., Kinchen, S. A., Williams, B., Ross, J. G., Lowry, R., Kolbe, L. (2002, October). Youth risk behavior surveillance in the United States of America. *Journal of School Health, 72*(8), 313–328.

Gunnar, M. (2000). Early adversity and the development of stress reactivity and regulation. In C. Nelson & N. Mahwah (Eds.), *The effects of adversity on neurobehavioral development: Minnesota symposia on child psychology* (Vol. 31, pp. 163–200). Minneapolis: Lawrence Erlbaum Associates.

Gunnar, M. (2001). Effects of early deprivation: Findings from orphanage-reared infants and children. In C. Nelson & M. Luciana (Eds.), *Handbook of developmental cognitive neuroscience* (pp. 617–630). Cambridge, MA: MIT Press.

Halterman, J. (2001). Iron-deficient children may have impaired cognitive performance. *Pediatrics, 107,* 1381–1386.

Harmatz, M. G., Well, A. D., Overtree, C. E., Kawamura, K. Y., Rosal, M., & Ockene, I. S. (2000). Seasonal variation of depression and other moods: A longitudinal approach. *Journal of Biological Rhythms, 15*(4), 344–350.

Harmon, D. B. (1951). *The coordinated classroom.* Research paper. Grand Rapids, MI: The American Seating Company.

Harner, D. P. (1974, March–April). Effects of thermal environment on learning. *CEFP Journal, 12*(2), 4–6.

Hastings, N. (1995). Seats of learning? *Support for Learning (England), 10*(1), 8–11.

Hattie, J. (1992). Measuring the effects of schooling. *Australian Journal of Education, 36*(1), 5–13.

Hayes, B. K., Foster, K., & Gadd, N. (2003, June). Prior knowledge and subtyping effects in children's category learning. *Cognition, 88*(2), 171–199.

Hayes, B. K., Goodhew, A., Heit, E., & Gillan, J. (2003, December). The role of diverse instruction in conceptual change. *Journal of Experimental Child Psychology, 86*(4), 253–276.

Heilman, K. (2000). Emotional experience: A neurological model. In R. Lane & L. Nadel (Eds.), *The cognitive neuroscience of emotion* (pp. 328–344). New York: Oxford University Press.

Helfer, M., Kempe, R., & Krugman, R. (1997). *The battered child.* Chicago: University Press.

Herz, R. S., Eliassen, J., Beland, S., & Souza, T. (2004). Neuroimaging evidence for the emotional potency of odor-evoked memory. *Neuropsychologia, 42*(3), 371–378.

Heschong, L., & Heschong Mahone Consulting Group. (1999). *Daylighting in schools: An investigation into the relationship between daylighting and human performance.* A study performed on behalf of the California Board for Energy Efficiency for the Third Party Program administered by Pacific Gas & Electric, as part of the PG & E contract 460–000. For a copy, e-mail Lisa Heschong at info@h-m-g.com.

Heschong Mahone Group. (2003). Windows and classrooms: A study of student performance and the indoor environment. A study performed on behalf of the California Energy Commission administered by Pacific Gas & Electric, October, contract P500-03-082-A-7. Available: www.h-m-g-.com/downloads/Daylighting/A-7_Windows_Classroom_2.4.10.pdf.

Hobson, A. (1994). *The chemistry of conscious states.* Boston: Little, Brown & Co.

Hodges, J., & Tizard, B. (1989). Social and family relationships of ex-institutional adolescents. *Journal of Child Psychology and Psychiatry, 30,* 77–97.

Hoffman, A. (1996). *Schools, violence, and society.* Westport, CT: Praeger Publishers/Greenwood Publishing Group, Inc.

House, J., Landis, K., & Umberson, D. (1988). Social relationships and health. *Science, 241,* 540–545.

Howard, P. J. (1994). *The owner's manual for the brain: Everyday applications from mind-brain research.* Austin, TX: Leornian Press.

Huesmann, L. R., Moise-Titus, J., Podolski, C. L., & Eron, L. D. (2003, March). Longitudinal relations between children's exposure to TV violence and their aggressive and violent behavior in young adulthood: 1977–1992. *Developmental Psychology, 39*(2), 201–221.

Hutchinson, S., Lee, L. H., Gaab, N., & Schlaug, G. (2003, September). Cerebellar volume of musicians. *Cerebral Cortex, 13*(9), 943–949.

Huttenlocher, P. (1994). Synaptogenesis in the human cerebral cortex. In G. Dawson & K. W. Fischer (Eds.), *Human behavior and the developing brain* (pp. 137–153). New York: Guilford Press.

Huttenlocher, P., & Dabholkar, A. (1997). Developmental anatomy of the prefrontal cortex. In N. Krasnegor, G. Lyon, & P. Goldman-Rakic (Eds.), *Development of the prefrontal cortex: Evolution, neurobiology and behavior* (pp. 69–84). Baltimore: Paul H. Brookes Publishing Company.

Ito, T. A., Larsen, J. T., Smith, N. K., & Cacioppo, J. T. (2001, October). Negative information weighs more heavily on the brain: The negativity bias in evaluative categorizations. In J. Cacioppo et al. (Eds.), *Foundations in social neuroscience* (pp. 576–597). Cambridge, MA: MIT Press.

Ivry, R. (1997). Cerebellar timing systems. *International Review of Neurobiology, 41,* 555–573.

Ivry, R., & Fiez, J. (2000). Cerebellar contributions to cognition and imagery. In M. Gazzaniga (Ed.), *The new cognitive neurosciences* (pp. 999–1012). Cambridge, MA: MIT Press.

Izard, C. (1998). *The face of emotion.* New York: Appleton-Century-Crofts.

Izard, C. E., Kagan, J., & Zajonc, R. B. (Eds.). (1984). *Emotions, cognition, and behavior.* Cambridge, Eng.: Cambridge University Press.

Jensen, E. (2000). *Arts with the brain in mind.* Alexandria, VA: Association for Supervision and Curriculum Development.

Jernigan, T. (2003, January 20). *Maturation and the human brain.* Talk given at the Learning Brain EXPO, San Diego, CA.

Johnson, M. (2001, July). Functional brain development in humans. *Nature Reviews Neuroscience, 2*(7), 475–483.

Johnson, T., & Johnson, R. (1999). *Learning together and alone: Cooperative, competitive and individualistic learning.* Boston: Allyn and Bacon.

Jonides, J. (1995). Working memory and thinking. In E. Smith & D. Osheron (Eds.), *An invitation to cognitive science* (pp. 215–265). Cambridge, MA: MIT Press.

Kagan, J. M. (1994). *Galen's prophecy.* New York: Basic Books.

Kasamatsu, K., Suzuki, S., Anse, M., Funada, M. F., Idogawa, K., & Ninomija, S. P. (2002, November). Menstrual cycle effects on performance of mental arithmetic task. *Journal of Physiology, Anthropology, and Applied Human Science, 21*(6), 285–290.

Kelso, S. (1997). *Dynamic patterns.* Cambridge, MA: MIT Bradford Book.

Kempermann, G. (2002, February 1). Why new neurons? Possible functions for adult hippocampal neurogenesis. *Journal of Neuroscience, 22*(3), 635–638.

Kempermann, G., Kuhn, H. G., & Gage, F. H. (1998). Experience-induced neurogenesis in the senescent dentate gyrus. *Journal of Neuroscience, 18,* 3206–3212.

Kesslak, J., Patrick, V., So, J., Cotman, C., & Gomez-Pinilla, F. (1998, August). Learning upregulates brain-derived neurotrophic factor messenger ribonucleic acid: A mechanism to facilitate encoding and circuit maintenance. *Behavioral Neuroscience, 112*(4), 1012–1019.

Kilgard, M. P., & Merzenich, M. M. (1998). Cortical map reorganization enabled by nucleus basalis activity. *Science, 279,* 1714–1718.

Kilgard, M. P., & Merzenich, M. M. (2002, March 5). Order-sensitive plasticity in adult primary auditory cortex. *Proceedings of the National Academy of Sciences USA, 99*(5), 3205–3209.

Killgore, W. D., Oki, M., & Yurgelun-Todd, D. A. (2001, February 12). Sex-specific developmental changes in amygdala responses to affective faces. *Neuroreport, 12*(2), 427–433.

Kilpatrick, L., & Cahill, L. (2003, December). Amygdala modulation of parahippocampal and frontal regions during emotionally influenced memory storage. *Neuroimage, 20*(4), 2091–2099.

Kim, J., & Diamond, D. (2002). The stressed hippocampus, synaptic plasticity and lost memories. *Nature Reviews Neuroscience, 3*(6), 453–462.

Kim, S., Ugirbil, K., & Strick, P. (1994). Activation of a cerebellar output nucleus during cognitive processing. *Science, 265,* 949–951.

Kimura, D. (2000). A scientist dissents on sex and cognition. *Cerebrum, 2*(4), 69.

Kirsch, I. (1999). The response expectancy: An introduction. In I. Kirsch (Ed.), *How expectancies shape experiences* (p. 7). Washington, DC: American Psychological Association.

Klausberger, T., Magill, P., Marton, L., Roberts, D., Cobden, P., Buzsaki, G., & Somogyi, P. (2003). Brain-state and cell-type specific firing of hippocampal interneurons in vivo. *Nature, 421, 844–848.*

Kohn, A. (1993). *Punished by rewards.* New York: Houghton Mifflin.

Kolb, B., & Taylor, L. (2000). Facial expression, emotion and hemispheric organization. In R. Lane & L. Nadel (Eds.), *The cognitive neuroscience of emotion* (pp. 62–83). New York: Oxford University Press.

Koob, G., & LeMoal, M. (1997). Drug abuse: Hedonic homeostatic dysregulation. *Science, 278,* 52–58.

Koob, G., & LeMoal, M. (2001). Drug addiction, dysregulation of reward and allostasis. *Neuropsychopharmacology, 24,* 94–129.

Kopp, B., & Wolff, M. (2000, January). Brain mechanisms of selective learning: Event-related potentials provide evidence for error-driven learning in humans. *Biological Psychology, 51*(2–3), 223–246.

Koretz, D. M., Linn, R. L., Dunbar, S. B., & Shepard, L. A. (1991, April 5). *The effects of high-stakes testing on achievement: Preliminary findings about generalizations across tests.* Paper presented at the American Educational Research Association, Chicago.

Kosslyn, S. (1992). *Wet mind.* New York: Simon and Schuster.

Krock, L. P., & Hartung, G. H. (1992, April). Influence of post-exercise activity on plasma catecholamines, blood pressure and heart rate in normal subjects. *Clinical Autonomic Research, 2*(2), 89–97.

LaBerge, D. (1995). *Attentional processing.* Cambridge, MA: Harvard University Press.

Lackney, J. (1994). *Educational facilities: The impact and role of the physical environment of the school on teaching, learning and educational outcomes.* Multi-disciplinary model for assessing impact of infrastructure on education and student achievement using applied research. Milwaukee, WI: Center for Architecture and Urban Planning Research, University of Wisconsin–Milwaukee.

Lackney, J. (2001). *The state of post-occupancy evaluation in the practice of educational design.* Paper presented at the Environmental Design Research Association, EDRA 32, Edinburgh, Scotland.

Lambert, L., & Walker, D. (1995). Learning and leading theory: A century in the making. In L. Lambert, D. Walker, D. Zimmerman, M. Gardner, & P. Slack (Eds.), *The constructivist leader* (pp.1–27). New York: Teachers College Press.

Land, C., & Riccio, D. (1998). Nonmotonic changes in the context shift effect over time. *Learning and Motivation, 29,* 280–287.

Landing, B. H., Shankle, W. R., Hara, J., Brannock, J., & Fallon, J. H. (2002, May–June). The development of structure and function in the postnatal human cerebral cortex from birth to 72 months: Changes in thickness of layers II and III co-relate to the onset of new age-specific behaviors. *Pediatric Pathology and Molecular Medicine, 21*(3), 321–342.

Lane, R., & Nadel, L. (Eds.). (2000). *The cognitive neuroscience of emotion.* New York: Oxford University Press.

LeDoux, J. (1994). Emotion, memory, and the brain. *Scientific American, 270*(6), 50–57.

LeDoux, J. (1996). *The emotional brain.* New York: Simon and Schuster.

LeDoux, J., Blair, H. T., Tinkleman, A., & Moita, M. A. (2003, April). Associate plasticity in neurons of the lateral amygdalae during auditory fear conditioning. *Annals of the New York Academies of Sciences, 985,* 485–487.

Lemasters, L. K. (1997). *A synthesis of studies pertaining to facilities, student achievement, and student behavior.* Blacksburg, VA: Virginia Polytechnic and State University. (ERIC Document Reproduction Service No. ED 447 687).

Leppämäki, S., Partonen, T., Lönnqvist, J. (2002). Bright-light exposure combined with physical exercise elevates mood. *Journal of Affective Disorders, 72*(2), 139–144.

Leshowitz, B. (1989). It is time we did something about scientific illiteracy. *American Psychologist, 44,* 1159–1160.

Leslie, F. M., Belluzzi, J. D., Lee, A. G., & Oliff, H. S. (2004, July). Age-dependent effects of nicotine on locomotor activity and conditioned place preference in rats. *Psychopharmacology, 174*(3), 389–395.

Lieberman, J. (1991). *Light: Medicine of the future.* Santa Fe, NM: Bear and Co.

Lieberman, M. (2000). Intuition: A social cognitive neuroscience approach. *Psychological Bulletin, 126,* 109–137.

Linden, D. E., Bittner, R. A., Muckli, L., Waltz, J. A., Kriegeskorte, N., Goebel, R., Singer, W., & Munk, M. H. (2003, November). Cortical capacity constraints for visual working memory: Dissociation of FMRI load effects in a fronto-parietal network. *Neuroimage, 20*(3), 1518–1530.

Linton, S., Hellsing, A. L., Halme T., & Akerstedt, K. (1994, October). The effects of ergonomically designed school furniture on pupils' attitudes, symptoms, and behavior. *Applied Ergonomics, 25*(5), 299–304.

London, W. (1988, April). Brain/mind bulletin collections. *New Sense Bulletin, 13,* 7c.

Lou, Y., Abrami, P., Spence, J., Paulsen, C., Chambers, B., & d'Apollonio, S. (1996). Within-class grouping: A meta-analysis. *Review of Educational Research, 66*(4), 423–458.

Louwman, M. W., van Dusseldorp, M., van de Vijver, F. J., Thomas, C. M., Schneede, J., Ueland, P. M., Refsum, H., & van Stavern, W. A. (2000, September). Signs of impaired cognitive function in adolescents with marginal cobalamin status. *American Journal of Clinical Nutrition, 72*(3), 762–769.

Lozoff, B., Brittenham, G., Wolf, A., McClish, D., Kunhert, P., Jimenez, E., Jimenez, R., Mora, L., Gomez, I., & Krauskoph, D. (1987). Iron-deficiency anemia and iron therapy effects on infant developmental test performance. *Pediatrics, 79,* 981–995.

Lupien, S. J., Gillin, C. J., & Hauger, R. L. (1999, June). Working memory is more sensitive than declarative memory to the acute effects of corticosteroids: A dose-response study in humans. *Behavioral Neuroscience, 113*(3), 420–430.

Lyons, D. M., & Levine, S. (1994). Socioregulatory effects on squirrel monkey pituitary-adrenal activity: A longitudinal analysis of cortisol and ACTH. *Psychoneuroendocrinology, 19*(3), 283–291.

Mack, A., & Rock, I. (1998). *Inattentional blindness.* Cambridge, MA: MIT Press.

MacLaughlin, J. A., Anderson, R. R., & Holic, M. F. (1982, May). Spectral character of sunlight modulates photosynthesis of previtamin D3 and its photo-isomers in human skin. *Science, 216,* 1001–1003.

Magee, J., & Cook, E. (2000). Somatic EPSP amplitude is independent of synapse location in hippocampal pyramidal neurons. *Nature Neuroscience, 3,* 895–903.

Maki, P. M., Rich, J. B., & Rosenbaum, R. S. (2002). Implicit memory varies across the menstrual cycle: Estrogen effects in young women. *Neuropsychologia, 40*(5), 518–529.

Maquet, P. (2001, November 2). The role of sleep in learning and memory. *Science, 294,* 1048–1052.

Maree, J., & Ebersohn, L. (2002). Emotional intelligence and achievement: Redefining giftedness. *Gifted Education International, 16*(3), 261–273.

Markakis, E. A., & Gage, F. H. (1999, April). Adult-generated neurons in the dentate gyrus send axonal projections to field CA3 and are surrounded by synaptic vesicles. *Journal of Comparative Neurology, 406*(4), 449–460.

Martin, A., & Van Turenout, M. (2002). Searching for the neural correlates of object priming. In D. Schacter & L. Squire (Eds.), *Neuropsychology of memory* (pp. 239–247). New York: Guilford Press.

Marx, A., Fuhrer, U., & Hartig, T. (1999). Effects of classroom seating arrangements on children's question asking. *Learning Environments Research, 2*(3), 249–263.

Marzano, R. (2003). *What works in schools: Translating research into practice.* Alexandria, VA: Association for Supervision and Curriculum Development.

Marzano, R., Pickering, D., & Pollock, J. (2001). *Classroom instruction that works.* Alexandria, VA: Association for Supervision and Curriculum Development.

Matthews, R. C. (1977). Semantic judgments as encoding operations: The effects of attention to particular semantic categories on the usefulness of interim relations in recall. *Journal of Experimental Psychology: Human Learning and Memory, 3*(8), 160–173.

Maughan, R. J. (2003, December). Impact of mild dehydration on wellness and on exercise performance. *European Journal of Clinical Nutrition, 57*(2), S19–23.

Maurer, D., & Lewis, T. (2001) Visual acuity and spatial contrast sensitivity: Normal development and underlying mechanisms. In C. Nelson & M. Luciana (Eds.), *Handbook of developmental cognitive neuroscience* (pp. 237–249). Cambridge, MA: MIT Press.

McDaniel, M., Waddell, P., & Einstein, G. (1988). A contextual account of the generation effect: A three factor theory. *Journal of Memory and Language, 27,* 521–536.

McEwen, B., & Lasley, E. (2002). *The end of stress as we know it.* Washington, DC: The Dana Press.

McEwen, B., & Schmeck, H. (1994). *The hostage brain.* New York: Rockefeller University Press.

McGaugh, J. (1992). Neuromodulatory systems and the regulation of memory storage. In L. Squire & D. Schacter (Eds.), *Neuropsychology of memory* (pp. 386–401). New York: Guilford Press.

McGaugh, J., Roozendaal, B., & Cahill, L. (2000). Modulation of memory storage by stress hormones and the amygdaloid complex. In M. Gazzaniga (Ed.), *The new cognitive neuroscience* (pp. 1081–1098). Cambridge, MA: MIT Press.

McGivern, R. F., Andersen, J., Byrd, D., Mutter, K. L., & Reilly, J. (2002, October). Cognitive efficiency on a match to sample task decreases at the onset of puberty in children. *Brain and Cognition, 50*(1), 73–89.

McLachlan, J. C. (2003). Using models to enhance the intellectual content of learning in developmental biology. *International Journal of Developmental Biology, 47*(2–3), 225–229.

McNaughten, D., & Gabbard, C. (1993, December). Physical exertion and immediate mental performance of sixth-grade children. *Perceptual and Motor Skills, 77*(3), 1155–1159.

McNay, E. C., McCarty, R. C., & Gold, P. E. (2001, May). Fluctuations in brain glucose concentration during behavioral testing: Dissociations between brain areas and between brain and blood. *Neurobiology of Learning and Memory, 75*(3), 325–337.

Mednick, S. C., Nakayama, K., Cantero, J. L., Atienza, M., Levin, A. A., Pathak, N., & Stickgold, R. (2002, July). The restorative effect of naps on perceptual deterioration. *Nature Neuroscience, 5*(7), 677–681.

Meier-Koll, A. (1999, April). Lateralized ultradian rhythms of the right and left brain: Temporal variations of tactile discrimination tested in German subjects. *Journal of Biosocial Science, 31*(2), 221–231.

Merzenich, M., Byl, N., Wang, X., & Jenkins, W. (1996). Representational plasticity underlying learning: Contributions to the origins and expressions of neurobehavioral disabilities. In T. Ono et al. (Eds.), *Perception, memory, and emotion: Frontiers in neuroscience* (pp. 45–61). Oxford, Eng. and Tarrytown, NY: Pergamon Books.

Michalon, M., Eskes, G., & Mate-Kole, C. (1997, January). Effects of light therapy on neuropsychological function and mood in seasonal affective disorder. *Journal of Psychiatry & Neuroscience, 22*(1), 19–28.

Middleton, F., & Strick, P. (1994). Anatomical evidence for cerebellar and basal ganglia involvement in higher cognitive function. *Science, 266,* 458–461.

Miller, E. (2001). The prefrontal cortex and cognitive control. *Nature Reviews Neuroscience, 1,* 59–65.

Miller, G. (1956). Human memory and the storage of information. *IRE Transactions of Information Theory, 2–3,* 129–137.

Mills, D. L., Alvarez, T. D., St. George, M., Appelbaum, L. G., Bellugi, U., & Neville, H. (2000). Electrophysiological studies of face processing in Williams syndrome. *Journal of Cognitive Neuroscience, 12,* 47–64.

Milner, P. (1999). *The autonomous brain.* Mahwah, NJ: Lawrence Erlbaum Associates.

Misner, D. L., Jacobs, S., Shimizu, Y., De Urquiza, A. M., Solomin, L., Perlmann, T., De Luca, L. M., Stevens, C. F., & Evans, R. M. (2001, September 25). Vitamin A deprivation results in reversible loss of hippocampal long-term synaptic plasticity. *Proceedings of the National Academy of Sciences USA, 98*(20), 11714–11719.

Mohanty, A., & Flint, R. (2001, March). Differential effects of glucose on modulation of emotional and nonemotional spatial memory tasks. *Cognitive, Affective & Behavioral Neuroscience, 1*(1), 90–95.

Moscovitch, M. (1995). Recovered consciousness: A hypothesis concerning modularity and episodic memory. *Journal of Clinical and Experimental Neuropsychology, 17,* 276–290.

Nadel, L., & Land, C. (2000, December). Memory traces revisited. *Nature Reviews Neuroscience, 1*(3), 209–212.

Nader, K., Schafe, G., & LeDoux, J. (2000, December). The labile nature of consolidation. *Nature Reviews Neuroscience, 1*(3), 216–220.

Neave, N., Menaged, M., & Weightman, D. R. (1999, December). Sex differences in cognition: The role of testosterone and sexual orientation. *Brain and Cognition, 41*(3), 245–262.

Neisser, U., & Harsch, N. (1992). Phantom flashbulbs: False recollections of hearing the news about Challenger. In E. Winograd & U. Neisser (Eds.), *Affect and accuracy in recall: Studies of "flashbulb" memories* (pp. 9–31). Cambridge, Eng.: Cambridge University Press.

Nelson, P., & Soli, S. (2000). Acoustical barriers to learning: Children at risk in every classroom. *Language, Speech & Hearing Services in Schools, 4,* 356–361.

Nettles, S., Mucherah, W., & Jones, D. (2000). Understanding resiliencies: The role of social resources. *Journal of Education for Students Placed at Risk, 5*(1–2), 47–60.

Nieto, S. (2003, May). What keeps teachers going? *Educational Leadership, 60*(8), 15–18.

Nissen, M., & Bullemer, P. (1987). Attentional requirements of learning: Evidence from performance measures. *Cognitive Psychology, 19,* 1–32.

Ohman, A., Flykt, A., & Lundqvist, D. (2000). Unconscious emotion: Evolutionary perspectives, psychophysiological data and neuropsychological mechanisms. In R. Lane, et al. (Eds.), *Cognitive neuroscience of emotion* (pp. 296–327). New York: Oxford University Press.

Overman, W., & Bachevalier, J. (2001). Inferences about the functional development of neural systems in children via the application of animal tests in cognition. In C. Nelson & M. Luciana (Eds.), *Handbook of developmental cognitive neuroscience.* Cambridge, MA: MIT Press.

Overton, D. A. (1984). State-dependent learning and drug discriminations. In L. L. Iverson, S. D. Iverson, & S. H. Snyder (Eds.), *Handbook of psychopharmacology, Volume 18* (pp. 59–127). New York: Plenum.

Padgett, D. A., MacCallum, R. C., & Sheridan, J. F. (1998, September). Stress exacerbates age-related decrements in the immune response to an experimental influenza viral infection. *Journals of Gerontology Series A: Biological Science and Medical Science, 54*(4), B347–353.

Padgett, D., & Sheridan, J. (2002). Social stress and the reactivation of latent herpes simplex virus type 1. In J. Cacioppo, et al. (Eds.), *Foundations in social neuroscience* (pp. 1185–1193). Cambridge, MA: MIT Press.

Palmer, L. (2003, July 25). *Smart Start program: Evidence from two schools: Vestibular stimulation improves academic performance.* Lecture at Learning Brain EXPO, Chicago.

Parmelee, A., & Sigman, M. (1993). Perinatal brain development and behavior. In M. M. Haith & J. Campos (Eds.), *Infancy and biology of development, Vol. 2: Handbook of child psychology.* New York: Wiley.

Paus, T., Zijdenbos, A., Worsley, K., Collins, D., Blumenthal, J., & Giedd, J. (1999). Structural maturation of neural pathways in children and adolescents: In vivo study. *Science, 283,* 1908–1911.

Pekkarinen, E., & Wiljanen, V. (1990, July–August). Effect of sound-absorbing treatment on speech discrimination in rooms. *Audiology, 29*(4), 219–227.

Perry, B. (1997). Incubated in terror: Neurodevelopmental factors in the "cycle of violence." In J. Osofsky (Ed.), *Children in a violent society* (pp.124–149). New York: Guilford Press.

Pert, C. (1997). *Molecules of emotion.* New York: Charles Scribner's Sons.

Petrides, K., Frederickson, N., & Furnham, A. (2004). The role of trait emotional intelligence in academic performance and deviant behavior at school. *Personality & Individual Differences, 36*(2), 277–293.

Phelps, E. A., O'Connor, K. J., Cunningham, W. A., Funayama, E. S., Gatenby, J. C., Gore, J. C., & Banaji, M. R. (2000, September). Performance on indirect measures of race evaluation predicts amygdala activation. *Journal of Cognitive Neuroscience, 2*(5), 729–738.

Piegneux, P., Laureys, S., Delbeuck, X., & Maquet, P. (2001). Sleeping brain, learning brain: The role of sleep for memory systems. *Neuroreport, 12,* A111–A124.

Pine, K., & Messer, D. (1998). Group collaboration effects and the explicitness of children's knowledge. *Cognitive Development, 13*(1), 109–126.

Pinker, S. (1994). *The language instinct: How the mind creates language.* New York: William Morrow & Co.

Polan, H., & Hofer, M. (1999). Psychobiological origins of infant attachment and separation response. In J. Cassidy & P. Shaver (Eds.), *Handbook of attachment theory and research* (pp. 162–180). New York: Guilford Publishing.

Poldrack, R. A., Clark, J., Pare-Blagoev, E. J., Shohamy, D., Creso Moyano, J., Myers, C., & Gluck, M. A. (2001, November 29). Interactive memory systems in the human brain. *Nature, 414,* 546–550.

Pollitt, E., & Gorman, K. (1994). Nutritional deficiencies as developmental risk factors. In C. Nelson (Ed.), *Threats to optimal development: The Minnesota Symposia on Child Psychology, 27* (pp. 121–144). Hillsdale, NJ: Erlbaum Associates.

Pollitt, E., Gorman, K., Engle, P., Rivera, J., & Martorelli, R. (1995). Nutrition in early life and the fulfillment of intellectual potential. *Journal of Nutrition, 125,* S1111–S1118.

Pollitt, E., Watkins, W., & Husaini, M. (1997). Three-month nutritional supplementation in Indonesian infants and toddlers benefits memory function eight years later. *American Journal of Clinical Nutrition, 66*(6), 1357–1363.

Pouget, A., Dayan, P., & Zemel, R. (2000). Information processing with population codes. *Nature Reviews Neuroscience, 1*(2), 125–132.

Quartz, S. R., & Sejnowski, T. J. (2002). *Liars, lovers and heroes: What new brain research reveals about how we become who we are.* New York: Harper Collins.

Ramachandran, V. S. (1990). Visual perception in people and machines. In A. Blake, & T. Troscianko (Eds.), *AI and the eye.* New York: John Wiley & Sons.

Ramakrishna, T. (1999). Vitamins and brain development. *Physiology Research, 48*(3), 175–187.

Reber, A. (1993). *Implicit learning and tacit knowledge.* New York: Oxford University Press.

Redish, E. F. (2004). A theoretical framework for physics education research: Modeling student thinking. In proceedings of the Varenna summer school, "Enrico Fermi" course CLVI, Italian Physical Society.

Reif, F. (1987). Interpretation of scientific or mathematical concepts: Cognitive issues and instructional implications. *Cognitive Science, 11*(4), 395–416.

Reik, W., Dean, W., & Walter, J. (2001). Epigenetic reprogramming in mammalian development. *Science, 293,* 1089–1093.

Renard, L. (2003, May). Setting new teachers up for failure . . . or success. *Educational Leadership, 60*(8), 62–64.

Repetti, R., & Wood, J. (1997). Effects of daily stress at work on mother's interactions with preschoolers. *Journal of Family Psychology, 11,* 90–108.

Reynolds, D., Nicolson, R. I., & Hambly, H. (2003, February). Evaluation of an exercise-based treatment for children with reading difficulties. *Dyslexia, 9*(1), 48–71.

Rickard, H., Rogers, R., Ellis, N., & Beidleman, W. (1988). Some retention, but not enough. *Teaching of Psychology, 15,* 151–152.

Rilling, J., Gutman, D., Zeh, T., Pagnoni, G., Berns, G., & Kilts, C. (2002, July 18). A neural basis for social cooperation. *Neuron, 35*(2), 395–405.

Rojas, I., Padgett, D., Sheridan, J., & Marucha, P. (2002, February). Stress-induced susceptibility to bacterial infection during cutaneous wound healing. *Brain, Behavior and Immunity, 16*(1), 74–84.

Roozendaal, B. (2003, December). Systems mediating acute glucocorticoid effects on memory consolidation and retrieval. *Progress in Neuropsychopharmacology Biological Psychiatry, 27*(8), 1213–1223.

Rosenzweig, E., Redish, D., McNaughton, B., & Barnes, C. (2003, April 28). Hippocampal map realignment and spatial learning. *Nature Neuroscience, 10,* 1038–1053.

Russell, J., Hendricson, W., & Herbert, R. (1984, November). Effects of lecture information density on medical student achievement. *Journal of Medical Education, 59*(11 Pt 1), 881–889.

Ryan, C. S., McCall, R. B., Robinson, D. R., Groark, C. J., Mulvey, L., & Plemons, B. W. (2002, January–February). Benefits of the comprehensive child development program as a function of AFDC receipt and SES. *Child Development, 73*(1), 315–328.

Saklofske, D., & Kelly, I. (1992). The effects of exercise and relaxation on energetic and tense arousal. *Personality and Individual Differences, 13,* 623–625.

Sakuragi, S., Sugiyama, Y., & Takeuchi, K. (2002, May). Effects of laughing and weeping on mood and heart rate variability. *Journal of Physiological Anthropology and Applied Human Science, 21*(3), 159–165.

Sampaio, R., & Truwit, C. (2001). Myelination in the developing human brain. In C. Nelson & M. Luciana (Eds.), *Handbook of developmental cognitive neuroscience* (pp. 205–220). Cambridge, MA: MIT Press.

Sanders, G., Sjodin, M., & de Chastelaine, M. (2002, February). On the elusive nature of sex differences in cognition: Hormonal influences contributing to within-sex variation. *Archives of Sexual Behavior, 31*(1), 145–152.

Sanes, J., & Lichtman, J. (2001, November). Induction, assembly, maturation, and maintenance of a postsynaptic apparatus. *Nature Reviews Neuroscience, 2*(11), 791–805.

Sapolsky, R. (1990). Stress in the wild. *Scientific American, 262,* 116–123.

Sapolsky, R. (1992). *Stress, the aging brain, and the mechanisms of neuron death.* Cambridge, MA: MIT Press.

Sauro, M. D., Jorgensen, R .S., & Pedlow, C. (2003, December). Stress, glucocorticoids, and memory: A meta-analytic review. *Stress, 6*(4), 235–245.

Schab, F. R. (1990). Odors and the remembrance of things past. *Journal of Experimental Psychology, Learning, Memory, and Cognition, 16,* 648–655.

Schacter, D. L. (1992). Understanding implicit memory. *American Psychologist, 47*(4), 559–569.

Schacter, D. L. (1996). *Searching for memory.* New York: Basic Books.

Schacter, D. L. (2001). *The seven sins of memory.* New York: Houghton Mifflin.

Schacter, D., & Tulving, E. (1994). *Memory systems.* Cambridge, MA: MIT Press.

Schmahmann, J. (1997). *The cerebellum and cognition.* San Diego, CA: Academic Press.

Schmolk, H., Buffalo, E., & Squire, L. (2000). Memory distortions develop over time: Recollections of the O. J. Simpson trial verdict after 15 and 32 months. *Psychological Science, 11,* 39–45.

Schroth, M. L. (1992). The effects of delay of feedback on a delayed concept formation transfer task. *Contemporary Educational Psychology, 17,* 78–82.

Schultz, W. (2000, December). Multiple reward signals in the brain. *Nature Reviews Neuroscience, 1*(3), 199–207.

Schultz, W., Dayan, P., & Montague, R. (2002). A neural substrate of prediction and reward. In J. Cacioppo et al. (Eds.), *Foundations in social neuroscience* (pp. 541–554). Cambridge, MA: MIT Press.

Schultz, W., & Dickinson, A. (2000). Neuronal coding of prediction errors. *Annual Review Neuroscience, 23,* 473–500.

Schwartz, P., Rosenthal, N., & Wehr, T. (1998, October). Serotonin 1A receptors, melatonin, and the proportional control thermostat in patients with winter depression. *Archives of Psychiatry, 55*(10), 897–903.

Sedikides, C. (1992). Mood as a determinant of attentional focus. *Cognition and Emotion, 6,* 129–148.

Sejnowski, T. (2002, January). The brain and learning [presentation]. At the Learning Brain Expo, San Antonio, TX.

Shannahoff-Khalsa, D. (1993, June). The ultradian rhythm of alternating cerebral hemispheric activity. *International Journal of Neuroscience, 70*(3–4), 285–298.

Shaywitz, B. A., Shaywitz, S. E., Pugh, K. R., Constable, R. T., Skudlarski, P., Fulbright, R. K., Bronen, R. A., Fletcher, J. M., Shankweiler, D. P., Katz, L., et al. (1995, February 16). Sex differences in the functional organization of the brain for language. *Nature, 373,* 607–609.

Shimamura, A. (2002). Relational binding theory and the role of consolidation. In L. Squire & D. Schacter (Eds.), *Neuropsychology of memory* (pp. 61–72). New York: Guilford Press.

Shors, T., Weiss, C., & Thompson, R. (1992). Stress-induced facilitation of classical conditioning. *Science, 257,* 537–539.

Shulman, G., Corbetta, M., Buchner, R. J., Fiez, F., Meizen, F., Raichle, M., & Peterson, S. (1997). Common blood flow changes across visual tasks: Increases in subcortical structures and cerebellum but not in nonvisual cortex. *Journal of Cognitive Neuroscience, 9*(5), 624–647.

Siegel, D. (1999). *The developing mind.* New York: Guilford Press.

Siegfried, T. (1997, August 18). Scientists aren't too depressed about learning from mistakes. *Dallas Morning News,* p. 9D.

Silverman, S. (1993). Student characteristics, practice, and achievement in physical education. *Journal of Educational Research, 87*(1), 54–61.

Slavin, R. E. (1994). Quality, appropriateness, incentive, and time: A model of instructional effectiveness. *International Journal of Educational Research, 21*(2), 141–157.

Smaldino, J., & Crandell, C. (2000). Classroom amplification technology: Theory and practice. *Language, Speech & Hearing Services in Schools, 4,* 371–375.

Soetens, E., Caesar, S., D'Hoodge, R., & Hueting, J. (1995). Effect of amphetamine on long-term retention of verbal material. *Psychopharmacology, 119,* 155–162.

Sousa, N., Lukoyanov, N., Madeira, M., Almeida, O., & Paula-Barbosa, M. (2000). Reorganization of the morphology of hippocampal neuritis and synapses after stress-induced damage correlates with behavioral improvement. *Neuroscience, 97,* 253–266.

Sowell, E., Thompson, P., Holmes, C., Jernigan, T., & Toga, A. (1999). In vivo evidence for post-adolescent brain maturation in frontal and striatal regions. *Nature Neuroscience, 2,* 859–861.

Sowell, E. R., Delis, D., Stiles, J., & Jernigan, T. L. (2001, March). Improved memory functioning and frontal lobe maturation between childhood and adolescence: A structural MRI study. *Journal of the International Neuropsychological Society, 7*(3), 312–322.

Sporns, O., Tononi, G., & Edelman, G. (2000, October–November). Connectivity and complexity: The relationship between neuroanatomy and brain dynamics. *Neural Networks, 13*(8–9), 909–922.

Squire, L. (1992). Memory and the hippocampus: A synthesis from findings with rats, monkeys, and humans. *Psychological Review, 99*(2), 195–231.

Stickgold, R., James, L., & Hobson, J. (2000). Visual discrimination requires sleep after training. *Nature Neuroscience, 3,* 1237–1238.

Suomi, S. (1999). Attachment in rhesus monkeys. In J. Cassidy & P. Shaver (Eds.), *Handbook of attachment* (pp. 181–197). New York: Guilford Press.

Sutoo, D., & Akiyama, K. (2003, June). Regulation of brain function by exercise. *Neurobiology of disease, 13*(1), 1–14.

Tanaka, S. (2002, June–July). Dopamine controls fundamental cognitive operations of multi-target spatial working memory. *Neural Networks, 15*(4–6), 573–582.

Taylor, H. L., & Orlansky, J. (1993). The effects of wearing protective chemical warfare combat clothing on human performance. *Aviation, Space, and Environmental Medicine, 64*(2), A1–41.

Taylor, S. E. (1991, July). Asymmetrical effects of positive and negative events: The mobilization–minimization hypothesis. *Psychological Bulletin, 110*(1), 67–85.

Temple, E., Deutsch, G. K., Poldrack, R. A., Miller, S. L., Tallal, P., Merzenich, M. M., & Gabrieli, J. D. (2003, March 4). Neural deficits in children with dyslexia ameliorated by behavioral remediation: Evidence from functional MRI. *Proceedings of the National Academy of Sciences, USA, 100*(5), 2860–2865.

Thompson, R. (1993). *The brain.* New York: W. H. Freeman Company.

Thornton, C. (2000). *Truth from trash: How learning makes sense.* Cambridge, MA: MIT Press.

Tomporowski, P. (2003, March). Effects of acute bouts of exercise on cognition. *Acta Psychologica, 112*(3), 297–324.

Tong, L., Shen, H., Perreau, V. M., Balazs, R., & Cotman, C. W. (2001). Effects of exercise on gene-expression profile in the rat hippocampus. *Neurobiology of Disease, 8*(6), 1046–1056.

Tonge, B. J. (1990). The impact of television on children and clinical practice. *Australian and New Zealand Journal of Psychiatry, 24*(4), 552–560.

Tremblay, L., & Schultz, W. (2000). Modifications of reward expectation–related neuronal activity during learning in primate orbitofrontal cortex. *Journal of Neurophysiology, 83,* 1877–1885.

Tremblay, R., Japel, C., Perusse, D., McDuff, P., Boivin, M., Zocolillo, M., & Montplaisir, J. (2002). The search for the "age of onset" of physical aggression: Rousseau and Bandura revisited. In J. Cicioppo, et al. (Eds.), *Foundations in social neuroscience* (pp. 965–978). Cambridge, MA: MIT Press.

Twenty years of citation superstars. (2003, September/October). *ScienceWatch, 14*(5), 1.

Uchino, B., Cacioppo, J., & Kiecolt-Glaser, J. (1996). The relationship between social support and physiological process: A review with emphasis on underlying mechanisms and implications for health. *Psychological Bulletin, 119,* 488–531.

Van Dyke, D. C., & Fox, A. A. (1990). Fetal drug exposure and its possible implications for learning in the pre-school and school-age population. *Journal of Learning Disabilities, 23*(3), 160–163.

Van Honk, J., Kessels, R. P., Putman, P., Jager, G., Koppeschaar, H. P., & Postma, A. (2003, October). Attentionally modulated effects of cortisol and mood on memory for emotional faces in healthy young males. *Psychoneuroendocrinology, 28*(7), 941–948.

Van Praag, H., Kempermann, G., & Gage, F. H. (1999, March). Running increases cell proliferation and neurogenesis in the adult mouse dentate gyrus. *Nature Neuroscience, 2*(3), 266–270.

Wagner, A. (2003). Cognitive control and episodic memory. In L. Squire & D. Schacter (Eds.), *Neuropsychology of memory* (pp. 174–192 & 273–286). New York: Guilford Press.

Walberg, H. (1999). Productive teaching. In H. C. Waxman & H. Walberg (Eds.), *New directions for teaching practice and research* (pp. 75–104). Berkeley, CA: McCutchen Publishing Corp.

Wallis, J. D., Anderson, K. C., & Miller, E. K. (2001, June 21). Single neurons in prefrontal cortex encode abstract rules. *Nature, 411,* 953–956.

Wang, X., Zhong, P., Gu Z., & Yan, Z. (2003, October 29). Regulation of NMDA receptors by dopamine D_4 signaling in prefrontal cortex. *Journal of Neuroscience, 23*(30), 9852–9861.

Weinstein, C., & Mayer, R. (1986). The teaching of learning strategies. In M. C. Wittrock (Ed.), *Handbook of research on teaching* (3rd ed., pp. 315–327). New York: Macmillian.

Whalen, P. (2003, July 18). *The amygdala: Why do you have one and why care?* Presentation at Learning Brain Expo, Chicago.

Wheeler, M., & Buckner, R. (2003, May 1). Functional dissociation among components of remembering:

Control, perceived oldness and content. *Journal of Neuroscience, 23*(9), 3869.

Whitelaw, A. (2003, Spring) Neuroscience in architecture. *AIA Journal of Architecture, 2,* 4–5.

Wilson, H. (1993). Theories of infant visual development. In K. Simons (Ed.), *Early visual development: Normal and abnormal* (pp. 560–572). New York: Oxford University Press.

Wilson, T., & Grim, C. (1991). Biohistory of slavery and blood pressure differences in Blacks today. *Hypertension, 17*(Suppl I), 1122–1128.

Winters, E. R., Petosa, R. L., & Charlton, T. E. (2003, June). Using social cognitive theory to explain discretionary, "leisure-time" physical exercise among high school students. *Journal of Adolescent Health, 32*(6), 436–442.

Wohlfarth, H. (1984). The effects of colour-psychodynamic environmental modification on disciplinary incidences in elementary schools over one school year: A controlled study. *The International Journal of Biosocial Research, 6*(1), 44–53.

Wohlfarth, H. (1985). The effects of colour-psychodynamic environmental modification on blood pressure and mood: A controlled study. *The International Journal of Biosocial Research, 7*(1), 9–16.

Wohlfarth, H., & Schultz, A. (1982). The effect of colour psychodynamic environmental modification upon psychophysical and behavioral reactions of severely handicapped children. *The International Journal of Biosocial Research, 3*(1), 10–38.

Wolfson, A., & Carskadon, M. (1998). Sleep schedules and daytime functioning in adolescents. *Child Development, 69,* 875–887.

Woodruff-Pak, D., Vogel, R., & Wenk, G. (2001, February 13). Galantamine: Effect on nicotinic receptor binding, acetylcholinesterase inhibition and learning. *Proceedings of the National Academy of Sciences USA, 98,* 2089–2094.

Wright, S., Horn, S., & Sanders, W. (1997). Teacher and classroom context effects on student achievement: Implications for teacher evaluation. *Journal of Personnel Evaluation in Education, 11*(1), 57–67.

Yamada, N., Martin-Iverson, M., Daimon, K., Tsujimoto, T., & Takahashi, S. (1995, June 15). Clinical and chronobiological effects of light therapy on nonseasonal affective disorders. *Biological Psychiatry, 37*(12), 866–873.

Yeh, S., Fricke, R., & Edwards, D. (1996). The effect of social experience on serotonergic modulation of the escape circuit of crayfish. *Science, 271,* 366–369.

Yurgelun-Todd, D. A., Killgore, W. D., & Young, A. D. (2002, December). Sex differences in cerebral tissue volume and cognitive performance during adolescence. *Psychological Reports, 91*(3 Pt 1), 743–757.

Zernike, K. (2001, August 5) The feng shui of schools. *New York Times,* Sec. 4A, p. 20.

Zull, J. (2002). *The art of changing the brain.* Sterling, VA: Stylus Publishing.

Follow-Up
Resources

Many excellent follow-up resources are available to further your understanding of brain research.

You can stay in touch with the latest brain research and get classroom-tested classroom-practical strategies. Send an email to the author at: info@jlcbrain and put "Newsletter" in the subject line. You'll receive a complimentary monthly newsletter that you can share with your staff.

Eric Jensen conducts practical, research-based staff development programs from one to six days in length. He also offers a challenging brain-based certification program for staff developers and consultants. These results-oriented programs develop cost-efficient, long-lasting training resources. The six-day workshop mirrors this book's content. The five-day training develops presentation skills, and the three-day program enhances special educator skills. Call (858) 642-0400, or e-mail diane@jlcbrain. com. For more information, go to www.jensen-learning.com.

Eric Jensen has written two dozen other books on learning and the brain. To get a catalog or to purchase, go to www.jensenlearning.com.

INDEX

About the Author

Eric Jensen is a former teacher and a current member of the Society for Neuroscience and New York Academy of Sciences. He has taught at all levels, from elementary through university. In 1981, Jensen cofounded SuperCamp, the nation's first and largest brain-compatible learning program, now with more than 50,000 graduates. He has written more than two dozen books on learning and the brain, including *Brain-Based Learning, Arts with the Brain in Mind,* and *Enriching the Brain.*

Jensen was the first to organize conferences that link neuroscientists with educators and he is currently completing his Ph.D. He is deeply committed to making a positive, significant, and lasting difference in the way people learn. Currently, Jensen does staff development, conference speaking, and weeklong in-depth training sessions.

Contact him at (858) 552-0110 (9–6 PST) or e-mail diane@jlcbrain.com.For more information, go to www.jensenlearning.com.

Related ASCD Resources: The Brain and Learning

At the time of publication, the following ASCD resources were available; for the most up-to-date information about ASCD resources, go to www.ascd.org. ASCD stock numbers are noted in parentheses.

AUDIO
The Adolescent Brain: A Work in Progress by Pat Wolfe (CD: #503257; tape: #203164)

How People Learn by John Bransford (CD: #504099; tape: #204065)

Teaching Matters: Active Brains, Engaged Minds by Robin Fogarty (CD: #503286; tape: # 203193)

Using Mental Models to Enhance Student Learning by Charlotte Danielson (CD: #504114; tape: #204080)

MULTIMEDIA
The Human Brain Professional Inquiry Kit by Bonnie Benesh (#999003)

NETWORKS
Visit the ASCD Web site (www.ascd.org) and click on About ASCD, then on Networks for information about professional educators who have formed groups around various topics, including "Brain-Compatible Learning." Look in the Network Directory for current facilitators' addresses and phone numbers.

ONLINE COURSES
Go to the ASCD's Home Page (www.ascd.org) and click on professional development to search for ASCD Professional Development Online courses on the Brain and Learning.

PRINT PRODUCTS
Educational Leadership: How the Brain Learns (entire issue, November 1998) (#198261)

Brain-Based Learning Electronic Topic Pack (#197194)

Brain Matters: Translating Research into Classroom Practice by Patricia Wolfe (#101004)

How to Teach So Students Remember by Marilee Sprenger (#105016)

Teaching to the Brain's Natural Learning Systems by Barbara K. Givens (#101075)

VIDEOTAPES
The Brain and Learning (4 videos) (#498062)

The Brain and Mathematics (2 videos) (#400237)

The Brain and Reading (3 videos) (#499207)

For more information, visit us on the World Wide Web (www.ascd.org), send an e-mail message to member@ascd.org, call the ASCD Service Center (1-800-933-ASCD or 703-578-9600, then press 2), send a fax to 703-575-5400, or write to Information Services, ASCD, 1703 N. Beauregard St., Alexandria, VA 22311-1714 USA.